A Recast Partnership?

A Recast Partnership?

Institutional Dimensions of Transatlantic Relations

Edited by Simon Serfaty

THE CSIS PRESS

**Center for Strategic
and International Studies**

Washington, D.C.

Significant Issues Series, Volume 30, Number 1
© 2008 by Center for Strategic and International Studies
Washington, D.C.
Printed on recycled paper in the United States of America
Cover design by Robert L. Wiser, Silver Spring, Md.
Cover photograph: © Corbis

12 11 10 09 08   5 4 3 2 1

ISSN 0736-7136
ISBN 978-0-89206-518-9

Library of Congress Cataloging-in-Publication Data

A recast partnership? : institutional dimensions of transatlantic relations / edited by Simon Serfaty.
    p. cm.
Includes bibliographical references and index.
ISBN 978-0-89206-518-9 (pbk. : alk. paper)
    1. European Union countries—Foreign relations—United States. 2. United States—Foreign relations—European Union countries. 3. European Union countries—Foreign relations. 4. European Union countries—Politics and government—21st century. 5. North Atlantic Treaty Organization. I. Serfaty, Simon. II. Center for Strategic and International Studies (Washington, D.C.) III. Title.

JZ1570.A57U65 2008
341.242'2—dc22

2007050001

CONTENTS

PREFACE

Forty years ago, at the peak of the Cold War, Henry Kissinger was concerned over the "troubled" state of the transatlantic partnership—"the most constructive American foreign policy since the end of World War II," he wrote at the time. "Increasingly sharp disputes among allies," he wrote, raised the "danger of being mired in the prudent, the tactical, or the expedient" and in the process threatened to "confuse creativity with a projection of the present into the future." A few years later, on April 23, 1973, Kissinger, now secretary of state, called for new initiatives—"a fresh act of creation" that would respond to "new problems and new opportunities" in ways that would be "equal to that undertaken by the postwar generation of leaders of Europe and America" after 1945. Many of the essays that follow do just that, and each of their authors, all leading authorities within the totality of the Euro-Atlantic community, assesses where we are, questions where we are heading, and reflects on how best to proceed.

The goal we share in and through these essays is not to "reinvent" either the North Atlantic Treaty Organization or the European Union, the two main institutional dimensions of the transatlantic partnership. That is not only unnecessary; it is also self-defeating: These institutions have served their members exceptionally well during and since the Cold War. Rather, what we propose is to renew them, and, better yet, to recast them in ways that can make each better suited for the other and both more effectively prepared to help their 32 members address the security, economic, political, and societal issues they all face in common.

That we would dare, or hope, to do so now, in 2008—the 35th year of Kissinger's so-called Year of Europe—has to do with the emerging state of the states, on both sides of the Atlantic, and the possible consequences of their condition for the institutions to which they belong or hope to join. What is dimly heard over the anguish of the moment echoes the 1970s, when a devalued U.S. leadership, struggling to find a way out of an imagination war in Vietnam, was challenged by a restless nation at home, by rebellious allies in Europe, and by relentless and brutal adversaries around the world. The United States was then said to be declining, and the Atlantic Alliance, as well as the then–European Community, were dismissed as fading or worse. Within a few years, however, after the election of new leaders—Margaret Thatcher in 1979, Ronald Reagan in 1980, François Mitterrand in 1981, Felipe Gonzales in 1982, Helmut Kohl in 1983, and Jacques Delors and even Mikhail Gorbachev in early 1985—America was back, and the Alliance, reconciled with a relaunched Europe, stood ready to defeat its inept and exhausted adversaries. These leaders were the architects of this remarkable era—a quick and peaceful end of the wars of the twentieth century that will astound historians for decades to come. Now, a new group of political architects is emerging to organize the institutional finality of the Euro-Atlantic partnership: If not now, when?

In Germany and in France, as well as in Britain, the replacement of worn-out and often-discredited leaders has ended the political agony that surrounded their last years in office. Despite the serious domestic challenges faced in all three countries, it can be expected that Angela Merkel, Nicolas Sarkozy, and even Gordon Brown are likely to remain in place for the next 6 to 10 years. On the whole, these new leaders are political pragmatists who can relate to each other, and they also appear ready to work with the United States—which is confirmed by their interest in engaging the outgoing U.S. president even as each eagerly awaits his successor. With elections in Spain and Italy due in 2008, the political framework is being recast for all of Europe and its most significant interlocutors, the United States and Russia, both also scheduled for elections in 2008.

Admittedly, these new leaders will have to bring some relief to a prolonged malaise that has featured but not been limited to the sluggish state of their economies and the disarray of their respective societies, as eloquently discussed by Michael Brenner in chapter 2 of this volume. However, there has already been some improvement, thanks, ironically enough, to the legacies of the former leaders, who have not received the credit they deserve: Gerhard Schröder, who started the economic reforms that Merkel is now pursuing; Tony Blair, who was the first to confront serious acts of post–9/11 terror in a European capital, which Brown is now also facing; and even Jacques Chirac's last prime minister, Dominique de Villepin, who introduced many of the policies his successor is now endorsing. With Germany again acting as the economic locomotive it is meant to be, EU growth achieved a six-year high in 2006, more than 1 full percentage point ahead of the United States, with encouraging signs in most of the major EU members as 2007 came to an end: the first budget surplus expected in Germany since 1989; the lowest levels of unemployment in France since 1982; and 40 consecutive quarters of economic expansion in Britain, where growth still remains ahead of euro-zone growth.

Along with becoming politically more confident and economically more robust, the states of Europe have also grown institutionally more cohesive. For much of the past decade, the EU was a convenient alibi used by national governments to redirect their citizens' discontent, thus facilitating an institutional crisis that exploded when voters in France and the Netherlands rejected the Constitutional Treaty in mid-2005. That debate was settled in June 2007 with a so-called simplified treaty that was floor-managed by Merkel but prepared by Sarkozy and ultimately endorsed by Brown. Now, at last, the EU can return to debating what it must do instead of carrying on a discourse over what it should be. That proposition, too, will be tested during the latter half of 2008, as the French prepare for and assume their six-month presidency of the EU.

The French presidency, which may be the last such EU presidency, looms as a defining moment for Europe: Much of what will follow will depend on what is achieved during those six months—how (meaning with whom) and to what ends (meaning without or against whom). The Lisbon Treaty, which is scheduled for ratification by all EU members before the next European Parliament elections in June 2009, provides a good basis on which to build a European Union that can be a more assertive power in the world without failing to become a more cooperative U.S. partner in a strong and cohesive NATO. The treaty includes a full-time president of the European Council, who will be able to serve for as long as five years and will gradually become the face of the 27-member union, while a smaller Commission continues to act as a quasi-legislative branch, and a reinforced Parliament begins to reduce the current democratic deficit that has kept the EU institutions away from European citizens. On paper at least, the new regime should move the Union closer to becoming a virtual "regional state"—as described by Vivien Schmidt in chapter 4—whose rules of governance are not shaped by a Constitution but by treaties—meaning "We, the Heads of State and Heads of Government" rather than "We, the People" or, in Blair's old formula, "a superpower rather than a super state."

Properly used, the new treaty can be an effective conduit for further initiatives in the defense and security areas. As is well known, U.S.-EU and EU-NATO policy harmonization has repeatedly suffered from divisions within the EU, not only among EU members but also between (and within) various EU institutions, thereby leaving the EU, as Jolyon Howorth expresses it in chapter 5, "in a real sense, leaderless." The new EU's "high representative for foreign affairs and security policy" will combine the security responsibilities of the European Council and Commission into one person and one instrument, thus providing the United States, and also NATO, with the mythical single telephone number to call. Should such a phone call be placed at some appropriate time in 2009, what they might talk about, and how, will also be largely determined in 2008, with an early preview during the NATO summit scheduled for Bucharest in the spring.

That summit, too, will have a significance that therefore transcends the issue most likely to define it: another round of NATO enlargement. By the time of the summit, the U.S. presidential primaries for both political parties will likely have delivered their verdict, thereby creating increasingly cacophonic sounds in a world that will find it difficult to listen to what outgoing President George W. Bush says while trying to anticipate what either of his possible successors might do, or cease to do, a few months later. Under such circumstances, it will be useful to rely on a European voice that, even (and especially) when speaking in French, can be heard with an unusual American accent as, past Bush and beyond Iraq, the Europeans and their Union prepare for a new U.S. president. That might mean, at long last, an end to the tiresome bilateral quarrel that has often stood in the way of closer transatlantic ties—a condition explained by Benoît d'Aboville in chapter 7 of this volume.

Admittedly, there have been many other moments in the past when Europe, seemingly on the verge of being back with an Atlanticist disposition and global expectations, was held back or taken away from its senior partner across the Atlantic. Whether this moment will last during and beyond the coming year is not clear, therefore, and it may depend on circumstances over which neither the states of Europe nor their Union have much control—especially at a time when the populist forces examined by Ivan Krastev in chapter 3 are poised to seize every opportunity to sharpen their attacks on Europe for the alleged intrusiveness of its institutions. Nor, in this initial phase in 2008, is this moment alone likely to produce the "fresh act of creation" that Kissinger called for 30 years ago. But, at least, improved relations between the United States and France in NATO, and between Britain, France, and Germany in the EU, are a much-needed start.

Hans Binnendijk and Richard Kugler (in chapter 6), as well as Julian Lindley-French (chapter 8) and Franklin Kramer (chapter 9), provide many suggestions for making of this start a new beginning in and beyond 2009, when the 32 countries that are members of either NATO or the EU (and, for most of them, both) celebrate the 20th anniversary of their triumph during the Cold War: the fall of the Berlin Wall in November 1989. Together with the other contributors to this volume, they offer an agenda for action that aims at the ever-closer Euro-Atlantic partnership needed for the emerging multipolar system of the twenty-first century.

Simon Serfaty
February 2008

ACKNOWLEDGMENTS

This volume is the fourth in a series that began with *The European Finality Debate and its National Dimensions* (2003) and continued with *Visions of America and Europe: September 11, Iraq, and Transatlantic Relations* (with Christina Balis, 2004) followed by *Visions of the Atlantic Alliance: The United States, the European Union, and NATO* (2006). All of these volumes were published by the CSIS Press, and my thanks go, therefore, to its able and dedicated director, James Dunton, and his competent and thorough staff, including Roberta Howard Fauriol.

The essays included in this volume were written at the close of a two-year project that involved the organization of a considerable number of meetings and the participation of more than 100 experts representing 76 institutions in the United States and most members of the European Union and NATO. We cannot thank them all individually, but many of them will recognize the ideas and arguments presented in these essays: whether they opposed or endorsed our conclusions, their contributions helped us all improve and enrich our thinking. We, the authors, are indebted to each and all of them.

Meetings organized on behalf of this project were held on both sides of the Atlantic. For our discussion in Riga, held prior to the important NATO summit that took place in Latvia in November 2006, we are especially indebted to the Strategic Analysis Commission (SAC) and its chair, Zaneta Ozolina: their generous cosponsorship of the meeting, combined with their remarkable organizational skills, made the meeting the success it was. For our discussions in Berlin, held shortly after the NATO summit, we were helped by my good friend, Ralph Thiele, now director of Special Projects at the German Air Force Office in Cologne: as always, I was sensitive to his friendship and appreciated his guidance. In Brussels, where we met in June 2007, shortly before the EU summit that was to end the German presidency of the European Council, we relied on the generous, tireless, and simply indispensable support of the Transatlantic Policy Network: thanks go to James Elles, a member of the European Parliament since 1984 and TPN's founding father, and to Vivien Haig, its director-general. Few organizations have done as much as TPN for sustaining, renewing, and ultimately recasting the transatlantic partnership.

The entire project was made possible by a generous grant from the Commission of the European Union. Our thanks, personally and institutionally, go to Ambassador John Bruton, head of the European Commission Delegation to the United States. As always, the work was integrated into the CSIS Europe Program: our thanks go to the German Marshall Fund of the United States, whose support is a vital dimension of the program, now directed by Julianne Smith. Finally, every part of the program and the many papers and reports it produced, as well as the development of this volume, involved vital contributions by CSIS Europe Program fellow Derek Mix, whose leadership and commitment met the highest standards and to whom I am especially grateful.

PART ONE

Introduction

CHAPTER ONE

THE UNITED STATES AND EUROPE IN A MULTIPOLAR WORLD

Simon Serfaty

S ingle events cannot be predicted, but their consequences can, not only because the most significant such events modify behavior but also because they are parts of patterns they confirm, redirect, or even start. To this extent, the inability to anticipate conditions that lie a few months ahead does not deny the analyst foreknowledge of conditions that might emerge a few years or even decades in the future. Herein lies the logic of a discussion of conditions involving America and Europe 20 years into the future: Much of what is to come is already here.

To show foreknowledge, scenarios are designed to forecast plausible outcomes for discernible trends. They are based on everything-else-being-equal-like arguments, and they make of rationality a central dimension of all future decisions. Though irrational behavior can occur, it is unusual and is therefore a form of historic discontinuity.

Discontinuities point to departures from facts-based and history-taught patterns of rational state and state-sponsored behavior. By definition, these are few—so much so that most are not easily recognizable until they have actually occurred and until their consequences, once confirmed, demonstrate that they were not a mere aberration.

Forecasting is not predicting. Predictions assume certainty about what will be, whereas forecasts at best assert certainty about what will *not* be while acknowledging uncertainty about what may be. In other words, forecasting reduces the otherwise infinite range of futures ahead but does not pick any—although some may be deemed more likely than others. That alone is enough to provide foreknowledge on which to base expectations and, possibly, make decisions as well.

Inherent in the analyst's foreknowledge is an inescapable need for omissions that shrink current reality to make it more comprehensible, without, hopefully, distorting it. As it has been argued, "History is not a roll of Life Savers candy out of which you pick those colors that you like best." And if it is, "then what is most important about each candy is the hole that defines their substance."[1] So it is with fact-based reality: Choosing only those facts that fit one's preferences or expectations creates holes that void these facts of any relevance.

What follows in this chapter is a small outline of the gigantic mass of things to come. The aim is to set a mood rather than to assert a comprehensive set of facts. No longer is the history of the future impossible to discern. Indeed, some of these futures are already so well under way that, for all purposes, they are already here. Acknowledging them is not the least of our challenges.

A FUTURE THAT IS ALREADY HERE

To understand is to perceive trends and identify patterns; to forecast is to rely on that understanding and anticipate the most likely consequences of these trends and patterns.[2] The latter part of the twentieth century reinforced or originated several trends that are not likely to be reversed over the next two decades: the spread of globalization, meaning a steady erosion of time and space; the devaluation of national sovereignty, and the related growth of institutions and nonstate actors, including nongovernmental organizations and global firms; and the rise of terrorism with a global reach, including a continued spread of weapons of mass destruction to both state and nonstate entities. Examined separately, each trend defines a future that has already happened because it cannot be rolled back even if it can be contained. Together, these trends point to an international order based on a genuinely global devolution of power occurring in the midst of a new and possibly revolutionary security normalcy that regroups a confused, volatile, and uncertain mix of issues: transforming and failing nation-states, intrusive and evolving international organizations, terrorist groups and cells, pandemics and galloping migration, and global warming and scarce energy supply, to cite but a few. No one power, however peerless, no concert of powers, however inclusive, no broader multilateral institution, however capable, and no single architecture, however legitimate, can suffice to put in place this order and manage it.

The End of the Unipolar Moment

Since the Roman Empire, power has never stayed in place for long, and the history of interstate relations is the product of such movement—where to, and especially how—because the decline of every great power proved to be generally irreversible but rarely peaceful. That power would now be moving is therefore neither new nor surprising, but that it would be moving toward countries that used to be under the control or influence of the United States and, more broadly, the West not so long ago is both somewhat surprising and relatively new.

For a moment, after the three global wars that defined the twentieth century—two of them said to be "world" wars and one dubbed as "cold"—the preponderance of American power was unmatched and was assumed to stand beyond the reach of any competitor. What defined that preponderance late into the twentieth century were not merely the facts of America's superior capabilities but also their "completeness"—meaning an unsurpassed mixture of military, economic, and political tools that the United States could seemingly use at will on behalf of national goals that would serve humankind after 1991 as effectively as they had in 1917 and 1941 and since 1947. At the close of the twentieth century, no other country or group of countries could make any such claims of capabilities, intent, and efficacy. None had traveled historically as light and even as successfully as America, and, no less significantly, none had the full range of resources needed for primacy—not the European Union, institutionally unfinished; or China and India, still in phases of transformation that left them incomplete; or Russia, seemingly too worn out after two exhausting wars in 50 years; let alone Japan or any single European state, simply too small.

After the Cold War, balancing the United States was therefore not a main driver of the new unipolar order because on the whole its preponderance was not feared and its competence was not questioned. As compared to illusive counterweights, cooperative counterparts provided immediate gratification based on economic interests for most, societal compatibilities for many, political incentives for some, and regional security concerns for nearly all. For a select few allies, like the United Kingdom, or even former adversaries, like Russia, a reasoned will for followership also raised promises of enhanced influence that could balance, or at least moderate, their senior partner's excesses and, who knows, temptation of empire.[3] To that extent, the United States could be the sole controlling regulatory agent of a new world order, as was shown in the first Gulf War. This unipolar moment was expected to last as long as the United States continued to show the restraint that other preponderant powers had lacked in the past.[4] This is what Bill Clinton, America's first (and, as it came to be, only) post–Cold War president did, almost to an excess; but this is what George W. Bush ceased to do after the September 11, 2001, terrorist attacks, also to an excess.

The quick rise of new powers early in the twenty-first century is not the outcome of specific projects or an explicit vision but rather that of an unexpected U.S. decline.[5] Under different circumstances—meaning, in the absence of 9/11 and the events that followed—new powers would have eventually emerged, to be sure, but not as quickly. Most likely, their emergence would have come at the invitation (or at least with the encouragement) of the United States, a country whose people simply did not enjoy the imperial status they progressively inherited from Europe's suicidal wars in the twentieth century—tentatively (and not for long) after 1917, when President Woodrow Wilson entered a war he could win but could not end; more and more assertively after 1947, when President Harry Truman was determined to end the war the United States had just won; and seemingly conclusively after 1991, when American power reigned supreme. Now, however, the unipolar moment of U.S. preponderance is over. This is not a matter of legitimacy, stemming from the world's growing allergy to that moment, but one of diminished efficacy, based on the facts of a disastrous waste of America's power and good name in Iraq.[6]

This is not to suggest that American power has already lost its preponderance, or that it might no longer be a relevant let alone indispensable ingredient of a future world order. It is to say, however, that even when U.S. power is welcomed, it has ceased to be sufficient and has become instead dependent on the contributions or even goodwill of other countries. Worse yet, in those cases when American power might be sufficient, it is still not dissuasive because alternative alignments that were not available earlier can now be pursued, without and at the expense of the United States.

Whether the unipolar moment that followed the Cold War can be resurrected is doubtful. Hopefully, after Iraq, the United States will eventually regain its good name, as it did, in a remarkably short time, after the Vietnam War when the humiliation of retreat in 1975 did not stand in the way of triumph less than 15 years later. But beyond Iraq and for years to come, the use of American power will be constrained, at home and abroad, by the memories of a war that proved to be politically deceptive, strategically flawed, tactically inept, and historically catastrophic. Long after the redeployment and ultimate withdrawal of U.S. forces, the war and its consequences will continue to be felt, most notably in the region—no longer as the American war it was initially but as the civil war it became subsequently. Indeed, it is not too early to suggest that the United States–led occupation of Iraq will have an impact on conditions in the Middle East and beyond for the next two decades—surely for the worse before they can hopefully turn gradually better. How much worse, and how soon better, will depend on the terms of U.S. failure—a *retreat* defined by a precipitate and ill-managed evacuation of U.S. and coalition forces, or a *withdrawal*, which would be engineered under pretenses of a successful military surge and in cooperation with traditional allies and neighboring foes alike.

The Normalcy of Multipolarity

There is little if anything that is intrinsically wrong, generally threatening, and specifically harmful to U.S. interests in a return to multipolar normalcy—"multipolar" because there would be many more powers than one, and "normalcy" because so it has been most of the time in history. By comparison, bipolarity is dangerous and unipolarity is exhausting. With only two powers at the helm, any breakdown of order is possible cause for a global war that might be difficult to control, as was nearly shown during the Cuban missile crisis in 1962 and was still possible as the Soviet Union was nearing collapse nearly 30 years later (and as was shown in 1914, under conditions of distorted bipolarity). Under conditions of unipolarity, any crisis anywhere in the world is viewed by the preponderant state as a possible challenge to its primacy—raising tests of efficacy and, hence, durability that no single power has been able to endure for long since the Roman Empire, and which the United States has neither the vocation nor the temperament to duplicate. Admittedly, multipolarity is demanding, conceptually no less than politically. But it is also arguably less dangerous and certainly less exhausting for the power that must otherwise protect its primacy against the one or many states that sooner or later come to resent or fear it for its capacity to impose or deny changes they fear or seek. To that extent, unipolarity can only be a short-lived moment of geopolitical transition during which the preponderant power makes desperate uses of history, whether its own or that of its adversaries, to move from crisis to crisis while others gather strength and regroup.

How manageable, if not desirable, the new multipolarity might be depends on where power goes, and to what ends. To argue the opposite is an irrelevant abstraction. The identity of the new ascending powers matters—not only their capabilities but also their goals and values. As Stanley Hoffmann wrote of great powers three decades ago, "In practice, that is, in history, their substance matters as much as their form."[7] There is no more moral equivalency between, say, Russia's and Europe's postimperial funk—since the mid-1990s or in the 1950s, respectively—than there was equivalency between the United States and the Soviet Union during their years of preponderance within their respective blocs. For both, substance (meaning capabilities but also goals) and form (meaning institutions but also leadership or even reputation) can best define the alignments that are most likely to emerge as forces for stability or instability in the system as a whole.

Entering the twenty-first century, nearly all countries with the highest per capita gross domestic product still came from the Euro-Atlantic West, the fulcrum of technological change and its benefits for the past millennium. That condition is changing, however, as Asian powers are closing in on the United States and overtaking Europe at the center of the new multipolarity. Among those powers, China is the most notable on grounds of capabilities (actual and potential, economic and military), interests (increasingly global as a necessity and not merely as a choice), and saliency (with a universal intent defined by a self-belief in a civilizational mission). China is back: This is not only the world's view of China, it is also China's view of the world, meaning that as Chinese leaders take their country back into the world with an imperial zeal that is enacted with imperialist tones, their constituencies welcome its resurrection as a world power.[8]

The consequences of China's return to primacy for Europe and its relations with the United States cannot be overstated. Already, China's rise has had a direct impact on global wages, price levels, interest rates, and corporate profits—as well as on commodity prices, including but not limited to energy prices. Already, it has redirected the flows of transatlantic trade, with China replacing the United States as the biggest source of exports to the European Union, while the United States has become an avid consumer of anything made in China. Already, China's interest in strengthening its political influence in areas that are of vital significance to its economic and security needs has altered traditional geopolitical relations, especially in Africa and the Middle East, where it is emerging as an alternative donor of choice, at the expense of Europe and America, and the multilateral institutions they both continue to control. And already, such assertive visibility around the world has caused significant tensions between the United States and its European allies, and additional mistrust between them and Russia, over their respective relations with this Asian power.[9]

As a matter of facts, including demographics and resources, but also as a matter of global and self-perceptions, India, too, is a major pole in the emerging multipolar system. But the role India is expected to play is quite different: Rather than a rival or even a competitor, like China, it is a possible strategic partner of choice for other powers that view India as China's most logical counterweight. Whether the United States (or/and Europe) can achieve a privileged relationship with India is not clear, however—and it may even be doubtful. Admittedly, India's commitment to secular democracy and religious pluralism is compelling. But on two of the most pressing global issues of the moment, weapons of mass destruction and global warming, India is a central part of the problem more than it is a convincing part of any solution. Moreover, standing in the way of a credible alignment with the United States is Pakistan, which has fought three wars with India since 1947. Closer U.S. relations with India would not only move Pakistan closer to China, which last fought India in 1962. They would also add to Pakistan's instabilities inspired by radical Islamist forces that might in turn undermine India's secular society through conspicuous acts of terrorism—with, possibly, an assist from Iran, itself a target of choice for both the United States and China, though for reasons and in ways predictably different. In any case, India's doubts about the sustainability of American power combine with its complacency about the credibility of Chinese power to keep it at an equal distance from both. This will remain even more likely if the rest of the world continues to pay less attention to India, which is already one of the world's top dozen defense spenders, than the Indians expect on the basis of their growing strength; 76 percent of Indians believe that in 2020 India will be ahead of both the United States and China, a figure that exceeds China's perception of its own status relative to the United States (with no other power deemed of relevance as far as China is concerned).[10]

Among other bidders for global status, Russia still stands tall. Since 2005, it has emerged as an increasingly vocal critic of unipolarity and, given its residual bipolar frustrations, a determined critic of the alleged U.S. attempt to impose "one center of authority, one center of force, one center of decisionmaking" on the world.[11] We know now, but late, that after the Cold War it was shortsighted for the United States and other Western powers "to deny or forget a thousand years of Russian history, replete with wars of imperial aggrandizement, the Russification of ethnic minorities, and absolutist, authoritarian, and totalitarian rule."[12] While waging the Cold War against the Soviet Union, the West seemingly forgot about Russia; and this forgetting meant a neglect of both how weak Russia had become, after more than 70 years of inept, corrupt, and wasteful governance, and how strong it might become again, in the name of centuries of relentless expansionism in the West and away from the East. A decade after the Cold War, "Old Russia" longs for its imperial days because it believes it is able to revive and relive them. In Europe, Moscow's relations with its former dependencies are therefore increasingly reckless, and occasionally reminiscent of brutal and domineering Soviet practices. Elsewhere, the drive to be heard is unmistakable, which is equally reminiscent of those bipolar days when Foreign Minister Andrei Gromyko used to boast that "no significant question . . . can be decided without or in defiance of the Soviet Union."[13]

Given the degree of EU dependence on Russia for natural gas (46 percent) and oil (25 percent), but also given the degree of U.S. geopolitical interest in Russia since 9/11, Russian leaders may have more leverage on regional security issues now than they did at the peak of Soviet power—especially because they benefit from divisions within Europe and between Europe and the United States over how best to engage Moscow. Yet unlike both China and India, Russia's advantages may prove short lasting. With energy resources generally assumed to be finite and probably not renewable, the country's economic base is all the more fragile because it works to the exclusive advantage of the individual few at the expense of the many—more like Nigeria than Norway. Worse yet, demographic trends, including especially low fertility rates, are significantly exacerbated by what amounts to a self-induced genocide, whereby aberrant individual behavior and insufficient state policies make Russia one of the few industrial countries where life expectancy has been falling and is expected to continue to fall in coming years—more like Malawi than Italy. Such a dwindling human mass within Russia will be an increasingly significant factor in its relations with neighboring and overpopulated China, where falling demographics do not have the same immediate impact, and also therefore with Europe and the United States. In short, a "menacing combination of demography and geography" limits the scope and durability of Russia's influence, mutes its revisionist temptation in the former Soviet space, and confines its strategic options in the East.[14]

Finally, to complete this pentagonal structure, Europe is already a decisive power in the world but only so long as it acts as the European Union rather than as one national capital at a time. That, too, was shown convincingly during the war in Iraq, when neither Britain's tradition of followership within the coalition of the willing Tony Blair helped build nor France's flair for obstruction with a coalition of the discontents that Jacques Chirac helped conceive was able to redirect, improve, or even reinforce U.S. decisions and policies—least of all when the "mission" in Iraq was mainly military, in the spring of 2003, but also during the ill-conceived postwar years, when the "missions" of stabilization and reconstruction demanded nonmilitary capabilities that the EU could have provided but failed to offer even when asked.[15] In short, without their Union, the states of Europe will find it difficult to be taken any more seriously in the twenty-first century than the European city-states of pre-Westphalian days were in the eighteenth century. But absorbed into the ever-closer Union to which the states of Europe have been committed since March 1957, they stand as a power whose influence (as distinct from its specific capabilities) might most readily approximate and even surpass that of any other world power in the multipolar environment of the twenty-first century.

ASCENDING EUROPE?

How new alignments will emerge over the next two decades remains difficult to forecast. Traditionally, alignments in multipolar systems have been shaped by common, or at least compatible, interests as each power aligned with or against another power, depending on issues. There is no central conflict around which a concert might take form, unless over time the broader implications of 9/11 were to create a sense of community that is still missing today. In theory at least, each power can align with any other power. In practice, however, alliance handicaps limit each power's ability to move at will because of differences, including values, which surpass whatever interest otherwise prompts alignment.[16]

In the quest for allies, China may be the most "handicapped" power. Its alignment with any other global power would be of consequence for the others, thus causing the very polarization they would all prefer to avoid. The United States, too, faces significant handicaps—especially relative to China over security and economic issues and, to an extent, Russia—but prospects for a strategic partnership with India are also blurred because of the consequences it would have, especially for China.

In such a system, Europe's position can prove to be enviable. Admittedly, it is the power that is likely to have the fewest military capabilities and the least inclination to make use of them. That alone, however, is not enough to deny decisive influence in a multipolar environment. Moreover, in a context that is generally sensitive to the impact of soft power, a power whose recent history has kept it relatively free from the maelstrom of power politics and broadly distant from the appeal of military power would not face serious alliance handicaps. But for Europe to take advantage of its paradoxical condition—a power in the world without being a world power[17]—it will first have to return to, and achieve, an institutional finality that can be forecast even if it cannot be truly defined.[18]

Back to Finality

From the failure of the European Defense Community and the Rome Treaties to the failed Constitutional Treaty and the Lisbon Treaty of December 2007, the history of the European Union has been one of seemingly terminal setbacks and decisive renewals. Throughout, however, the dynamics of the process have remained the same: Deepen in order to widen, widen in order to deepen, and reform in order to do both. At age 50, the EU now stands as an ever closer union of 27 members that have relinquished ever greater pieces of their national sovereignty to an ever more intrusive institutional discipline known as the *acquis communautaire*. In recent years, however, this idea of Europe has become more of a political issue—which means a growing public ambivalence as more citizens disagree over what Europe is, question what it does, neglect what it has achieved, and differ over what they want out of it next.

With too much policy coming out of the European Union, and too much politics produced out of its members, anti-European populist pressures might grow to a point that would not only prevent further integration but might also threaten past achievements.[19] Integrating Europe is not only a matter of facts—a so-called *Europe des projets* defined by what its institutions do, and how well—it is also a matter of feelings—a *Europe des nations* in which citizens define what they want, and how much. As a result, EU finality will not be achieved without re-founding the European discourse that inspires the public commitment to the institutions of the Union—a sort of European nationalism that can supersede resurgent nationalisms in Europe. To restore such feelings is the central challenge that a new generation of political leaders will be confronting for the balance of this decade.

The required "new beginning" is not a matter of constitutional finality that would grow out of a bottom-up legitimacy—"We the people"—but rather an issue of institutional modalities negotiated by "We" the heads of state and government, and ultimately conducive to an unwritten constitution, *à l'anglaise*. For such modalities to be legitimate, there must also be renewed evidence of institutional adaptability and efficiency. Now, as before, the nation-states of Europe must fade if they are to be saved: The issues that European citizens care most about are mainly those that cannot be effectively tackled by national governments alone—including the need to remain competitive in a global economy, to which are linked all the questions that will determine Europe's future prosperity, as well as such other issues as immigration and homeland security that condition citizens' identity and safety.

At this point in its history, the European Union must repeatedly remind its citizens what it can do for them rather than ask them what they can do for the Union. Otherwise, lacking privileges and visible entitlements, Europe may quickly lose its luster among new and old members alike. Thus, with only one-fourth of the Europeans polled in the EU's five biggest members finding that life in their country has improved since it joined the EU, Europeans would now prefer less Europe if offered a choice. And yet, EU-wide public opinion polls also reveal that a majority of interviewees expect more and even faster integration over the next 15 years—including in areas that are explicitly opposed, like enlargement, a common economic policy and its corollary, a

European government for the economy, and, though less pronounced, a common social policy and a European army.[20]

Given such public ambivalence, the case for flexible integration may
become more and more compelling, thus creating partial communities
within the Union. In the past, a "multispeed" approach to integration
implicitly assumed that every member state would ultimately share every aspect of EU life, even if at first it did not or could not embrace
every new initiative or, as a new member, enforce all of the *acquis*. The
process would thus evolve at different speeds but in the same direction and toward the same goals—ever closer for all members, though
over time, as well as ever larger with more members, though in due
time. Whether such delayed convergence will remain a shared goal in
coming years is not clear. But so long as no state finds it possible to
leave the Union or some central EU dimension to which it has already
adhered, like the euro zone, and assuming that the Union continues
to find exclusion of any of its members not desirable, the prospects
for such convergence for most if not all the 27 current EU members
in a "finished" Union by some reasonable date in the future are realis-
tic, including completion of an economic and monetary union for all
members, as well as a common foreign policy relying on ever closer
security and even defense policies. However difficult it may be to join
the EU, it is even more difficult to leave it; and however painful it may
seem to live within the EU, it will remain even more painful to try to
prosper without it.

In short, notwithstanding recurring announcements of its impending death, Europe is here to stay as an ever-closer community of shared
political, social, and cultural values that define an identity that is both
compatible with but distinctive from that of its closest parallel, namely,
the American Union (table 1.1).[21]

For diehard Euroskeptics in the United States, however, the idea
of *finalité* is closer to the literal meaning of the French word as they
issue periodic warnings of Europe's impending death. Their obituar-
ies are often written with the selective memories of past sins that are
used to substantiate predetermined forecasts of future decline and
decadence—sins of appeasement, anti-Semitism, and, inevitably, anti-
Americanism.[22] Woven into those memories are a host of selective
economic data and demographic extrapolations that add up into an
irreversible descent into irrelevance—a depopulated Europe in which
"there won't be many Germans in Germany or Italians in Italy," and a

Table 1.1. The European Union: A Union in Search of an Identity

Political Values	Social Values	Cultural Values
Rule of law	Welfare	Enlightenment
Separation of church and state	Tolerance	Historicity
Pluralism and parliamentarism	Leisure	Christianity

deindustrialized Europe that caters to its new Asian or Arab masters.[23] On neither of these accounts do the numbers tell the whole story, and for every set of numbers there is usually another set that tells the opposite story anyway—especially if the related data are to be adjusted for national or cultural distortions, such as the balance between welfare and leisure, or soft and hard power. The goal for the 27 EU members is not to outpace the U.S. economy but to keep pace in ways that face up to, and gain from, global pressures to an extent that provide broad satisfaction for citizens. In and of itself, the fact that Europeans welcome a shorter workweek and expect longer paid holidays than Americans do, or that their growth in gross domestic product is not as robust, is no more significant than the same facts applied to the United States relative to the Asian powers. Admittedly, low fertility rates (with an EU average below 1.5 live births per woman) could become a serious drag for a continent that is also getting so much older (with an EU-wide median age range moving close to 50 years) that the working-age population threatens to be insufficient to satisfy either the European labor markets or the European welfare states. But in an enlarged Europe that remains opened to the outside world, steady flows of immigrants should release such demographic pressures until past 2025, by which time fertility rates are expected to improve for many of the main countries involved.[24]

For the past 35 years, enlargement has been both a consequence of and a cause for Europe's continued success—a master key to unlock the limits to its economic growth and political reach. For the EU to throw away that key and permanently close the door on further enlargement would diminish its prospects for its members' affluence, as well as for their influence on nonmembers.

Admittedly, conditions have changed over time. At first, enlargement alternated between rich and poor countries—with the rich old members expected to help provide for the poor new ones: Britain and Denmark for Ireland (1973), followed by Greece (1980), and Spain and Portugal (1986); and Austria, Finland, and Sweden in 1995 for the former Warsaw Pact and Soviet republics in 2002—which were almost all poor or very poor—plus Romania and Bulgaria in 2007. Because most of the remaining applicants are intrinsically poor, this pattern is over; Norway is one of the very few remaining rich European countries that might still join over the next decade, assuming it becomes willing at last. The key to enlargement is no longer the *acquis* only, which had to do with the applicant's preparedness for membership, but the *non-acquis*, meaning the members' receptiveness to ever more exacting needs for solidarity with, and equality among, all member states. These needs have become considerable. They require a reformed and enlarged budget—meaning fewer entitlements (especially with regard to agriculture) and more revenues, meaning higher contributions from the richer members and even, conceivably, a small Eurotax that would give the European Commission its own revenue base—as the first Commission president, Walter Hallstein, already sought more than four decades ago. (At first, a Eurotax could be designed for the explicit purpose of waging a regional war on poverty, for example, or for a common fight for the environment, thus reinforcing a sense of solidarity among EU citizens; later, a Eurotax could also serve new budget line items for security and defense issues, or even a reserve for human- or God-made EU-based disasters.)

EU membership negotiations have historically been long and contentious, especially when the applicant happened to be large and heavily populated. Like Britain in the 1960s, but also like Spain during and after the 1970s and Poland in the 1990s, Turkey is such a candidate for membership—crowded, large, and demanding. In future years, both sides may be tempted to end the negotiations—as was the case with Britain in early 1963. In most EU countries, it is viewed as simply too big, too poor, too diffuse, too dangerous, too unstable—and frankly, too Muslim—to join any time soon. Yet for the EU to say No to Turkey, or for Turkey to say No to the EU with any semblance of finality would have lasting consequences for all, especially if it were to occur abruptly and without alternative plans for another kind of intermediate or even long-term association. That is not merely about the EU; it is also about nearly each EU member where can be found sizable Muslim minorities that await their inclusion as full-time citizens of their respective countries. The two issues are intimately linked; to keep Turkey at the margin of the EU—with, but not in, Europe—would deny the multicultural integration of its members—Muslims in Europe but not European Muslims. Or, to put it differently, to assume that Turkey will remain outside Europe indefinitely is tantamount to assuming that little progress will be made by the EU and its members to integrate its growing Muslim population.

Membership is not everything, however. With further EU enlargement likely to be delayed so long as the Turkish application has not been settled—as happened during the long debate over Britain's membership—some variations of reinforced association may be extended not only to Turkey but also to other neighboring nonmember countries: by opening EU markets to their exports, releasing its assistance for the more needy among them, and extending other forms of privileged relations with states that respond to basic humanitarian norms, including observer status in relevant bodies like the Committee of Permanent Representatives or even ad hoc participation in councils of ministers on issues for which they have particular relevance or interest.

Historians will marvel at Europe's ability to renew and recast itself during the second half of the twentieth century. As a rising power in the world, the EU has interests in, and influence over, areas that cover and even exceed the area of its members' former empires. That influence is enhanced by a reputation that the states of Europe have renewed over the past 50 years, when other regions in the world found the lessons they taught, and the values they embraced, worthy of emulation: that history can be made to change its course, away from war; that geography can be helped to change its ways, without war; that democracy can be adapted to local conditions; and that globalization can be lived without compromising cultural traditions. Europe's appeal does not merely spring from the advantages of an unfinished single market standing and growing next to large underdeveloped areas in the East and the South. America's intimacy with the new Europe is real, but it breeds a form of misplaced and misleading familiarity that equates the European Union and the United States and makes the latter sensitive to the former's power and influence only to the extent that they parallel its own.[25]

In this context, the abstract idea of American power and European weakness, which flourished during the unipolar moment, is especially flawed under multipolar conditions. All together rather than one at a time, a powerful EU relies on capabilities that emanate from its members and include preventive security tools like trade policy, economic aid, and public diplomacy that are competitive with those available to the United States or any other great power. Admittedly, military capabilities and political unity are lacking, but the next few years will show whether Europe and its Union can also regain a taste for the former while it reconciles itself with the need for the latter in order to move up to the next level: as a power in the world that can also stand as a world power with the *Wehrwille* that France misplaced during the debacle of June 1940, Germany lost in Stalingrad in December 1942, and Britain subsequently exhausted—a "war will" that would not be a will for war but a will to win, not against or at the expense of each other but together as a Union that has ceased to be a choice but has become an imperative.

Balancing Power, Influence, and Indifference

Deep into America's bipolar confrontation with the Soviet Union, suggestions that the United States was, or should be, concerned with such Old World ideas as the balance of power were profoundly distasteful and dismissed as, literally, un-American.[26] As Henry Kissinger noted in the mid-1960s, "It is part of American folklore that while other nations are concerned with equilibrium, we are concerned with the legal requirements of peace. . . . We have a tendency to offer our altruism as a guarantee of our reliability." It is to that tendency—"a failure in the U.S. philosophy of international relations," that Kissinger attributed the nation's failure in Vietnam.[27] Yet, notwithstanding such early attempts to "Europeanize" America's foreign policy discourse, any suggestion that the world was moving toward a new multipolarity was deemed to be adversarial and even anti-American as recently as the start of the war in Iraq. It is "troubling," said Condoleezza Rice in late 2003, that "some [in Europe] have spoken admiringly—almost nostalgically—of multipolarity as if it were a good thing, to be desired for its own sake."[28]

Unipolarity is a condition to which Americans can relate more naturally, because history and geography kept them safe in splendid indifference until they were moved into, and assumed, a position of supreme influence. "Superiority" is an easy concept to grasp and even justify. It can be measured, unlike such self-limiting goals as "parity" or "sufficiency"—let alone alien concepts like "balance" and "equilibrium." Unipolarity is a condition that places a premium on power over diplomacy and encourages a unilateralist temptation that ignores the constraints of alliances—meaning a commitment to consultation before decisions are made, and the need to defer decisions so long as consultation has not produced the needed consensus. In a unipolar world, power talks but rarely listens; what you can do for me matters less than what I can do to you.

Bipolarity is a condition the United States learned to accommodate after 1945. It favors alliances as the most effective way to prevent the other superpower from extending its reach until it is predictably rolled back: The broader the scope of the confrontation, the wider the network of related alliances. However, in a bipolar world, power still remains indifferent to diplomacy, not only because of the gap between the superpowers and their allies but also because of the stalemate written into a two-power structure. With bipolarity, power informs but rarely consults; what I do for you matters more than what you can do with me.

By comparison, multipolarity is defined by power but cannot afford to neglect diplomacy, given the inability of the one to surpass or even equal the many: Do not ask what you can do for me, but do ask what you must do with me. Combinations in a hostile and dangerous multipolar world are different from the cooperative arrangements favored by the United States in a unipolar or bipolar world that is destined to match the American standards of harmony and order. An alliance, in this kind of environment, is "undiluted," the kind of entangling alliance "charged with perplexities" that was warned against in Washington's and Jefferson's farewell admonitions to America.[29] Not the least of these perplexities is the significance of every dimension of power, meaning that superior military capabilities do not suffice to define influence and that military inequalities are not enough to create instabilities. The United Kingdom is a common example; for much of the nineteenth century, it was a world power even though it never was a power in Europe, whose order it managed effectively though with fewer capabilities than any of its rivals.

As discussed above, the five most likely poles of global power are known. That the United States will remain preponderant is likely, but that it will also dominate is most unlikely. In the poetry of geopolitics, preponderance and dominance do not rhyme. The former, which is about capabilities, does not follow from the latter, which has to do with questions of will, leadership, and resilience. Moreover, standing in the way are also many poles of regional influence that lack global reach in either area of hard or soft power but whose decisions can nonetheless affect decisively the global order. The list of these influentials is long, and it tends to fluctuate as circumstances no less than capabilities seem to define their rank and status. Under conditions of unipolarity, these states can seek leverage with a strategy of followership, eager to reap the rewards that the strong will grant its weaker, privileged partner—or, at the very least, avoid retributions with a strategy of benign indifference that abstains from any proactive opposition to the dominant power. In a bipolar environment, some of these states chose to maximize their leverage with a strategy of nonalignment—meaning some distance from both superpowers, though not necessarily equidistant. In a multipolar environment, these pivot states can seek and even achieve regional dominance. They deserve a diplomatic care, an attention for domestic details, a respect for history, and an awareness of geography that America does not understand well and for which Americans do not care much.

In a bipolar system, competition over the allegiance of a nonaligned pivot state (or even the defection of an aligned pivot state) was an extension of the rivalry between the two superpowers. For example, the alliance between the Soviet Union and nonaligned India, signed in early August 1971, responded to the U.S. opening to Communist China, which Kissinger had initiated with a secret visit to Beijing via Pakistan three weeks earlier. In other words, there was no new U.S. policy toward China but rather a new U.S. policy toward the Soviet Union in China—and the response was not a new Soviet policy toward India but a new policy toward the United States in India. Such motivation set strict limits on the two superpowers' bilateral initiatives, as was to be shown during the war between Pakistan and India. With the global balance at stake, the U.S. attempt at normalization with China (and its "tilt toward Pakistan") paralleled Moscow's tilt toward India in the midst of growing tensions with China.

The pivot state was neither of these up-and-coming major states, however, but Pakistan, because India was presumed to seek Soviet support not only to liberate East Pakistan but also to dismember and destroy West Pakistan.[30] Should such aims be fulfilled, the demonstration of U.S. impotence would serve as diplomatic clarification for China, whose support for Pakistan would have also been strategically exposed in and beyond the region. Changes in specific regional relationships could thus affect relations between the two superpowers, but no new influential was likely to gain a global stature any time soon, as proved to be the case for both India and China, neither of which truly affected the ultimate outcome of the Cold War.

Three decades later, Pakistan remains a pivot state, but its maneuvers in the midst of growing internal instabilities are fundamentally different. In coming years, Pakistan's drift into Islamic radicalism would have global consequences that no major global power could either afford or tolerate, including India, the country now most openly cultivated by the United States to balance China. However, a U.S.-Indian alliance would have a significant impact on South Asia and even beyond if it were to be perceived as an anti-Islamic alliance—akin to the Holy Alliance of Old Europe.

Iran is another decisive pivot state, though hardly for the same reasons—and for more reasons than its interest in achieving nuclear status. Unlike Pakistan, Iran is mounting a bid for regional preponderance that neither its neighbors nor the global powers are willing to accommodate collectively but cannot prevent individually. Indeed, Iran has emerged as a laboratory for the new multipolarity; how its bid is countered, and by whom, will condition the stability of the entire region. Other pivot states include Turkey, relative to Europe (including Russia) and the Middle East, which raises, as discussed above, the question of EU membership for this Muslim country; South Korea and North Korea, assuming their unification after a collapse of North Korea late in the 2010s, relative to Japan and China and thus, by implication, to the United States; and oil-rich Nigeria, where a resumption of ethnic conflicts in an oil-exporting country that is half-Muslim would have serious consequences outside West Africa.

In coming years, the greatest challenge to statecraft will be to devise a global order that accounts for the regional volatility that evolves around these pivot states—all countries that shaped many serious Cold War crises—while responding to the aspirations and interests of new ascending powers and easing the plight of failing states and their populace. "It's diplomacy, stupid"—the next generation of statesmen will have to struggle with a geopolitical cartography that is likely to become more complex as the number and diversity of players grow while the nature and focus of the threats expand. That is an art Europeans practice well—and it is one that Americans will have to master quickly.

A EURO-ATLANTIC AXIS OF STABILITY

After the Soviet collapse, illusions of a new world order ended on September 11, 2001, and the post-9/11 delusion of a unipolar world order ended with the war in Iraq. Gone, now, is the rigid bipolar simplicity of the Cold War, when the threat was readily identifiable and detestable. But gone, too, is any of the short-lived and largely unsuccessful approaches to world order adopted by three American presidents since 1991: preponderance first, indifference next, and omnipotence last.[31] In place of any sort of order, there is now a complex, volatile, dangerous, and hostile world beset with threats that are shared unevenly and unleashed unpredictably. There is little to love about this world, which hardly meets U.S. and European expectations, but it is one from which there is no exit, which hardly fits either the U.S. temperament or the changed mood of a recast Europe.

In paving the way for the future, history stutters. Neither in 1815 nor in 1919 did a new world order require global assembly. For better (after 1815) and for worse (after 1919), the world was said to evolve around a mainly European structure that needed to be restored rather than recast. Neither in 1945 nor in 1991 was there much interest in restoring a past order. But on neither of those occasions did a new world order have to be developed out of such a disjointed set of values and perceptions, aspirations and ambitions, personalities and attitudes, cultures and histories, public intrusiveness and disaffection as can be found now. In the current milieu, even history is a poor guide. For the policymaker, lessons learned from the past no longer seem entirely suitable; for the analyst, concepts refined in the past no longer appear specifically relevant.

Three sets of challenges prevail—each urgent, all overlapping, and each likely to be transformed for either the much better or much worse over the next decade. First, a traditional power equation demands that, past the Cold War, the preponderant state(s) make room for the ascending power(s), which await(s) changes in a status quo that no longer reflects the changing distribution of power. Historically, this has never been easy; great powers have fought to preserve their status or deny that of their emerging rivals, which is what prompts some to insist that some form of U.S. confrontation with China, its most direct challenger, is all but inevitable.

Second, however, since 9/11 this global transfer of power and the calculations it entails have been altered by an altogether different set of issues, which stand short of the traditional ways of war but transcend past ideas of terrorism. These issues point to such a fundamental divide as to overwhelm any design for regulated order, either through the primacy of the one or equilibrium among the many.

Third and finally, there is the new agenda imported by the better half of the word from its global suburbs in the lesser half. This is an agenda that shows little distinction between the domestic and the international. Inside and across boundaries, it covers the provision of social services, health care, education, emergencies, pandemics, human rights, and much more. From without, it is about global warming, energy and commodity supplies, space exploration, and much more. Whether these distinctive agendas might converge and be addressed within a single architecture is doubtful. Assuming that it might, what that architecture would look like for such different worlds cannot be forecast let alone predicted. Considered together, these worlds and these agendas point to a new Hobbesian anarchy that mixes the traditional issues of the past—issues of power, states, and equilibrium—with new issues of affluence, rights, and values.

Under these conditions, neither time nor distance provides reliable safeguards—enough time to be late, as Americans used to be, and enough distance to be indifferent, as Europeans have become. Each threat is lived in real time and feared with urgency. Because anything can happen anywhere at any time, events are less predictable than ever, and the presumption of rationality is increasingly challenged or at least blurred: If life defines death as its most sacred meaning, what is there to deter or contain, and how is one to defend or compel? Give me death, or give me—give me what? These, whoever "they" might be, are Dostoyevsky's new Possessed, recognizable for their "great revulsion at life"; these, wherever they are, are Frantz Fanon's new "wretched of the earth" whose "suppressed fury" defines their willingness to kill and be killed.[32] The risk is that for their intended victims in the West, the struggle will cease to be between power and principles and become a struggle between the politics of power and the politics of force; even more dangerously, prospects of horrific attacks may become so convincing as to have reason give way to emotions as the subjective interpretation of alleged facts makes an illusion of objectivity.

Many of these risks were shown on the way to, and during, the war in Iraq. But the war, as well as its aftermath, also confirmed two simple truths for both the United States and Europe. First, the very nature of the new international system—defined by the transformation of the threat no less than by the rise of new powers—defines the limits of America's power and leadership; preponderance does not equal omnipotence, and in the emerging new system, even the United States will not be able to endure for long without primary allies of choice. Second, Iraq also confirmed that there is little room in the new world for the states of Europe unless they act in unison, as a Union from which they gain the collective weight they all lack individually. After half a century of growing intimacy, America and Europe have run out of alternative partners of choice—if not with each other, with whom? After half a century of community building, the states of Europe should have known better—if not as a Union, how? Whatever is said on either side of the Atlantic about the other, and whatever either side might expect about other parts of the world, there is a Euro-Atlantic community of compatible values, overlapping interests, and common goals. And this community forms the basis for a shared commitment to an international order that accommodates the new security normalcy conceived in 1991 with the passing of the communist illusion, born with the anarchical sounds of the terrorist attacks of September 2001, and recast during the failed war in Iraq since 2003.

In the midst of significant political changes in the United States and Europe, the test of Euro-Atlantic finality is a test of will for and in each of the countries that is part of this community, and a test of efficacy for the two institutions that define it. But on the eve of the tremendous economic, societal, and security challenges that lurch ahead, this is also a test of vision that demands that this group of states act as an axis of stability for a multipolar environment the like of which has not been seen in at least a century. For this axis to emerge, both NATO and the EU will have to take each other seriously. This is a reality that neither America nor Europe can escape, as they both learned during their costly debate over Iraq, and it is also a reality for which both Europe and America need to prepare: If not together, how; if not now, when?

Notes

1. Mark Mazower, "The Dangers of Pick'n'Mix History," *Financial Times*, January 10, 2005. Also see Peter Drucker, "The Futures That Have Already Happened," *The Economist*, May 21, 1989, 19–21.

2. The literature that covers the many issues raised by these few words is considerable and varied. See, e.g., Isaiah Berlin, *The Hedgehog and the Fox: An Essay on Tolstoy's View of History* (New York: Simon & Schuster, 1953), 19; John Lewis Gaddis, "International Relations Theory and the End of the Cold War," *International Security* 17, no. 3 (Winter 1992/93): 5–58; Robert Jervis, "The Future of World Politics: Will It Resemble the Past?" *International Security* 16, no. 3 (Winter 1991/92): 39–73; and Eric Hobsbawm, *On History* (New York: New Press, 1997), 1–9.

3. Stephen G. Brooks and William C. Wohlforth, "Hard Times for Soft Balancing," *International Security* 30, no. 1 (Summer 2005): 72–106. There should be no confusion between the facts of America's "imperial" power and the goals of an "imperialist" policy. After the Cold War, the United States was an anti-imperialist imperial power. Simon Serfaty, *The Vital Partnership: Power and Order* (Lanham, Md.: Rowman & Littlefield, 2006), 21–23.

4. "Regulation is the process by means of which a system attempts to maintain or preserve its identity over time as it adapts to changing conditions." Morton A. Kaplan, *System and Process in International Politics* (New York: John Wiley & Sons, 1957), 89.

5. The same might be said about the first half of the twentieth century, when the rise of both the United States and the Soviet Union was conditioned by the unexpected collapse of the traditional European Great Powers after World War I. This was an accomplishment, wrote Raymond Aron, that "required an almost incredible combination of stupidity and bad luck." Raymond Aron, *The Century of Total War* (Boston: Beacon Press, 1955), 96. And yet, as argued by the historian Geoffrey Barraclough, the course for "the dwarfing of Europe" was charted even before the war in 1914. Geoffrey Barraclough, *An Introduction to Contemporary History* (London: Penguin Books, 1966), 73.

6. The total cost of all the wars waged by the United States since the Revolutionary War—with the two exceptions of World War II and the Vietnam War, but including the War of 1812, the Mexican War, the Civil War, the Spanish-American War, World War I, the Korean War, and the Gulf War—was $560 billion (in 1990 dollars), which is the estimated amount of the direct costs incurred by the United States in Iraq during the first four and a half years of the war). *Statistical Abstract for the United States*, quoted by Deborah McGregor, "Bush Feels Heat from Republican Party over Iraq Policy," *Financial Times*, July 13, 2004.

7. Stanley Hoffmann, "Obstinate or Obsolete? The Fate of the Nation-State and the Case of Western Europe," *Daedalus* 95, no. 3 (Summer 1966): 862–916.

8. The Bertelsmann Foundation, *Who Rules the World? World Powers and International Order—Conclusions from an International Representative Survey* (Berlin: Bertelsmann Foundation, 2006). Though Chinese respondents viewed their country as the second-leading world power, far behind the United States, they placed it nearly on par with the United States, which would still be on top, by 2020.

9. Joseph Quinlan, *The Rise of China: A Brief Review of the Implications on the Transatlantic Partnership,* Report to the German Marshall Fund of the United States (Washington, D.C.: German Marshall Fund, 2007).

10. Bertelsmann Foundation, *World Powers in the 21st Century: The Results of a Representative Survey in France, Germany, India, Japan, Russia, the United Kingdom and the United States* (Berlin: Bertelsmann Foundation, 2006), 17. India's assumption is that China's ability to sustain its growth over the next two decades is more at risk than its own. In fact, of course, there are risks for both. National Intelligence Council, *Mapping the Global Future,* Report of the National Intelligence Council's 2020 Project (Washington, D.C.: National Intelligence Council, 2004), 53.

11. Vladimir Putin, speech at the 43rd Munich Conference on Security Policy, Munich, February 10, 2007.

12. Ariel Cohen, *A New Paradigm for U.S.-Russian Relations: Facing the Post–Cold War Reality,* Heritage Foundation Backgrounder 1105 (Washington, D.C.: Heritage Foundation, 1997), 11.

13. Quoted by S. Neil McFarlane, "The Soviet Conception of Regional Security," *World Politics* 37, no. 3 (April 1985): 312.

14. Zbigniew Brzezinski, *The Geostrategic Triad: Living with China, Europe, and Russia* (Washington, D.C.: CSIS Press, 2001), 58 ff. Julie DaVanzo and Clifford Grammick, *Dire Demographics: Population Trends in the Russian Federation* (Santa Monica, Calif.: RAND, 2001). See also chapter 3 in this volume by Ivan Krastev.

15. Simon Serfaty, *Architects of Delusion: Europe, America, and Iraq* (Philadelphia: University of Pennsylvania Press, 2008).

16. George Liska, *Nations in Alliance: The Limits of Interdependence* (Baltimore: Johns Hopkins University Press, 1962), 16–17.

17. Simon Serfaty, "A New Deal in U.S.-EU-NATO Relations," CSIS Initiative for a Renewed Transatlantic Partnership, July 21, 2004. See also chapter 5 in this volume by Jolyon Howorth.

18. "I have never doubted," wrote Jean Monnet at the close of his life, "that one day this process will lead us to the United States of Europe; but I see no point in trying to imagine today what political form it will take. . . . No one can say." So it was then, and so it remains today. Jean Monnet, *Memoirs* (Garden City, N.Y: Doubleday, 1978), 523–524.

19. Vivien Schmidt, *Democracy in Europe: The EU and National Polities* (New York: Oxford University Press, 2006). See also chapter 2 in this volume by Michael Brenner and chapter 4 by Vivien Schmidt.

20. Armando Garcia-Schmidt and Dominik Hierlemann, *EU 2020: The View of the Europeans—Results of a Representative Survey in Selected Member States of the European Union* (Berlin: Bertelsmann Foundation, 2006). Also see George Parker, "Polls Reveal 44% Think Life Has Got Worse since Joining EU," *Financial Times*, March 19, 2007.

21. Commission of Strategic Analysis, *The Future of Europe* (Riga: Commission of Strategic Analysis, 2007), 3.

22. Consider, e.g., George Will's discussion of Europe's "truly remarkable phenomenon of anti-Semitism without the Jews" or "Christian anti-Semitism without the Christianity." George Will, "Final Solution, Phase 2," *Washington Post*, May 2, 2002.

23. Robert J. Samuelson, "The End of Europe," *Washington Post*, June 15, 2005. For demographic projections, however, Walter Laqueur holds an undisputable record with his endorsement of vague "UN projections" that by 2300 there will be a mere 59 million Europeans left—"with many European countries . . . reduced to about 5 percent of their current population and . . . Italy to less than 1 percent." Walter Laqueur, *The Last Days of Europe: Epitaph for an Old Continent* (New York: St. Martin's Press, 2007), 27. Also see Atlantic Council of the United States, *The Transatlantic Economy in 2020: A Partnership for the Future* (Washington, D.C.: Atlantic Council of the United States, 2004), 9–10.

24. Jeremy Rifkin, *The European Dream* (New York: Penguin Books, 2004), 72. Nicole Gnesotto and Giovanni Grevi, eds., *The New Global Puzzle: What World for the EU in 2025?* (Paris: Institute for Security Studies, 2006), 19.

25. Michael Brenner, *Toward a More Independent Europe*, Egmont Paper 12 (Brussels: Royal Institute for International Relations, 2007), 10. Also see Jolyon Howorth, *Security and Defense Policy in the European Union* (London: Palgrave, 2007).

26. Arnold Wolfers, *Discord and Collaboration: Essays on International Politics* (Baltimore: Johns Hopkins University Press, 1962), 117.

27. Henry A. Kissinger, *American Foreign Policy*, expanded ed. (New York: W. W. Norton, 1974), 91–92. For Kissinger's reflection on the "U.S. philoso-

phy," see Richard M. Pfeffer, *No More Vietnams? The War and the Future of American Foreign Policy* (New York: Harper & Row, 1968), 13.

28. Remarks by Condoleezza Rice, International Institute for Strategic Studies, London, June 26, 2003. So pointed was Rice's remark that then–French foreign minister Dominique de Villepin found it necessary to respond, later that summer, that "the French vision of multipolarity does not aim in any way to organize rivalries or competition, but rather responsibilities, stability, and initiatives." "Discours d'ouverture de M. Dominique de Villepin," Onzième conférence des ambassadeurs, Paris, August 28, 2003.

29. Charles Burton Marshall, *The Exercise of Sovereignty* (Baltimore: Johns Hopkins University Press, 1965), 58–59.

30. See Raymond L. Garthoff, *Détente and Confrontation: American and Soviet Relations from Nixon to Reagan* (Washington, D.C.: Brookings Institution Press, 1985), 263 ff. The Shanghai Cooperation Organization, which brings together China, Russia, and four landlocked Central Asian states, can serve to assert some distance from both the EU and the United States, and it might even play some role in the economic development of Central Asia. But it neither solves nor even dampens the rivalry between Russia and China, which is likely to continue to surpass that between either of these states and both the United States and the EU.

31. See Zbigniew Brzezinski, *Second Choice* (New York: Basic Books, 2007).

32. Geir Kjetsaa, *Fyodor Dostoyevky: A Writer's Life*, trans. from Norwegian by Siri Hustvedt and David McDuff (New York: Viking, 1987), 255–257. Frantz Fanon, *The Wretched of the Earth*, preface by Jean-Paul Sartre and trans. by Constance Farrington (New York: Grove Press, 1963), 17–18.

PART TWO

The State of the States

CHAPTER TWO
_____

THE STATES OF EUROPE AND THEIR DISCONTENT

Michael Brenner

The European Union has been suffering from a malaise. A mood of disquiet pervades the continent's political elites. Its symptoms are flagging confidence and anxiety about the future. This apprehension is only partially alleviated by the uptick in the continental economies, a hard-won consensus on a Reform Treaty, and a leadership change in major capitals. This state of mind stems from disarray on a still-daunting agenda of constitutional reform, reinvigorating the continental economies, solving the awkward Turkish puzzle and, not least, dealing with encroachments from the world beyond Europe's borders. And all of this is in an atmosphere made tense by continuing friction among member governments, most of which are struggling with thorny domestic problems and a disaffected populace. Hence, the European project seems to be adrift. For those attached to the idea of an ever-closer union, the outlook is glum. For those who want the Union to get on with doing its stipulated tasks well, the picture is not much brighter. For Euroskeptics of every stripe, it is a field day.

A feature of this anxious season is an obsessive quest for the collective European identity. Rediscovered in the postwar years, it once again is elusive.[1] The arduously acquired surety of who and what Europe is now is dimmed—a victim of enlargement, of the distancing in time of negative reference points, of success and of failure:[2] success in fostering a pacific, self-absorbed citizenry devoted to enjoying the fruits of prosperity in a stable community; failure in the elites' inability either to reassure that the good times will continue in the face of exposed vulnerabilities or to muster the spirit to deal with the forces that are making the future look hazardous. The sources of a free-floating neurosis are diversity (of immigrant religion and culture), disparities (of wealth and economic security), demographics (of an inverted age pyramid), and dependency (for energy and security) on others.

Europe's external environment feeds these anxieties. From the world outside the community come the waves of globalization, in its several manifestations: the immigrants; the terrorist creeds and passions; the oil and gas; and, not least, the omnipresence of the United States.

The compelling question is: What is the nature of the European collectivity and how do Europeans conceive of it? Is Europe simply a loose component of some more nebulous entity called the West or an autonomous entity, however Western, that has its own political persona, purposes, and allegiances? Providing answers that are persuasive —to publics as well as political elites—is the sine qua non for meeting Europe's obligation to itself and to the rest of the world.

CONUNDRUM

The twin issues of the European Union's legitimacy in the eyes of its citizenry and their sense of collective identity lie at the heart of the issue. They are intertwined. Political authority, as distinct from the exercise of power, does not exist without some common bond among those who are subject to its actions, and they with their rulers. That bond takes many, diverse forms; all have as their denominator at least a modicum of a consciously shared social existence. Collective self-conception can be as basic as obedience to the same authority and acceptance of its rules. For example, the spread of Roman citizenship in the last phase of the empire engendered a semblance of legal equality that carried in its train a sense of allegiance to those persons and institutions that promulgated and applied the law. Whatever else the empire's diverse citizens felt they were (for most non-Italians, those other identities did cut deeper), they were citizens/subjects of Rome. The Ottoman and Habsburg empires, at their apogee, offer analogous examples. In this barebones political system, a Hobbesian-like appreciation of public order validates the rule of those who established it—however ruthless the means.

A similar implicit calculus is observable in every *polity*. The near-universal wish to live free of an extant or existential fear of threat to life and property creates a bias toward whatever or whomever provides it. Habits of mind and behavior reinforce it, as does the material well-being that it permits or facilitates. Deeper sentiments of solidarity temper it. What bearing do these observations have on the current anxious state of the European Union? Three come to mind. First, the present vague sense of a common European identity among the populaces of EU member states may well be adequate for continued performance of functions now mandated to authorized bodies. They, and the treaties on which they are grounded, are associated so closely with the prevailing prosperity and peace as to be taken for granted, taken to be worthy, and given the benefit of most doubts.[3] This assessment gains strength among those national publics who have been engaged together in the enterprise longest, those who are most clearly beneficiaries in terms of material and security interests, and those who harbor the weakest residues of national identity and/or have little or only modest respect for the governing competence of their national elite. Italy in the past was an example of the last. Bulgaria, Romania, and even Poland (despite its nationalism) may well take the same path.

Second, the corollary is that the existing state of imagery and conception may not serve adequately to allow the European Union to cope with further enlargement, for the inclusion of new countries dilutes the value of collective experience. It forces attention on what is novel and different. It exacerbates difficulties in making extant procedures work, and it opens questions of ultimate purpose long elided or shrugged off as irrelevant. Moreover, the present way of doing things, a matter of custom as much as rules, may not conform to the traditions of newer members. That is the say, the commitment to conciliation and compromise that, in turn, enables a technocratic modus operandi is not necessarily natural for countries where the premises of collective action have recently undergone radical alteration and continue to undergo close scrutiny. Neither is there reason to expect its citizens to have so thoroughly domesticated the nationalist impulse. Most certainly, the zero-sum mentality is much more active among recent and would-be member publics. In short, identity should be appraised in relative terms: Is it proportionate to the needs of the public enterprise?

One can make a strong case that the European Union, as currently constituted, lives within an ideational political space that affords it enough legitimacy to perform almost all its authorized functions. Ratification of the Constitutional Treaty would not have substantially en-

hanced that authority; accordingly, its demise has not hamstrung the
Union. The one area where it could have made some difference, albeit
a marginal one, is animating the Common Foreign and Security Policy
(CFSP). The Lisbon Treaty signed in December 2007 provides for a
somewhat diluted version of the innovations stipulated in the Constitution. The larger point is that for Europe to cope effectively with challenges that originate beyond its borders, it may require both a more
sharply delineated sense of self and the will to act that it engenders.

The problem can be stated in Weberian terms. The hallmark political behavior of the community is *rational instrumental*.[4] That refers to
the EU's legal structure: organizational formats, procedures, rule for-
mulation/promulgation/enforcement. Calculations of interests (mainly economic and institutional) and the methods for pursuing them
also can be so designated. The ensuing norms have become routinized
over time in *habitual* thinking and behavior. *Value instrumentalism*
figures in the equation insofar as general principles of public conduct
and collective enterprise, derived from a vague ethic of enlightened
humanism, provide normative reference marks. The shortcomings
of this ethos serving as the mainspring for external policies have become evident. Those values are not truly adequate guideposts for understanding or influencing much of the rest of the world. They need
to be combined with more traditional methods of political influence.
Europe, tested and shown wanting in the Balkan wars of the 1990s,
has yet to demonstrate a capacity for making that reconciliation. Any
further determination can only be made in the practice of concerted
strategies that, as of now, remain embryonic—beyond the commercial
realm. The weakness of the fourth element in Weber's typology of public behaviors, the *affective* (i.e., emotional), highlights the difficulties of
adding the external dimension to the community as constituted. Affect
is the basis for trust, thereby is a crucial underpinning to popular legitimacy, and thus is related to Europe's foreign policy capacity.[5] I shall
return to this crucial theme.

There is a paradox here: The situational logic that generates powerful inertial tendencies within the community loses much of its force
when Europe is challenged abroad. To date, those challenges have been
either of a secondary order or attenuated by American control over the
field of action. In the past, internal divisions have seriously hampered
attempts to breathe life into the CFSP while crisis management has
been hamstrung by discord, as witness Bosnia and the second Iraq war.

Though consequential, they still did not endanger core interests, much less call into question the survival of the Union, which for the most part kept operating as if nothing grave was occurring. One factor that kept pressures to a tolerable level was that there was no compelling need for the EU countries to move decisively. Bosnia was, in any tangible sense, marginal. Iraq, in the minds of most, did not pose a direct threat that menaced anything of cardinal importance. In the latter instance, the principal stake was indirect—relations with the United States. The sense of danger would be markedly higher if a conjectured threat were to arise that was direct, immediate, touched core interests, and did not permit member governments to hide behind the United States or if the United States itself was seen as a big part of the problem—for example, a postulated attack against Iran. In that event, the viability of Europe, as constituted, to meet a basic political responsibility would be put to a fateful test. The danger is less one of unraveling than of incapacity or paralysis.

Background

We need remind ourselves of those singular features that have facilitated the successful experiment that is the European community's construction. A sense of history tops the list. We all have been inculcated with the litany that the strategic objective of the enterprise was to relegate Franco-German enmity to the archives of national memory. The keen, gnawing awareness that all Europeans have been enveloped by their too-eventful history led to a broader, more radical conclusion. European history as a whole was as much the common enemy that galvanized political will as was the threat posed by Soviet communism. A high order of statesmanship by a remarkable cadre of European leaders sought a conscious break from that past. If America in the late eighteenth century was born against others' history, Western Europe in the mid–twentieth century succeeded in liberating itself from its own history. The shattering events of the first half of the century opened a way for the European peoples to profoundly change their ways of interacting.

Liberation entailed an emotional, philosophical, and intellectual distancing from those ingredients of political life that had been the hallmarks of public affairs. Internationally, it was the lethal rivalries of power politics. Domestically, it was ideologically driven factional conflict. The "civilian societies" of today's Europe (especially at its Western end) have transmuted themselves.[6] Their *polities* are suspended somewhere between a national past and a truly supranational future. This new Europe was made possible more by a process of political subtraction than political addition. That is to say, the domination of public affairs by prosaic concerns and tame ambitions is both effect and reinforced cause of the Europeans shedding those parts of their makeup that could impede the process of integration. Nationalist passion, ideological inspiration, the impulse to draw lines of all kinds between "us" and "them"—all have dried up. The societies that have evolved, due in good part to this phenomenon, are also noteworthy for a diminished sense of collective duty, an aversion to danger and sacrifice, and an introspection that borders on the self-centered. They are experiencing the banality of success. The affinity between the tepid politics of European societies accompanied by the low-key, incremental style of governance from Brussels (and Frankfurt) has been the central reality of Western European affairs for half a century. Progressively, it has embraced most of the continent. It entails a style of public life that diminishes the importance of group identity.

That is true in two principal ways. First, the need that persons have for group affiliations of any sort is exceptionally low by historical and comparative civilizational standards. Indeed, there never have been societies so lacking in collective affect. The reasons are familiar to anyone versed in the literature on postmodern society and/or able to discern the world around us. Like the hummingbird whose flying supposedly defies the laws of aerodynamics, Western—especially Western European—societies seemingly defy the principles of political sociology. We are treated to constant predictions that such a state of affairs is unsustainable, in terms of individuals' psychic health, communal stability, or both. Signs of a yearning for communitarian ties, for the succor afforded by ascriptive groupings, are repeatedly noted as harbingers of dramatic changes to come. But the former rupture does not happen, and the latter forecast proves false.

Second, today's ripples of anxiety about what Europe is, and is about, stem in good part from the economic insecurities associated with "globalization." They are aggravated by the campaigning of doctrinaire neoliberals who—for their own intellectual and economic reasons—pronounce the comfortable world Europe inhabits as untenable. In truth, it is not untenable in its essentials. Yet to the extent that this disconcerting idea gains currency, it sows doubts and aggravates worries among the populace about the ability of governments to protect their well-being. The affectively self-sufficient individuals of contemporary Europe can manage with minimal communal ties because their needs and wants have been largely secured by a paternalistic state. The coarser, less caring individualism of the Anglo-American type—the model for the militants of neoliberalism—would undercut that foundation of security. If that happens, the dearth of strong communal bonds could have serious individual and political consequences. They would register on community institutions. They would be manifest, too, in a weakened ability to act externally.

The European Union, as depicted above, appears to have achieved a viable state of public affairs—so long as we discount those newfound concerns originating in the international environment. There is no gainsaying, however, a growing dismay that "little Europe" cannot insulate itself from global forces. To fix on them, whether expressed tangibly by unassimilated immigrant communities or over the horizon, is to force attention on the identity issue. From one perspective, it is no different from the existential feelings of vulnerability experienced everywhere in the advanced liberal world. Reasons and roots, or the lack of the latter, are similar whether in America or Japan. The important difference in Europe is the greater blurring of national identity and the formlessness of Europe's political identity. They combine to heighten the spreading sentiment that Europe as constituted is neither enough of a self-defining, collective reference point nor an entity that can secure individuals in a globalizing yet intimidating world. They clearly are related. As noted above, a weak sense of "Europeanness" denies EU institutions the degree of legitimacy that would allow them to crystallize European interests and to affirm them externally.

Hence, the question: What are the bases for sharpening that identity? The conventional answers are easily dismissed. Common ethnicity, language, cultural distinctiveness, or religion does not exist to the necessary degree, or they are not salient enough to count for much. Foreign threats are lacking the immediacy, tangibility, and gravity to rally sentiment and thinking. Yes, Europeans, and most especially Western Europeans, know in their bones that they all are different from other civilizations, whether Asian, African, and/or Islamic. There are suspicions, too, that they are different from Russia, a sensation heightened by Russia's reversion to autocracy under Vladimir Putin. (It is reciprocated by a historically rooted Russian ambivalence as to its

cultural relationship to non-Orthodox Europe.) A sense of distinctiveness vis-à-vis the United States with regard to some social values (e.g.,
social violence) is emerging as well, albeit to a far lesser degree. But
lifestyle does not make for a collective identity that can support a political structure. The relationship with America does bulk large in this
picture, for two reasons: It helps to refine an understanding of what
the elements of European identity are, and to address how the terms
of that relationship affect what Europe needs to do for it to play a role
in the world commensurate with its interests, vulnerabilities, and potential influence. Here is a cardinal element of ideational reality that
affects every part of Europe's identity problem.[7]

For 60 years, Europe could afford to be strategically parochial, or
so it has thought—so long as America tended to matters elsewhere
around the globe, even if its manner of doing so did not always elicit
praise. This dominant/subordinate relationship continues to inflect
Europe-America interaction and impinges as well on Europeans' sense
of self, along with their aptitude for autonomous behavior. Such a long
hiatus in exercising normal powers of sovereignty, set in the broader
context of overweening American cultural and intellectual influence,
inescapably has created a culture of inequality.

The orientation of all European governments is perpetuated to some
degree by the overshadowing United States. Passivity and diffidence
are the common elements. The latter attribute assures that the former
only rarely turns into passive aggression. The inability of EU member governments to act effectively in concert contributes to this type
of behavior. A leaderless group of governments is fated to experience
all the liabilities and pitfalls of consensual policymaking and execution. Tough situations evoke avoidance behavior because no one has
the incentive to boldly identify it, for to do so is to volunteer to take up
a potentially onerous responsibility. Moreover, agreement among the
instinctively cautious is likely to be on a lowest-common-denominator
basis; thus, coping is the norm and risk aversion is strong.

There are complementary reasons, indigenous to Europe, for this
situation: inter alia, the continent's long peace, the attributes of European states' "civilian societies," a philosophy of politics that transposes
in diluted form the ethic of cooperation and compromise cultivated
internally onto the more tumultuous affairs of other regions. Indeed,
one hears from thoughtful Europeans the view that Europe is destined
to moderation and *Zurückhaltung* if it wants to ensure that the community

enterprise does not founder on the shoals of daunting, contentious external ventures. Still, we should recognize the confining effects of close association with a cosseting, protective, hyperactive, supremely self-confident America.[8]

The Middle East since 9/11

The maelstrom of crisis that is the Greater Middle East poses a dual challenge for the European Union while highlighting the paramount importance of European identity in determining how it addresses both. The West's triumph in the Cold War was celebrated as a vindication of constitutional democracy. It was a victory of values more than of power. Many foresaw that a postmodern mode of politics, grounded on conciliation and cooperation, would spread around the globe. Europe and America were envisaged as partners in a compact to foster a world system in their image. The sternest test of this conviction was the Middle East. It topped the list. By reason of its turbulence, its propinquity and its combination of major EU interests made that test compelling, daunting, and divisive. Overlapping crises in Palestine, Iraq, Iran, and Lebanon have become starker against the backdrop of the vivid threat of Islamic terrorism, for there are serious, not easily reconciled differences between a majority of Europeans and America about how to approach every one of the high agenda items. The inhibition of governments in Europe to broach them, and often even to hint at them, testifies to two distressing realities: Many European leaders do not believe, deep down, that Washington has mended its maverick ways and, therefore, it is hazardous to do or say anything that could provoke the beast; and America continues to denature Europe by its intimidating, looming presence.

Divergent assessments of risk and what to do about them expose intrinsic differences of outlook. The marked discrepancies in whether or how they translate into action, in turn, reveal the asymmetry of the relationship. One difference is the sense of mission, or lack of it, to promote the basic liberal values they share. Americans see themselves as having been not only born in a condition of enlightenment but also accorded the mission of lighting the path for the rest of the world. The United States' exceptionality lies in its superior virtue with the obligations attendant upon it. Whether as model or agent, the country's destiny is fulfilled abroad as well as at home. Respect, admiration, and ultimately emulation are presumed to conform to the natural order of things. Europe lacks an analogous sense of mission. It does not feel anointed by Providence or Destiny to do good in the world. Europeans' community was created arduously by pragmatic people inspired as much by a dread of repeating past errors as realizing a dream. Its focus was wholly introspective. Today, Europeans' pride in their signal accomplishment is tempered by the travails of the present. Leaders' aspirations tend to be limited, prosaic, and close to home. The exceptions were Tony Blair's talk of a democratizing mission and Jacques Chirac's references to France as a beacon unto the nations. But they bore no comparison, in terms of conviction or popular echo, to George W. Bush's proclamation of a crusade to spread liberty into the darkest corners of the globe. Blair looked more like he was hitching his legacy wagon to Bush's shooting star, and Chirac seemed to be indulging in flights of French fancy rather than convinced of his ability to refashion the world in France's or the West's image. Chirac's successor, Nicolas Sarkozy, shows no such disposition, his *tous azimuts* strategic metaphors notwithstanding. In short, what comes naturally to an American president is a reach of imagination and a formidable challenge to confidence for a European head of government.

The dedication to reconstruction of post-Saddam Iraq on a foundation of democratic politics and market economics is in line with Americans' optimistic, "can-do" mentality. To take on the formidable task of remaking a society with which there are no historical ties or cultural and religious affinities requires a self-confidence and a belief in social engineering that no European country could muster—or even would dream of. Some may have in the heyday of their imperial past. Chastened by those encounters, and shorn of illusion by searing experiences in the crucible of Europe's twentieth-century civil wars, they are leery of taking up the enlightened democrat's burden.

Most Europeans have found unpersuasive this belief in the pliability of alien societies and, therefore, the swiftness with which they can be transformed. History has instilled in them the idea that the past casts its shadow over the present in ways that set bounds on how far and how fast enduring change can be made, however desirable it may be. That line of analysis strengthens the case for a parallel European strategy for encouraging democratization in the Middle East. It has been argued that, if indeed "the United States has become so toxic in the Arab world, other parts of a differentiated West will have to take the lead."[9] Europeans' hesitancy about throwing themselves wholeheartedly into any parallel project is nearly universal—for readily recognizable reasons. For they confront a twofold dilemma, one of self-identity and one of diplomatic practicality. Pride in their signal accomplishment of building a harmonious Europe against the grain of all its history leads to mixed feelings about whether it can be replicated elsewhere. On the one hand, their experience supports belief in a set of radical propositions: that former bitter enemies can be reconciled (applicable to Palestine, Lebanon?); that transnational cooperation can be institutionalized; and that sectarian differences need not stand in the way of nurturing common bonds (relevant to Iraq?). The transformative power of the EU as idea and practice is impressive. Yet the resulting heightening of a sense of "Europeanness" also sharpens the distinction between their postmodern societies and the swirl of passion—religious, ideological, nationalist—that still dominates politics elsewhere, especially in the Muslim world.

As noted above, the incomprehension of those forces evokes both fear and sense of cultural distance. Indeed, *growing comprehension can have the effect of reinforcing both.* In this regard, the difference from Americans' optimism and doctrinal faith in their power to change the world for the better is glaring. At question is self-confidence, and confidence in the wider relevance of one's own experience. European doubts as to the latter derive in part from parochialism, in part from the waiver from larger international responsibilities they have enjoyed under the American imperium, and in part from a considered intellectual judgment that democracy of the Western variety is not a readily exportable item.

The second part of their dilemma lies in the contrasting assessments most Europeans make about what in fact they can do to promote democracy in other regions of the globe. They generally hold to the view that democratic polities are far harder to develop than is the installation of nominal democracies, and that it is too easy to confuse the two. Without the belief that the course of human political development is preordained, that there is a liberal teleology at work in the world, but rather that it is subject to the intricate play of complex social forces, progress in democracy building is conceived of as critically dependent on a preceding social evolution. Robert Cooper makes the point that "democracy is as much a social phenomenon as a political one. . . . This makes the export of democracy as a packaged system difficult, and in some cases impossible. The hardware of laws, constitutions, and armies can be explained and established with benign foreign help, but the software of unwritten rules has to be developed, invented, and copied locally."[10]

The preconditions for achieving a stable democracy are viewed as the weakening of kin and sectarian ties relative to national citizenship; a readiness to participate in the democratic process on a reasonably fair and equitable footing; and a populace who sees not only a road to power that will give them what they want but also that the same road is open to others who may well have a different set of desires. Most critical is an acceptance of institutional and legal checks that put a break on state power, whoever wields it. Most Europeans do not share the assumption that clever constitutional architecture in itself can ensure against the victors abusing that power. Moreover, they ascribe to the judgment of Reinhold Niebuhr, who admonished his fellow countrymen at the height of the Cold War that "success in world politics necessitates disavowal of the pretentious elements in our original dream . . . even when they appear to be universally valid; and a generous appreciation of the valid elements in the practices and institutions of other nations."[11]

The Morality Factor

These differences express themselves as well in attitudes toward the applicability of strict moral standards to the ends and, especially, the means of foreign policy. The prevailing European view of political morality as it pertains to international relations is more restrained, and discriminating, than the American sense of righteous mission to "improve" the world.[12] It is true that Europeans' achievement in creating a community of concord is seen as a moral enterprise as well as a realist one. Indeed, the Europe of the EU is inclined toward moral absolutism internally. That is not the standard it normally has set externally. There is in fact a gradation of standards that confirms roughly to geography.

Propinquity makes Europeans at once more alert to the dangers that could arise from inchoate conditions in their neighborhood and more confident that they can exert some beneficial influence. Expanding the definition of neighborhood beyond Europe challenges the EU's new-found foreign policy vocation in terms of political culture, self-image, and moral grounding. The belief that Europe does have major interests at stake in its expanded neighborhood is affirmed with reference to the Middle East in the landmark European Security Strategy, "A Secure Europe in a Secure World," adopted by the European Council in 2003. Yet it hesitates to put forth its own strategic ideas. This application of differential standards is not an expression of either expediency or moral relativism. Rather, it expresses an instinctive caution as to the possibly unsettling effects of imposing from without political ideals that ignore history, culture, and existing mores. Europeans do not feel they must observe a categorical imperative to judge, instruct, and lead others in campaigns of moral uplift, as do so many Americans. Postmodern Europe's moral sensibility is humanistic. It is uneasy with grand formulations. And it is leery that impulsive, premature exercises in democracy building can open the way to rabid sectarian forces whose commitment to democratic forms is opportunistic. The troubling outcomes of elections in Iraq, Lebanon, Palestine, and Iran add to those doubts. Therefore, they are more inclined to act on humanitarian grounds to alleviate distress and suffering in the here and now than to embark on architectonic projects to construct democracies from the ground up.[13] Even Europeans who call for a more forthcoming European commitment to the cause of democratic reform caution against unduly optimistic projects of nation building and state building. Timothy Garton Ash, reflecting on recent experience, concludes, "I don't yet see a single example of a post-intervention occupation which has successfully 'built' a self-governing free country. . . . Both in principle and in practice it's better that people find their own path to freedom, in their own countries, in their own time." He also has exhorted his fellow Europeans: "The main thing is to refuse the illusion of impotence."[14] Therein lies the rub. Composing these two admonitions is a formidable and diplomatic task. The inclination to eschew it is made all the stronger by American domination of strategic thinking in Europe and of the field of action.

Admittedly, these generalizations blur differences of national experience, belief, and conviction. They became starkest in the disagreements between Britain, on the one hand, and France and Germany, on the other, over intervention in Iraq. They are implicit in the kinds of qualifications each has set in supporting an assertive plan to spread democracy throughout the Middle East. British and French leaders blend idealism with realism in different ways, while German idealism still contends with its moral inhibitions about the use of coercive power. The big three are less hesitant, and in fuller agreement, on the proposition that the EU has something distinctive to offer in bringing about a peaceful settlement between Israelis and Palestinians: the moral and political lessons learned from their accomplishment in building a harmonious Europe against the grain of all their history. But efforts to apply these lessons to Palestine through concrete actions have been thwarted by the Europeans' inhibitions and the Israeli-American refusal to allow the EU play the role of mediator. Today, more than ever, European policy sails placidly in Washington's wake, as witness its unqualified endorsement of the hard line on Hamas.[15] The transformative power of the EU as idea and model *is* recognized. Its very considerable success in consolidating the liberal revolution in Central and Eastern Europe is a matter of pride. That second historic accomplishment is viewed as validating the community-building enterprise and the philosophy that guides it. However, the EU still wrestles with the normative issue stemming from the basic differentiation that is made between Europe and non-Europe—as reflected in its timid efforts in the Middle East and its acute discomfort at the prospect of Turkey becoming a member.

CONSTITUTIONAL INNOVATION AND LEADERSHIP CHANGE

The renewal of the attempt to rationalize the EU's institutions, brought to an abrupt halt in the spring of 2005, has rekindled hopes for improving the community's ability to exert influence on the world stage. As of now, those *structural* features that have bedeviled all attempts to fashion collective policies remain in place: the reliance on ad hoc agreement among member governments, as represented in the European Council; the fixed biannual rotation of the Council presidency; the granting of only limited powers of initiation and coordination to the Council secretariat; and the lodging of authority for the implementation of Union policies in two separate entities, the Office of the High Representative for the Common Foreign and Security Policy, answerable directly to the Council, and the commissioner for external relations, answerable to the Commission president.

Reforms embodied in the proposed EU Constitution were directed explicitly at remedying these shortcomings: a two-year term for the Council presidency, substantially enhanced powers and resources for the CFSP secretariat, and consolidation of the position of high representative with that of the commissioner for external relations. The draft accord on a reduced Constitution, the Reform Treaty, reached at the June 2007 summit meeting under the German presidency, restores most of the earlier projected reforms. The noteworthy differences involve the precise organizational role of the renamed "high representative for foreign affairs and security policy" in his capacity as chair of ministerial-level meetings within the Council.

The damage done to the CFSP during the interregnum between constitutional rejection and the resuscitation of a slimmed-down version will take time to repair. The EU experienced both an overall weakening of the community ethos and a rigidifying of practices that have long been a handicap. The erosion of popular support for new EU initiatives made leaders chary of committing themselves to policies and projects that entailed the pooling of resources and of any curbs on national prerogatives. Joint actions proposed in the name of Europe, justified in terms of both greater efficacy *and* establishing the EU as a world actor, were viewed with skepticism. It is instructive that the much-heralded move by Britain, France, and Germany to engage Iran in the hope of neutralizing the crisis over its nuclear program (thereby avoiding a dangerous confrontation between Washington and Tehran) was a striking instance of multilateral diplomacy. However, it was conceived and directed by the three partner governments acting on their own. It did not work through the CSFP machinery; Javier Solana was frozen out of the action. Only well along in the process did the initiative receive formal blessing from the EU and assign the high representative an auxiliary role. Cooperation among the three on so sensitive, consequential an issue certainly was welcome—especially in the wake of their bust-up over Iraq. But it has done little to strengthen the CSFP. Moreover, from today's perspective, it is evident that the Bush administration never was prepared either to lend the effort its support, except on its own restrictive terms, or to commit itself to the strategic dialogue with Iran that has been the sine qua non for reaching an understanding from the outset. Visions of a European diplomatic coup were a mirage. Most significant, the episode did little to earn Europe respect as a serious diplomatic player in the region, in the United States, or in the eyes of its citizenry.

On other matters, the inclination to undertake solo performances is still strong. Unilateralism has shown itself alive and well—from Blair's ignoring of his peers on a medley of Middle East issues to Sarkozy's reversion to French tradition in acting as *cavalier seul* in his Libyan escapade to passing by the Polish and Czech governments' bald affirmation of their right to reach independent agreements with the United States on the "missile shield."[16] This outbreak of unilateralist foreign policy behavior continues to erode much of the trust among leaders that is essential to making the European Union's still-cumbersome procedures work well enough to launch and sustain major enterprises.

The period of stasis that followed the crisis over the Constitution has had the general effect of darkening prospects that Europeans can come to terms with hard decisions over how to combine hard and soft power in dealing with an agenda of singularly complicated external challenges, above all the tangle of Middle East conflicts. Indeed, there may be a dilution of the Union's soft power. A divided Europe uncertain as to its identity and fretful about its future is a less attractive model and a less powerful magnet for others. A Europe beset by internal problems and dissonant debates is prone to a parochialism that ignores or devalues the significance of what is happening beyond its borders. Time, attention, and political capital are finite commodities. The contentiousness created by Poland's brusque attitude toward the tentative constitutional accord negotiated over the summer of 2007 was indicative of the heartburn produced in trying to assimilate some new members whose leaders are prideful, willful, and mercurial. Warsaw's attitude consumed enormous diplomatic energy while making the eventual accord an 11th-hour cliffhanger. Then, its backing away from the agreement prolonged the suspense and frayed nerves across the continent.

Once again, preoccupation with arranging the community's internal affairs left little political space for addressing mounting external problems vis-à-vis Russia as well as the rapidly deteriorating situation in the Middle East. Just as the mood about the EU was becoming more upbeat in anticipation of fresh impulse being given to the community project, the Polish affair dampened optimism. One can readily foresee this pattern repeating itself as the Turkish membership issue takes center stage for an extended performance. Hence, subjectively, the prevailing sentiments of disappointment and dispiritedness have been only partially cleared. The restoration of some vitality to continental economies will not suffice to offset them.

There is yet another feature of the present political environment in Europe that stands in the way of both the enhancement of Brussels institutions and self-assertion internationally: the widening gap between European publics and government leaders. The widespread feeling that the latter are inattentive and unresponsive to popular sentiment is much commented upon, primarily in reference to the constitutional issue. Less recognized is the discrepancy in attitudes toward world problems.[17] This is unmistakable with reference to trust in the United States generally and the related issues of Palestine and Iraq in particular. It is most striking in the strong revulsion against rendition/torture juxtaposed to the studied denial and avoidance behavior of leaders. Whereas governments offer active or tacit support to the American position, heavy majorities in nearly all European countries see it as counterproductive if not downright dangerous. This is true in Britain, the Netherlands, Denmark, Germany, and France, now that Sarkozy has tilted the Elysée towards the Bush White House. In theory, public opinion so disposed could potentially facilitate greater expression of European independence on foreign policy. The choice of leaders to move in the opposite direction lowers the trust and deference accorded decisionmakers, thereby further reducing their inclination to exercise a higher degree of autonomy.

As long as Europe's model is experienced as somehow flawed, its promotion abroad can be expected to sputter. Equally, a troubled and discordant Europe is hamstrung by a reduction in political resiliency. That is to say, readiness to embark on the venturesome project of global political engagement is measured not only in terms of available power assets (hard and soft) but also in terms of an ability to run the risks and absorb the setbacks attendant upon so bold and open-ended an undertaking. A robust EU would provide mutual reinforcement of commitment and the reassurance of shared purpose for member governments. A weak, distracted EU leaves each partner to face uncertainty and danger alone. This is at a time when vulnerabilities are more acutely felt due to a heightened sense of terrorist threats at home. The resulting hesitancy about courting danger is manifest in the widespread opposition within Germany to a more aggressive role for German forces serving in the International Security Assistance Force. Other European governments, Britain and the Netherlands excepted, are little more prepared to place their soldiers in harm's way. Wedding principle, prudence, and power in a credible, collective European foreign policy looks a distant prospect.

NEW LEADERS

The recent turnover in the leadership of all "Big 3" governments, as well as in Italy, obliges us to consider its significance for the community's evolution and, particularly, how it relates to the rest of the world. Three features of the situation are immediately recognizable. First, Gordon Brown and Nicolas Sarkozy are not principled believers in an enhanced EU. The former is a mild Euroskeptic; the latter is eclectic in his thinking and actions with regard to the community. Brown as British prime minister is no more sympathetic to the European enterprise, including economic and monetary union, than was Brown the chancellor. Sarkozy has tacked to all points of the compass, evincing no considered, coherent view of how France and French interests are linked to what the EU does or is. At different times he has pronounced a new European dream, a new French dream, and even a new Mediterranean dream. (Turkey explicitly has no place in the first of these.) Angela Merkel, by contrast, holds true to the German tradition of promoting the Union as a matter of principle and practice—Berlin's greater readiness to protect its own interest in that context notwithstanding.

On matters of external relations, Merkel is a staunch multilateralist—whether it is missile defense, Afghanistan, approaches to Israel/Palestine, or nuclear nonproliferation. In mid-2007, she, like the entire German political class, was upset by the French president's signing a set of nuclear cooperation–cum–arms export agreements with Mu'ammar Gadhafi. Uneasiness about prospects for the Franco-German couple as a constructive partnership in managing community affairs is accentuated by Sarkozy's manifest enthusiasm for New Labour's view of the world, as punctuated by the announcement of a commitment to hold monthly strategy sessions with Brown. But the three leaders do share one important idea about world affairs: their conviction that close ties to the United States are imperative. All hold to the proposition that maintaining Euro-American solidarity trumps developing a European political personality or fostering the CFSP. Indeed, there is a definite inclination to give Washington the benefit of the doubt even where skepticism exists about the probity of its judgment or the deftness of its diplomacy. Brown, Merkel, and Sarkozy are Atlanticist by instinct, by cultural attraction, by admiration of the American socioeconomic model, and, especially in Sarkozy's case, because that is where the action is.[18] So powerful are these sentiments that they seem impervious

to the Bush administration's serial failures, reckless tendencies, unilateralist recidivism, the president's unpopularity and lame-duck status, and—indeed—to popular opinion among their own constituents.
Sarkozy in particular has made a series of studied gestures to identify
himself personally, and France, with America on the fraught issues of
Iraq, Hamas, Iran, and the "war on terror."[19]

CONCLUSION

One marker of Europe's future as a world power is clear: There will be
no initiative from the American side to modify that key relationship.
More than any other factor, it continues to affect how Europe thinks
about the world around it. Washington enjoys too many advantages
from it to want significant behavioral changes. The practical benefits of
having what is potentially the world's second-strongest power center
unsure of its identity, deficient in will, and ready to find compensa-
tion in dependence on the United States are manifest. For the Bush
administration, this state of affairs perfectly suits the U.S. dedication
to exercise hegemonic dominance. It promises supporters and allies
on American terms when America wants them. On another plane,
Americans' sense of self, along with their sense of the country's exceptional place in the grand scheme of things globally, is gratified by two
aspects of these Euro-American realities. Emulation of what is thought
and done across the Atlantic is applauded as conforming to the natural
order of things.

   Moreover, the absence of a serious European challenge, political or
conceptual, spares Americans either critical self-examination of those
postulates so basic to the national persona or the exertions required to
keep down a rival. The family ties with Europe strengthen both feelings
because the unique virtues of American society are taken to be the ultimate expression of Western civilization's superiority generally—and
that attitude means it is up to the Europeans to change, for their own
sake and also for America's. If they are too timid, too fractious, and too
habituated to playing off an American lead, then the EU will fail to create its fair share of public goods. And an undersupplying Europe will
run the risk of being devalued by others as a force to be reckoned with
in international political and security affairs.

   This line of reasoning will prevail whoever occupies the White
House in 2009, contrary to much hopeful opinion in European

capitals. There is neither evidence from candidates' declarations and the discourse of the American foreign policy community nor a persuasive counter-logic to conclude otherwise. The next president surely will be less impulsively unilateralist and more calculating as to the advantages of bringing along allies. The White House will still face a set of pressing issues—Palestine, Iran, and most certainly Iraq in one dire strait or another. Each will engage major American interests. Each will require decisive action. Each will incline the U.S. administration to keep its own counsel and to rely ultimately on its own judgment. One need only monitor the discourse within the American foreign policy community to appreciate how natural it is for Americans to place themselves in the position of command, figuratively and literally. The dialogue is punctuated with "they must" and "we should make clear to them." The "they" is everyone from close allies to enemies to all those implicated in the matter at hand. Advice and guidance from others, including European capitals, will not be actively sought.

The global loss of trust in the United States has exacerbated the Europeans' predicament. A less effective American foreign policy aggravates regional problems. A less credible United States whose ideals are eroded by egregious acts delegitimizes the West as a whole. Together, they raise the stakes on Europe filling the gap in both effectiveness and legitimacy. The former challenge is neither recognized nor engaged as Europeans suffer from the residual instincts of reliance on Washington and from their own self-doubts. The latter depends on meeting two preconditions: crystallizing a collective political identity commensurate with prevailing sentiment, and reconciling this identity with the hard choices imposed by an unruly world that does not necessarily yield to the enlightened thinking that is the identity's core.

Perhaps most debilitating is the sense that what Europe decides and does—or even does not do—cannot determine its future. That is because a willful America pronounces on the matters that count most, because Europe is unable to counteract or deflect America, and thus in some profound way because Europe is irrelevant to the great issues of the day. There could be no better example of a self-fulfilling, if silent, prophecy.

Notes

1. The arduousness of the transformation that led to the Europe enjoyed today can be easily forgotten. The distress of the postwar years is brought back

by Tony Judt, *Postwar: A History of Europe since 1945* (New York: Penguin, 2005).

2. Two noteworthy reflections on the European "difference" are offered by Tony Judt, "The Future of Decadent Europe," and Giles Andreani, "Decadent Europe Revisited," as part of the Brookings Institution's U.S.-Europe Analysis Series, February 2006.

3. The upswing in positive feelings toward Brussels was recorded in a series of Eurobarometer polls and other polls taken in the spring and summer of 2007. The Eurobarometer figures were presented in *The Letter* (Fondation Robert Schuman), May 22, 2007.

4. Max Weber, *Economy and Society*, vol. 1 (Berkeley: University of California Press, 1978).

5. There is an inherent paradox to the philosophy of reason and reasonableness that sustains the European enterprise. It traces back to Enlightenment thinking. As Pierre Hassner wrote, the apprehension that "the universal rule of reason which was supposed to lead to the liberation of man could lead to a new form of oppression" became dreaded reality in the twentieth century. "Either technical, instrumental rationality could become an instrument of power, hence of domination, or became the claim of rational universality could mean the repression of identities and differences." Pierre Hassner, "Who Killed Nuclear Enlightenment?" *International Affairs* 83, no. 3 (May 2007): 455–467. The European project admirably has laid those fears to rest among member countries. Their success owes to the stress on values of humanism to temper any inclination toward a system of technocratic dictatorship, the high importance accorded reciprocity at all levels, and—not least—the progressive dilution of sectarian identities that has made repression of other identities a moot question. The realization that this success is a function of the whole package coming together sharpens the sense that universality in theory does not mean ease of emulation—tutored or organic—in practice. The Balkan strife, followed by the dismal experiment in imposed democratization in the Middle East, has solidified those prudential instincts.

6. The concept of sociopolitical postmodernism has a number of progenitors; among them are Christopher Coker, "Post-Modernity and the End of the Cold War," *Review of International Studies* 18 (July 1992): 189–198; and Stephen Toulmin, *Cosmopolis: The Hidden Agenda of Modernity* (Chicago: University of Chicago Press, 1990). Robert Cooper first outlined his thinking in "The Postmodern State and the World Order," *New Perspectives Quarterly* 14, no. 4 (1996): 48–56.

7. I expand on these themes in *Toward a More Independent Europe* (Brussels: Egmont Institute, 2007).

8. What emanates from America intrinsically has great trend-setting potential for two reasons. One is America's reality-based image as the home
of the new and better. Another is the country's exceptional assets for dis-
seminating what it originates: CNN, Hollywood, the English language. This
is a theme of thoughtful continental commentary on the braided strands
of American influence on European thinking. See, e.g., Hubert Védrine,
France in an Age of Globalization (Washington, D.C.: Brookings Institution
Press, 2003). Also see Bertrand Badie, *L'impuissance de la puissance* (Paris:
Fayard, 2004). This phenomenon is much discussed in terms of American
"soft power," popularized by Joseph S. Nye, whose formulation is presented
fully in *Soft Power: The Means to Success in World Politics* (New York:
PublicAffairs, 2005). Moreover, in the realms of economics and management, American institutions, especially its universities, are uniquely able
to confer status. It works in two ways: American thinking and its expound-
ers are most likely to get an attentive, sympathetic hearing; and the status attached to American institutions can be transferred to foreigners—as
individuals or as an institution—who associate with it. To be a producer
of a scarce good (and status is indeed a scarce good) is to be in a position of
power.

9. Dana H. Allin and Steven Simon, "America's Predicament," *Survival* 46,
no. 4 (Winter 2004–2005): 7–30; the quotation is on page 25.

10. Robert Cooper, "Military Occupation Is Not the Road to Democracy,"
New Statesman, May 3, 2004, 25–27. An approach that unduly stresses the
"hardware" of democracy characterizes the report issued by a panel of American experts assembled by the Council on Foreign Relations, *In Support of Arab
Democracy: Why and How*, Independent Task Force Report 54, ed. Madeleine
K. Albright and Vin Weber (New York: Council on Foreign Relations, 2005).
Among its recommendations is the admonition that "to reduce the possibility
that Islamist movements will overwhelm more open Middle Eastern political
systems, Washington should promote constitutional arrangements that would
restrain the power of majorities to trample the rights of minorities" (p. 5). For
a reflective consideration of the complications encountered in the fostering
of democracy by outside parties, see Thomas Carothers, *Critical Mission. Essays on Democracy Promotion* (Washington, D.C.: Carnegie Endowment for
International Peace, 2004).

11. Reinhold Niebuhr, *The Irony of American History* (New York: Charles
Scribner's Sons, 1951), 79.

12. On this theme, see the insightful analysis by Jack Miles, "Religion and
American Foreign Policy," *Survival* 46, no. 1 (Spring 2004): 23–37. The moral
compass of postmodern Europe seems more aligned with the New Testament.
Conciliation, harmony, redemption, and an abhorrence of violence are hall-

marks of contemporary political culture across much of Europe. Hence, there was more empathy with, or at least tolerance of, Jimmy Carter's piety and Bill Clinton's ebullient Baptist faith than with the hard-edged evangelical faith of George W. Bush, which Europeans neither comprehend nor respect.

13. The United States' project in Iraq stunned them in its audacity as much as it sowed anxiety over its unwanted effects. Democracy transplanted as a paternalistic act of the West runs the risk of being rejected as something alien to the culture and mores of its recipient. The Iraqi enterprise produced more shock and awe, for these reasons, in Western Europe than it did among Iraqis accustomed to the Sturm und Drang of incessant war, bombast, and blood. American hubris, American conceit, American power, and America's unwavering faith in its good intentions have engendered a mix of reactions. Apprehension and estrangement predominate. More recently, they have been mingled with grudging respect for the United States' perseverance in encouraging Iraqi democracy and its blunt talk to Egyptian and Saudi leaders—the exact portions varying from country to country, government to government, intellectual elite to intellectual elite. There is now an apparent current of thinking that EU ideals and interests together dictate that Europe associate itself, somehow, with the American effort to encourage the opening and liberalization of Arab/Muslim societies. The coalescence of support for such a project, and a consensus on how to execute it, must overcome the ingrained skepticism that, in part, is the residue of the bruising transatlantic exchanges. The multiple, often contradictory images of the United States and its world role held by Europeans are assayed with subtle insight by François Heisbourg, "American Hegemony? Perceptions of the US Abroad," *Survival* 41, no. 4 (Winter 1999/2000): 5–19.

14. This is one theme developed by Timothy Garton Ash in his call for a reenergized, reoriented Euro-American partnership in *Free World: America, Europe, and the Surprising Future of the West* (New York: Random House, 2004), 222–223.

15. Not a single European leader has voiced public criticism of the strategy to undercut the legally elected Hamas government by all means available. The violent Fatah-Hamas confrontation in Gaza, won by Hamas, was met with sighs of satisfaction because it provided some kind of moral cover for a politically counterproductive policy. See "Solana évoque un lien possible entre l'Iran, Gaza et le Liban," *Le Monde*, July 2, 2007. The revealing response is summed up by Ismael Haniyeh, "L'aveuglement des Européens est décevant," *Le Monde*, July 12, 2007. The European Union did not improve its position as a possible mediator by having Javier Solana meet with Fatah leaders on the very day that President Mahmoud Abbas arbitrarily changed the rules for legislative elections in a blunt effort to disadvantage Hamas.

16. Irritation over Sarkozy's repeated upstaging of his European partners is especially sharp in Berlin. See "Sarkozy's Stolen Victories: France Goes It Alone," *International Spiegel*, July 31, 2007.

17. All public opinion surveys confirm this assertion. See, e.g., the Harris Survey conducted for the *Financial Times* in June 2007, "European See US as Threat to Peace," *Financial Times*, July 1, 2007. Also see "Transatlantic Trends, Key Findings 2007," which reports the results of an extensive opinion survey by the German Marshall Fund of the United States, September 2007. On Hamas and Palestine, the official position of the British government was picked apart in a scathing report by an all-party House of Commons foreign affairs select committee. Ben Hall and Daniel Dombley, "Hamas Boycott Criticized in UK," *Financial Times*, August 13, 2007. Colin Powell's strongly stated conviction that opening a dialogue with Hamas was crucial for progress on Palestine went entirely unremarked upon, if not unnoticed, in European policy circles.

18. Sarkozy has close family ties with the New York financial community; Brown has close professional and personal ties there.

19. Sarkozy gave a fuller statement of his perspective on the world with special reference to Franco-American ties in his address to assembled French ambassadors in Paris, August 22, 2007.

CHAPTER THREE

THE AGE OF POPULISM

Ivan Krastev

The "American moment" has come to an end. "American power is vast and may yet grow," wrote European political thinker Pierre Hassner, "but the legitimacy of that power is waning, and with it the authority of both America's world and its model."[1] A majority of the people in the world now reject not only American foreign policy but also the American model of democracy and even the American way of doing business.[2] More troubling yet, this rejection is not just about George W. Bush, and it is difficult to imagine how America's ideological predominance can be recovered in the next decade, regardless of who might occupy the White House in January 2009. Admittedly, the United States will continue to shape the world, but more by representing some of "the others" to a variety of opponents than by serving as a model for all.

The "postmodern moment" in Europe has also ended. Post–Cold War Europe is history, and the European project feels adrift. On the continent, "the sources of a free-floating neurosis are diversity (of immigrant religion and culture), disparities (of wealth and economic security), and dependency (for energy and security) on others."[3] The European Union is no longer either an uncontested hegemon in European politics or an irresistible pole of attraction for its neighbors. The promise of a European order where nations grow together or else disappear altogether, where ideological conflicts melt away, and where cultures intermingle through increasingly free commerce and communication has turned out to be a mirage. At Europe's periphery, Russia's "sovereign democracy" and Turkey's "Islamic democracy" stand as alternative models of governance.

The "democratic moment," too, has been transformed. The idea of popular sovereignty has shown an influence that is more universal than that of democracy. Even the most undemocratic modern regimes must claim legitimacy, not from divine right, dynastic succession, or right of conquest but from the will of the people, however expressed. More popular sovereignty does not necessarily mean more freedom, however. The world is seeing an emergence of popular governments that are antiliberal in their domestic politics and aggressive in their foreign policy.

These three simultaneous crises of America's global hegemony, of the postmodern European order, and of the rise of populism as an unintended consequence of the late-twentieth-century wave of democratization are the key features of a new strategic context. While the West has been preoccupied with threats generated by failed states and international terrorist networks, the resurgence of the nation-state as the main international actor has become the true defining feature of the early twenty-first century.

WHAT ABOUT NATO?

In the post–September 11, 2001, world, NATO is almost everywhere, and it is prepared to do almost anything anywhere: to fight global terrorism in Afghanistan, to prevent genocide in Darfur, to train security forces in Iraq, to accept new members in the Caucasus, to become a global alliance—and more. NATO is viewed as a guarantee against the rise of immature great powers, the spread of weapons of mass destruction, the competition for diminishing fossil fuels, and the democratization of destruction as ever smaller groups gain access to ever greater destructive power. The NATO fatigue that was a distinctive feature of the early 1990s, and the skepticism about NATO that was a trademark of neoconservative unilateralism, have turned into a newly born enthusiasm for NATO. Coming after the failure of the U.S. "coalition of the willing" in Iraq and Europe's growing frustration with the ineffectiveness of the United Nations, such a renewed interest in NATO should come as no surprise. In all but the most extreme cases, unilateralism has become a relic of the past. In all but the most trivial of cases, the United Nations is paralyzed. Early in the twenty-first century, it is widely agreed in the Western strategic community that NATO is the institution best able to deliver when it comes to effective multilateralism.

NATO might very well be the best instrument for solving world problems, but it is not without problems of its own. For much of this decade, public support for NATO and NATO-led operations has declined dramatically in a number of key member states. The transatlantic divide over the U.S. war in Iraq has not yet been overcome, and, more important, member states continue to lack a common understanding of the new geopolitical context, as well as a common vision of a preferred world order. The state of the strategic debate within NATO can best be described as asymmetrical denial. Both American and European policy elites live in such a state, and what most separates Europe and America is that the parts of reality they deny are different.

Washington seems ready to accept the "end of the liberal moment." Recent debates for and against "democracy promotion" indicate a change of heart in the American policy community—meaning a drift away from "transformative diplomacy."[4] What the United States is still reluctant to accept, however, is the end of the unipolar world and the decline of U.S. power. Many of the new realists prefer to believe instead that unipolarity is not ending but merely being transformed. Whichever may be the case, most would agree that the United States is not as powerful as neoconservatives had originally believed but is still more powerful than critics in Europe conceive it to be—in other words, not omnipotent but still preponderant. In Robert Kagan's seductive formulation, "A superpower can lose a war . . . without ceasing to be a superpower if the fundamental international conditions continue to support its predominance."[5] As a result, most would also agree that, based on U.S. military supremacy and the strength of the American economy, U.S. predominance can be preserved.

Enter NATO. From a U.S. viewpoint, the best way to preserve American dominance in the world, preventing global anarchy in the process, is to transform the U.S. hegemony into a Western hegemony, using a Global NATO as a key tool for reshaping the strategic environment. The ideas for a Global NATO that were tested at the Riga Summit in November 2006 illustrate the rise of this vision. Predictably, these ideas were not enthusiastically endorsed by the European allies; Europe's initial reaction was one of fear and apprehension, rather than excitement and optimism.

Although the European Union no longer dreams about acting as a counterweight, its relations with the United States in a unipolar world have remained ambiguous. On the one hand, the EU was the principal beneficiary of the American moment in international politics, which created a strategic context in which EU enlargement to Central and Eastern Europe was possible. On the other hand, the EU often found its preferences for multilateralism and the primacy of international law muted under an intimidating U.S. hegemony. Clearly, mixed sentiments are still present in Europe: Anti-Americanism remains a significant element in the West European political environment, and Central European societies are also growing more skeptical of the United States.

Most Europeans would agree that the American unipolar moment is over but at the same time argue that the liberal moment is still alive. European publics continue to believe that the pressures of globalization will eventually bring about the transformation of modern societies and states into postmodern societies and states. However, there is also a substantial risk that the multipolar world of the twenty-first century will come to resemble the dangerous nineteenth-century world of power politics. In any case, it is likely that "the leaders of a post-American world will not meet in Brussels but in Beijing, Moscow, and Washington."[6] What many European policymakers prefer to ignore is that the EU's dominance in Europe is challenged by both Russia's project of "sovereign democracy" and the emergence of Turkey as a more democratic, but at the same time very traditional, nation-state that resists the charms of European postmodernity. Enter NATO, again. Europe needs NATO for the preservation of its "postmodern moment" at a time when the EU's soft power is in crisis and its process of enlargement is on hold.

POST-SOVIET RUSSIA VERSUS POSTMODERN EUROPE

Post–Cold War Europe is history. Russia has reemerged as a great revisionist power. Questions surround this reemergence. How serious is the Russian challenge? Is Russia a rising power or a declining power enjoying a temporary comeback? Is Russia a neo-imperial power aiming to dominate its weaker neighbors or a postimperial state trying to defend its legitimate interests? Does Moscow view the EU as a strategic partner or as a threat to its ambitions in Europe? How stable is Vladimir Putin's regime and what are the Kremlin's long-term interests and short-term fears?

Putin's Russia frightens the West because the West does not understand it. Russia is simultaneously a rising global power and a weak state that corrupt and inefficient institutions are weakening even further. Because Russia is more democratic but less predictable and less reliable than the Soviet Union, it is both rock solid and extremely vulnerable. To be sure, the country's economic growth has been impressive, but it is not sustainable. As to its foreign policy, it is a puzzle. The more capitalist and Westernized Russia becomes, the more anti-Western its policies seem to be.

Soaring oil and gas prices have made Russia more powerful, less cooperative, and more arrogant. Oil money dramatically boosted state finances, thereby decreasing dependence on foreign funding. With the third-largest hard currency reserve in the world, Russia is running a huge current account surplus and paying off the last of the debts it accumulated in the early 1990s. Russia's former reliance on Western credits has come full circle, as Europe now relies on Russian energy resources. Russia's military budget has increased sixfold since the beginning of the century, and Russia's intelligence network has penetrated all of Europe. Moscow has succeeded in regaining effective control over the entire territory of the Russian Federation. At least for now, Chechnya is pacified and public opinion polls show levels of support for President Putin that exceed 80 percent of all Russian citizens.

Russia's influence in global politics has also dramatically increased. Russia has succeeded in regaining the strategic initiative in Central Asia, where Putin invested much personal energy and political skill in making the Shanghai Cooperation Organization a more credible counterbalance to Western hegemony in the region. In mid-2007, the UN deadlock on the status of Kosovo was an especially vivid demonstration of the new reality—that Russia can no longer be ignored. In short, Russia is a rising power that no longer wishes to be lectured to but instead wants to deliver the lectures itself. "What to do with Russia?" is no longer an issue of concern, as it was for much of the 1990s; what is asked more pressingly is "What to do about Russia?"

Yet, Russia remains a highly vulnerable power. Its economic growth is largely the outcome of rising energy prices—energy exports fund about 30 percent of the Kremlin's budget—while levels of technological modernization remain comparatively low across the board. Russia is run as a classic oil regime, rife with corruption and inefficiency. Underinvestments in the development of new oil and gas fields diminish the chance that energy exports will increase in the future, and they also signal the likelihood of future shortages on the domestic market. Standards of living have increased, but Russia remains a poor country compared with the West. Social inequality is skyrocketing, and the quality of education continues to deteriorate. No Russian university ranks among the leading 50 universities in the world. Alcoholism and a collapsing health system are fueling a demographic catastrophe: The population has been shrinking by 700,000 annually for the past eight years, even though the country's HIV/AIDS epidemic has not yet peaked. Male life expectancy is among the lowest in the world. Regardless of its recent foreign policy initiatives, Russia remains quite isolated in the world. Over the long term, the rise of China and India is more of a threat than a benefit to Russia. Moreover, Russia is also extremely vulnerable to the rise of radical Islam. As global polls indicate, Russia's influence has not recovered since the collapse of the Soviet Union, and though Russia is back on the central stage in Europe, European public opinion has become increasingly skeptical and even hostile to Russian policies and to President Putin and his regime.[7] In short, Russia is a declining power whose resurgent assertiveness rests on a crumbling foundation.

The nature of the Kremlin's regime also remains a puzzle. Putin's Russia is not a pedestrian authoritarian state. It is not a "Soviet Union lite," notwithstanding a national anthem that is the same as the old Soviet one. Nor is Russia a transition democracy. The Kremlin does not think in terms of the rights of individual citizens but of the needs of the population as a whole. This concept of "population" is a contrast to both to the notion of "rights" that is at the core of liberal democracy and the idea of "the people" that is at the core of nationalist programs. In Putin's Russia, the rights of the citizen-voter give way to the rights of the consumer, the tourist, and the figures of authority and wealth.

"Russia," writes Dmitri Trenin, "is reminiscent of Germany in the 1920s, with its vibrancy and intense feeling of unfair treatment by others; France in the 1940s, when it was trying to heal its traumas; or Italy in the 1960s, as far as the nexus of power, money, and crime is concerned."[8] Indeed, Russia is reminiscent of very old Europe. It features nostalgia for the old European nation-state and for a European order organized around a balance of power and the principle of non-interference in the domestic affairs of other states. Russia's view of the European order is a mixture of nostalgia for the time of the "concert of Europe" and envy of present-day China, which manages to balance openness to the West with rejection of Western interference in its domestic politics. For the Kremlin, the end of the Cold War meant a return to the pre–Cold War European order. For Western Europe, the end of the Cold War meant the rise of the postmodern European state. The EU dreams about cosmopolitan democracy, while Russia longs for the Congress of Vienna.

"What came to an end in 1989," wrote Robert Cooper, summarizing Europe's consensus, "was not just the Cold War or even . . . the Second World War. . . . What came to an end in Europe (but perhaps only in Europe) were the political systems of three centuries: the balance of power and the imperial urge."[9] The European policy elite assumed that the end of the Cold War meant the emergence of a new European order. The key elements of this postmodern European order are a highly developed system of mutual interference in each other's domestic affairs and security based on openness and transparency. The postmodern system does not rely on balance of power; nor does it emphasize sovereignty or the separation of domestic and foreign affairs. It rejects the use of force as an instrument for settling conflicts and deliberately promotes increases in mutual dependence and vulnerability between European states.

In the 1990s, Russia was not a postmodern state but was part of this new European order. The Treaty on Conventional Forces in Europe and the activities of the Organization for Security and Cooperation in Europe (based on intrusive inspections and active monitoring) were the West's major instruments for integrating Russia into the postmodern system. Russia's acceptance of these instruments made it appear to be a modern state that had accepted the postmodern imperatives of openness and interdependency. Russia's weakness created the illusion that Moscow had ideologically subscribed to this system—but the reality turned out to be very different. At the first opportunity, Russia chose to build its statehood according to European practices and ideologies of the nineteenth century, rather than the twenty-first.

The contrasting nature of political elites in Russia and Europe today is one more reason for concern over the future of the relationship. Unlike the late Soviet elites, who were bureaucratic, risk-averse, and even competent when it came to international relations and security policies, the new Russian elite consists of the winners of the zero-sum games of the transition. They are highly self-confident, risk prone, and immensely wealthy. Europe does not know how to deal with these people. European political elites that made their careers practicing compromise and avoiding conflicts are facing elites that are proud of not taking hostages. It is not an accident that the Russian word for top advisers, "siloviki," like the words "sputnik" and "perestroika," is one of the few Russian words that no longer requires translation in any European language.

The real source of an emerging confrontation between Russia and the EU is not competing interests or values. It is political incompatibility. Russia's challenge to the EU cannot be reduced to the issue of energy dependency and Moscow's ambition to dominate a "near abroad" that also happens to be the EU's "new neighborhood." At the heart of the current crisis is not a clash between democracy and authoritarianism; history demonstrates that democratic and authoritarian states can easily cooperate. Rather, at the heart of the crisis is the clash between the postmodern state, embodied by the EU, and the traditional modern state, embodied by Russia. In this context, the confrontation between Russia and the EU is very different from that between Russia and the United States. To survive, the EU needs its own Russia policies, which cannot simply be an extension of the U.S. policy toward Russia, whatever it is or might become. At the same time, the EU needs NATO (meaning the United States) to compensate for its relative military weaknesses relative to Russia.

THE POPULIST CHALLENGE

The transformation of the "democratic moment" has also received too little notice. The Western policy community, obsessed with threats emanating from failed states and transnational terrorist networks, has failed to recognize the complex nature of the global wave of democratization that started after the end of the Cold War and has underestimated its impact on the security dilemmas faced by both Europe and the United States. NATO has neglected security threats stemming from the democratization of major parts of the world, and from the transformation of democratic regimes among the Alliance's own member states. The world has entered the age of the populist revolutions. As observed by Zbigniew Brzezinski,

What is distinctive about our time is that the United Sates and Europe, the most advanced part of the world, face a massive and unprecedented global awakening, . . . what French society as a whole experienced during the French revolution—a sudden stirring of political awareness, unleashed passions, fermenting excitement, and escalating aspiration. Today, that sense of revolution is the political reality worldwide and it is altogether new, though it has been developing over a number of decades. . . . Through the world, we see similar trends in the rise of radical populism, which carries with it the potential for political extremism. This radical populism organized through the Internet and fueled by the images of human inequality that are disseminated globally by the electronic media, is also stimulated by the new political reality.[10]

Many of today's threats are associated with the global process of democratization and its concomitant effect of creating multiple, overlapping interdependencies. The current wave of democratization is fundamentally different from the previous three waves analyzed by Samuel Huntington and others because, among other factors, there is no longer any legitimate ideological alternative to democracy and the spread of market economics.[11] Yet, the failures of decolonization have resulted in a proliferation of weak or failed states.

The politicization of cultural and religious identities, much more than the rise of religiosity, is a distinctive feature of the new populist condition. The clash between the principles of democratic majoritarianism and liberal constitutionalism characterizes this new wave of democratization, which in many parts of the world has taken the form of populist revolution. The age of populism is also the age of global comparison and global media networks. People compare their standard of living with that of the most developed countries. The information revolution has profoundly changed the media environment, and the terms of national debates are no longer exclusively determined by nation-states. Even more important, the populist revolution is also taking place in countries that are considered part of the West. The rise of populist leaders such as Pim Fortuyn in the Netherlands, the victory of the "No Vote" in the referenda on the EU Constitution in France and the Netherlands, and populist governments in Poland and Slovakia are all developments signaling that the new political reality can have a grave security impact.

The Western policy community is at a loss about how to deal with the rise of populism. The populist revolution weakens key institutions of liberal democracy, such as the independent judiciary, central banks, and the independent media. Populist leaders gain the support of the people on the back of their mistrust for political elites. During the Cold War, foreign policy and security issues were effectively excluded from the domain of electoral politics due to the nature of the security threat. The failure of the popular and strong Italian Communist Party to enter government during the entire Cold War period is a strong illustration of the strength of Cold War constraints on Western European democratic politics. In the post–Cold War reality in Europe, in which economic and many other policy decisions are taken out of the domain of electoral politics—as many key decisions are made in Brussels—foreign and security policy has once again come center stage. The fall of the government of José-Maria Aznar in Spain, in the immediate aftermath of the Madrid bombings in March 2004, is a demonstration that elections can be won by foreign policy-minded majorities. It is not possible to understand the nature of global threats, therefore, if we fail to understand the nature of the populist revolution.

In 2006, the worldwide survey conducted by Gallup International captured the radical nature of the new populist situation.[12] Though 79 percent of all respondents around the world were said to accept democracy as the best form of government, 48 percent of those same respondents also claimed that elections in their countries are neither free nor fair—with only 30 percent in agreement that their countries are governed by the will of the people. Democratic disappointment is particularly strong in Western Europe, where a majority of respondents agreed that while elections are free and fair, the will of the people is neglected. This is a historical impasse: Millions of people are brought into democratic politics, but the newly born democratic institutions quite often fail to meet voters' expectations. The popular will has become the only legitimate source of power, but worldwide acceptance of democracy is accompanied by declining trust in the institutions of representative democracy in the West and the rise of populist leaders in the rest.

The rise of the political Islam that is intensively discussed is just one of the manifestations of the new populist revolution. The complexity of the populist phenomenon is linked to the fact that populism is difficult to define and generalize. It is antiliberal but not antidemocratic. It can come from the left, as is the case in Latin America, or from the right, as is the case in Europe. The distinctive feature of populism is the perception of politics as a clash between elites and the people. Populists oppose not only ruling elites, but also the political and security related consensuses they represent. Populism expresses itself in the form of direct and unmediated relationships between elites and the people. It favors instruments of direct democracy, such as referenda, and manifests itself in rebellion of the represented against those who claim to represent them. In the West, the rise of populism reflects the new relationship between elites and publics. It marks a loss of elites' grasp on power. At the same time, post–Cold War Western European democracies suffer from a decline in ideological politics, a crisis of mass political parties, and the emergence of a freer and much more provocative media.

Central Europe is a prime example of the new populist condition. Populism and illiberalism are tearing the region apart. Hungary is in a state of "cold civil war" between a manipulative postcommunist government (one that admitted to lying "morning, noon, and night") and the populist anticommunist opposition that keeps its doors open to the extreme Right. The Slovak government is a strange coalition of Robert Fico's soft populists, Jan Slota's hard nationalists, and Vladimir Meciar's Meciarists—an unimpressive mixture of nationalism, provincialism, and welfarism. In the Czech Republic, there is no major problem with the government—the "problem" instead is that for almost eight months in 2006–2007 political parties in the country failed to form a government. In Romania, the president and the majority in Parliament wage an open political war, with secret police files from the communist era and files on corruption from the postcommunist era as weapons of choice. In Bulgaria, extreme nationalism is surging, and the mainstream parties and governmental institutions seek to accommodate it rather than fighting it.

But it is in Poland that is situated the capital of illiberalism in Central Europe. From 2005 to 2007, Poland was ruled by a coalition of three parties: the post-Solidarity revanchists of the Law and Justice Party, the postcommunist provincial troublemakers of the Self-Defense Party, and the heirs of pre–World War II chauvinist, xenophobic, and anti-Semitic groups that form the League of Polish Families. With Poland more divided than ever, the quality of its public debate was embarrassing. Parallels between such political turmoil in Central Europe and the crisis of democracy in interwar Europe are irresistible, including the growing tensions between democracy and liberalism, the rise of "organized intolerance," public demands for direct democracy, and the proliferation of charismatic leaders capable of mobilizing public anger.

However tempting such analogies may be, they are exaggerated. In present-day Central Europe, unlike Europe in the 1930s, there is no ideological alternative to democracy. The economies of the countries in the region are not stagnating—they are booming. Standards of living are rising and the unemployment is declining. The membership of Central European countries in the EU and NATO acts as a safeguard to democracy and liberal institutions. More than 15 years after the collapse of communism, and a few years after gaining institutional membership in the West, the streets of Budapest and Warsaw are flooded not by ruthless paramilitary formations in a search of a "final solution" but by restless consumers in search of a good sale. What is witnessed in the region is a populist rhetoric without any, or at least without many, populist policies, especially when it comes to the economy. Regardless of the fact that populist leaders blame neoliberal policies for the suffering of the people, they are not eager to change these policies. For the moment at least, the economic policies of Poland's or Slovakia's populist governments did not and do not, respectively, differ substantially from their liberal predecessors' policies. In short, Central Europe is not back in the 1930s. But does this mean that the populist epidemics in NATO's new members lack security implications?

THE NEGLECTED THREAT

The rise of populism has been neglected by security analysts and military planners. Populism was initially viewed as a transitional phenomenon that lacks security implications. But, in the view of this author, it is exactly the rise of populism in different parts of the world that should be at the top of the agenda of the Western strategic community. In the words of the American strategist Steve Ropp, "The potential rise of populism . . . should not be viewed by policy planners as posing just another specific type of security threat. For unlike the traditional, irregular, catastrophic, or disruptive ones normally considered in the future scenarios, populism poses a potential challenge to the underlying political substructure that has given us the collective material capability and moral legitimacy to deal with all these threats."[13]

The rise of populism also presents a major conceptual challenge to the democratic peace theory that was the ideological framework behind NATO's strategy in the 1990s. As demonstrated on the basis of rigorous statistical analysis by two outstanding scholars of international relations, Edward Mansfield and Jack Snyder, since 1815 democratizing states have been more prone to start wars than either established democracies or authoritarian regimes.[14] In other words, whereas democratic peace theory is correct when claiming that liberal democracies do not fight one another, it is also equally true that populist democracies (electoral democracies with weak or broken constitutional constraints) are more prone to start a war than any other regime.

The rise of populism both inside and outside the West will have, and has already had, a profound impact on the security dilemmas that NATO faces. The rise of populism and the emergence of populist governments among NATO member states can block the decisionmaking process in the Alliance, thus making it a useless instrument. The withdrawal of Italian and Spanish troops from Iraq after changes of government in those countries indicates the new strategic uncertainty. The decision of those governments marked a break with Cold War democratic politics that kept security issues, and particularly NATO, outside electoral politics. Imagine, at some NATO Summit, the French delegation led by Jean Marie Le Pen, the Polish delegation led by Andrzej Lepper, and the Bulgarian delegation led by Volen Siderov—all extreme anti-NATO nationalists who reached the second round of their respective presidential elections just a month ago. In Europe, it is no longer possible to take for granted the democratic foundations that the old Cold War environment guaranteed. Key foreign policy decisions in the future will possibly be made via referenda dominated by violent nationalists or diehard pacifists rather by political elites behind closed doors.

Forces for change are afoot that render assumptions about constancy null and void. In the new populist context, elites and foreign policy experts are losing their grasp on the making of foreign policy in the NATO member states, and public opinion is more able to directly determine its conduct. The decision of the French Parliament that further enlargements of the EU should be decided by popular referenda is a clear illustration of this new trend. The result will be that foreign policy will move away from pragmatic centrism. The rise of instant and constant media with large blocks of time and space to fill, in combination with the seductive power of "Big Ideas" and conspiracy theories, contributes to the populist turn.[15] The principal beneficiary of the populist shift in foreign policy decisionmaking in some of the NATO member states are nationalists and isolationists, two groups that can mobilize emotions in public opinion. What can be expected is a higher degree of unpredictability in the foreign policies of the member states, including a unilateral use of vetoes on critical Alliance missions. A dysfunctional NATO could result from the rise of populism in the member states. The rise of populism in the member states will also profoundly affect the attractiveness of the Alliance, wearing away its status as a "club" that many want to join.

The rise of populism outside NATO's member states also presents a threat in at least six respects. In the first place, in future interventions in many parts of the world where there is populist mobilization, NATO forces will face increasing difficulties controlling the situation on the ground and reaching lasting deals with local forces. This will increase the likelihood of civil wars. The war in Iraq confirmed Raymond Aron's earlier observation that "permanent insecurity represents the victory of the rebels over the pacifying forces. . . . The rebels win if they manage to survive. The pacifying forces lose unless they gain complete victory."[16] Second, the rise of populism and populist governments will increase the likelihood of the nationalization of natural resources and will intensify resource wars. Hugo Chávez's Venezuela is an illustration of this tendency. Third, the rise of populism is accompanied and strengthened by the rise of nuclear nationalism. An unintended consequence of a decade of humanitarian wars in the 1990s was the urge for nuclear weapons. What can be observed today is the coupling of the classical idea of sovereignty with the idea of possessing nuclear weapons. This is pushing the world into an age of nuclear sovereignty.

Fourth, the uncertainty provoked by the behavior of NATO's populist allies in different parts of the world is another negative impact of the rise of populism. The ongoing conflict between Georgia and Russia is a case in point. NATO cannot ignore the legitimate security concerns of the Georgian government and withdraw its support from Georgia without inviting a crisis of confidence and losing its geopolitical standing in the Caucasus. Any distancing of NATO from Georgia would play into the hands of Moscow's hegemonic aspirations for its postcolonial presence in the post-Soviet space. At the same time, NATO's strategic relationship with Russia cannot be held hostage to the populism of the

government in Tbilisi. Fifth, the rise of anti-Americanism as one of
the political manifestations of the global populist revolution presents a
further dilemma in the global security equation. Anti-Americanism is
a complex and contextual phenomenon for which attempts at general-
ization can be counterproductive. At the same time, it is not possible to
remain blind to the fact that the global rise of anti-Americanism is one
of the by-products of the global populist revolution. In security terms,
the presence of widespread and politicized anti-American sentiments
will dramatically increase the costs of U.S. involvement in many parts
of the world (consider Latin America and the Middle East) and at the
same time will create incentives for Europeans to minimize their involvement in U.S.-led operations. Sixth and finally, the emergence of
anti-Western populist alliances is a significant threat. The recent alliance between Tehran, Caracas, and Damascus portends the likely
emergence of more such alliances. These are not the antihegemonic
alliances predicted by the realists but alliances rooted in the political
mobilization of popular emotions. Chávez's cooperation with Tehran
does not increase Venezuela's security. It increases the global popular-
ity of the self-proclaimed leader of the Bolivarian revolution.

What is striking in the new political environment are the threatening similarities among the three discourses that shape global politics
today: anticorruption, antiterrorism, and anti-Americanism. All three
are "empty boxes," easily filled with vague anxieties and cynically designed political strategies; each is a response to the growing gap between elites and publics; and each is symptomatic of a political world
where democracy has no ideological alternative but where many are
nonetheless disillusioned with what democracy is capable of delivering. All three are manifestations of the fate of politics in the age of
populism.

Western liberal democracy adopted a high profile in promoting
an anticorruption agenda, trying to channel anti-elite sentiments for
the purpose of supporting democracy and open markets. The United
States tried to convince people that their corrupt governments are the
problem; but forced by the global "war on terror," Washington allowed
discredited but useful governments to label their domestic opponents
as terrorists and to curb civil rights, in return for their support. In the
case of anti-Americanism, threatened local elites attempt to gain legitimacy by convincing frustrated publics that the United States is the
root cause of everything that is going wrong in their own countries and

in the world. The clash of these three discourses is at the heart of the populist condition.

The death of grand ideological narratives and the predominance of Third Way centrism profoundly transformed modern democratic politics. Elections lost their former role of presenting a grand choice between worldviews—more and more are taking the form of "ritual killings of governments in power." The new populist majorities perceive elections not as an opportunity to choose between policy options but as a revolt against privileged minorities. In this context, populism is not characteristic of certain political parties but the new condition of political life in many parts of the world.

CONCLUSIONS

NATO won the Cold War. NATO reshaped post–Cold War Europe. At the beginning of the twenty-first century, in the eyes of the Western strategic community, NATO is the institution that most closely embodies effective multilateralism. Based on the notion that "NATO, almost alone among the alphabet soup of multilateral organizations, actually has a track record of working,"[17] the hope with regard to the new global threats to the world order is that "as the world's premier multinational military organization, comprising many prosperous nations with a vested interest in maintaining global stability, NATO is uniquely suited to meeting such demands."[18] The refrain that "all we need is NATO . . ." is the newest mantra in the Western strategic community. But can NATO meet all these expectations?

In a strategic context characterized by the simultaneous crises of America's global hegemony, of the postmodern European order, and of the rise of populism as the unintended consequence of the wave of democratization at the end of the twentieth century, the fate of NATO can be questioned. In its search for relevance, NATO faces three major challenges. First, NATO member states should agree on a common understanding of the new strategic context in which their Alliance will operate. Second, NATO as an institution should regain the support of public opinion in the member states and should adapt to the profound changes in the process of democratic decisionmaking that are under way in the member states. And, third, NATO should reform itself to prevent dysfunction in the decisionmaking process resulting from the emergence of populist governments within the Alliance.

In mid-2007, public opinion polls suggest that support for NATO and NATO-led operations have dramatically decreased in some key member states—old and new members alike. The case of Turkey is particularly alarming. Turkish society over the last five years has become the most anti-American public in the world.[19] There is a growing risk of one or a few member states vetoing some of the ongoing operations of the Alliance. A transatlantic crisis over the installation of elements of an American antimissile defense shield in Poland and the Czech Republic can hardly be ruled out. The cost of using a veto in NATO has been significantly reduced with the end of the Cold War. The specter of referenda on foreign policy issues haunts European policy elites.

The only way out of this strategic and institutional impasse is policy thinking that is outside the current paradigm. The shift in strategic context urges policymakers to reconsider the usefulness of some of the options for NATO's future. More specifically, the reorganization of NATO into a two-pillar alliance—a coalition between the EU and the United States instead of an Alliance of 26 member states standing aloof from a Union of 27 states—is an idea whose time has come.

The growing danger posed by the rise of populism in security decisionmaking should be an incentive to reassess the attractiveness of this previously feared option. The cost for a single country to block common decisions is higher for the member states of the EU than for those of NATO. The EU Lisbon Treaty signed in late 2007 may make that cost even higher. A two-pillar alliance will promote the EU's foreign policy and defense identity, which is critical for effective responses to the challenges of Russia. NATO as a two-pillar alliance will increase the attractiveness of EU membership for Turkey.

Redefining NATO as a partnership between the United States and the EU, plus those NATO countries that are not EU members as well as those EU countries that are not NATO members, would reconcile the United States' urgent need to redirect the Alliance from Europe to the rest of the world and the EU's urgent need to preserve its postmodern hegemony on the old continent. In Europe there is only one player with the capacity and the interest to be a global player: the European Union.

To conclude, the age of the populist revolutions has begun, and it is not possible to understand the nature of the global threat if we fail to understand the nature of these revolutions. NATO has neglected the security risks emanating from the transformation of democratic regimes within the Alliance's own member states. During the Cold War, foreign policy and security issues were de facto excluded from the domain of electoral politics due to the nature of the security threat. Now these issues are at the center of electoral politics in both the old and new democracies of Europe. The only way for NATO to go global without becoming the victim of a populist backlash in its member states is by transforming itself into a two-pillar alliance.

Notes

1. Pierre Hassner, "The Fate of a Century," *The American Interest* 3, no. 2 (July–August 2007): 36.

2. Pew Global Attitudes Project, "Global Unease with Major World Powers," June 27, 2007.

3. This is a quotation from chapter 2 in this volume by Michael Brenner.

4. See, e.g., "Symposium: Debating Democracy," *The National Interest,* no. 90 (July/August 2007): 8–13.

5. Robert Kagan, "End of Dreams, Return of History," *Policy Review* 144 (August–September 2007): 24. For an opposite view, see chapter 1 in this volume by Simon Serfaty.

6. Kagan, "End of Dreams," 24.

7. Pew Global Attitudes Project, "Global Unease."

8. Dmitri Trenin, "Russia Redefines Itself and Relations with the West," *Washington Quarterly* 30, no. 2 (Spring 2007): 103.

9. Robert Cooper, *The Breaking of Nations: Order and Chaos in the Twenty-First Century* (London: Atlantic Books, 2003), 16.

10. Zbigniew Brzezinski, Christopher J. Makins Lecture, May 31, 2006, given at the British Ambassador's Residence in Washington; http://www.acus.org/docs/060531-CJM_Lecture_Brzezinski.pdf.

11. Samuel P. Huntington, *The Third Wave: Democratization in the Late Twentieth Century* (Norman: University of Oklahoma Press, 1991).

12. Gallup International Association, "Voice of the People 2006: What the World Thinks on Today's Global Issues," March 2006.

13. Steve C. Ropp, *The Strategic Implications of the Rise of Populism in Europe and South America* (Carlisle, Pa.: Strategic Studies Institute of the U.S. Army War College, 2005), v.

14. Edward Mansfield and Jack Snyder, Electing to Fight: *Why Emerging Democracies Go to War* (Cambridge, Mass.: MIT Press, 2005).

15. Stephen Halper and Jonathan Clarke, *The Silence of the Rational Center* (New York: Basic Books, 2007), 73–87.

16. Raymond Aron, *The Dawn of Universal History: Selected Essays from a Witness to the Twentieth Century* (New York: Basic Books, 2002), 33.

17. John C. Hulsman, "The Future of NATO," in Issues 2006 (Washington, D.C.: Heritage Foundation, 2006); and John C. Hulsman, *The Candidate's Briefing Book* (Washington, D.C.: Heritage Foundation, 2006), 155.

18. Ivo Daalder and James Goldgeier, "Global NATO," *Foreign Affairs* 85, no. 5 (September–October 2006): 105.

19. More than four out of five (83 percent) of Turks hold an unfavorable view of the United States—the second highest percentage after the Palestinians among the 47 nations polled, and a dramatic increase since 2002 (54 percent). Pew Global Attitudes Project, "Global Unease."

PART THREE

The State of the Union

CHAPTER FOUR

THE EU AS A SUPRANATIONAL REGIONAL STATE

RETHINKING WHAT THE EU IS
AND WHERE IT IS GOING

Vivien A. Schmidt

During the past few years, the European Union has been going through a major institutional crisis, linked to the failure of
the Constitutional Treaty. A new treaty may well resolve the
immediate cause of the crisis, but the underlying sources of the crisis
remain. The EU has had a tremendous impact on its member states'
national democracies. Although the "democratic deficit" has long been
seen to be a problem at the EU level, the real problem is at the national
level. This is because national leaders and publics have yet to come to
terms with the institutional impact of the EU on the traditional workings of their national democracies, in particular with regard to representative politics.

In the process of European integration, the EU has served to alter
not only national policies but also national polities, as the locus of
governmental power and authority has shifted upward to the EU, as
the focus of interest access and influence has moved from national
capitals to Brussels, and as national partisan politics have been marginalized by the EU's interest-based politics. But although the EU's very
institutional presence has greatly affected national governance practices, such effects are not the source of a national democratic deficit
per se. After all, European integration has served to promote member
states' democratic purposes in a host of ways, primarily by enabling
them to achieve collectively what would be harder to attain individually in regional peace, economic prosperity, and world power. And it
provides for citizen voice, access, and influence through a number of
different avenues.

The real problem results not so much from the new Europeanized governance practices as from how these practices clash with old ideas about national democracy in the absence of a new legitimizing discourse about European integration, let alone new mechanisms for citizen participation. National leaders continue to project traditional visions of national democracy as if nothing has changed, even though everything has changed; worse, they engage in blame shifting or credit taking on the EU-related policy issues while remaining silent on the EU-related polity issues except at defining moments, when it may be too late—as in the cases of the referenda on the Constitutional Treaty in France and the Netherlands in mid-2005. Most important, all this contributes to the current crisis of national politics, which is where the democratic deficit related to the EU has its most serious effects.

In what follows, I first ask: What is the EU? This is necessary because, without knowing what the EU is, we cannot fully understand its effects on its member states. As will be seen, the EU is characterized not as a future nation-state but as a supranational *regional state* that differs from the democratic nation-state in terms of sovereignty, boundaries, identity, economy, and governance, and in which democracy is based on a different balance of legitimizing mechanisms. I then go on to focus on the EU's impact on national politics, in particular with regard to how the EU's *policy without politics* makes for national *politics without policy*. The chapter concludes by considering the question: Can the democratic deficit be resolved?

THE EU: DEMOCRATIC LEGITIMACY IN A REGIONAL STATE?

To understand the impact of the EU on national politics, we first need to know what the EU is. The EU bears little resemblance to the nation-state. It has for a long time been described as sui generis. But, more recently, it has been portrayed as a "neomedieval empire," which nicely evokes the indeterminateness of the EU's borders but does not do justice to its formalized internal governance system. And it has been portrayed as a future republic or a future superstate, both of which are admirable projections of possible futures but do not sufficiently reflect the present.[1] By contrast, I see the Union as a "regional state," characterized by shared sovereignty, variable boundaries, a composite identity, a highly differentiated economy, compound governance, and fragmented democracy.[2] The EU's characteristics as a regional state not only make it very different from any nation-state; it also creates difficulties for its member states, particularly in its impact on representative democracy.

Sovereignty, Boundaries, Identity

As a regional state, the EU is characterized by shared or "pooled" sovereignty, which is linked not only to recognition from the outside (as with all nation-states) but also to acceptance from the inside, from its member states, policy area by policy area.[3] First, though the internal building of EU sovereignty began with the end to tariff barriers and took great leaps forward with the single market and the single currency, the EU's external recognition as a sovereign region is already evident in international trade, competition policy, and the euro zone but certainly not, as yet, in security and defense or in foreign policy. It is important, however, that even these areas have been Europeanizing, despite the fact that they represent some of the last vestiges of nation-state sovereignty for member state leaders, and disagreements do flare up from time to time—most notably in the case of the Iraq war. Interestingly, national publics have consistently been most in favor of Europeanization in these very areas (as shown in Eurobarometer surveys year after year). Public support of EU common defense and security policy, for example, fluctuated between 68 and 79 percent in the EU-15 between 1992 and 2005, for an average of 73.4 percent.[4]

Second, the EU has variable boundaries not only in territory but also in policies. Where the EU's territorial *finalité* will be is not known: Will it stop at the Balkans, Ukraine, Georgia, Turkey—or even the United States, 50 years hence (although, of course, only if it abandons capital punishment)? But the EU's policies other than those related to the single market also have highly variable geometry: Schengen borders do not encompass the United Kingdom and Ireland but include nonmembers like Iceland, Norway, and most recently Switzerland. Denmark is not a member of the European Security and Defense Policy, but all members can opt in or out of missions. The euro zone encompasses only 15 of the EU-27, with some member states semipermanent outsiders because of official opt-outs (namely, the United Kingdom and Denmark) and others only temporary outsiders (the new member states).[5] Even more significantly for the nation-state integrity of the EU's member states, European integration has led to a "process of nation state boundary transcendence, resulting in a process of de-differentiation of European polities" after a history of five centuries of progressive differentiation into nation-states.[6] This also applies to the very boundaries of the welfare state, despite the clear lack of EU jurisdiction in this area.[7]

This variability in policy boundaries, which will only increase as the EU grows wider through future enlargements and deeper through future policy developments, has two potential benefits. These will be operative, however, only if the future is conceptualized with the EU as regional state (rather than future nation-state) in mind, and only if a greater variation in potential institutional arrangements is accepted within the EU as well as with bordering countries. Within the EU, such institutional arrangements could encompass "structured" or "enhanced" cooperation—already written into the Nice and Constitutional treaties—or even "core groups" that would engage deeper integration in particular policy areas for member states that need and/or desire an "ever closer union"—say, in macroeconomic policy for the countries in the euro zone, in security policy for the bigger military players, and even in pensions policy for similar kinds of welfare states. With bordering countries, policy boundary variability could facilitate the membership process at a time when this is politically difficult, because the issue of membership would no longer be an immediate matter of "in" or "out" but would become a longer-term question of "in which areas" or "out of which areas." This would enable countries like Turkey in particular to become a part of the EU slowly but surely, policy area by policy area, avoiding the "big bang" of membership in 10, 15, or 20 years—by which time Turkey could be seen as a perfectly acceptable partner even to Austria. Failing this, over the next decade or so, Turkey will likely have become completely turned off by an accession process that involves an ever-growing number of *acquis communautaires* negotiated without them in the EU, even if Turkey were not in the end turned down.

Third, the EU's identity is composite, with its citizens maintaining a stronger identification and sense of belonging within the member states than with the EU. Eurobarometer polls have shown time and again, however, that although European citizens' primary sense of identity is centered in their own member state, close to a majority have a composite European identity, with the European second to the national. But although the EU's *being* is therefore quite weak compared with the national level, its *doing* is strong, given how much member states have engaged in building the EU through policymaking in an ever-increasing number of domains.[8] Political community, after all, need not be based primarily on ethnocultural identity but rather on "the practices of citizens who exercise their rights to participation and communication," as Jürgen Habermas has argued.[9]

The major problem for the EU's identity, however, is not so much its *being* or its *doing* as its *saying*, because the EU depends upon its member states to speak for it. This they have neither done very well, given widespread blame shifting and credit taking on policy issues, nor very much, given their silence on polity issues. The difficulty for the EU is not just that national leaders are also engaged in the task of building national identity, and therefore are less likely to consider building that of the EU. It is also that there is a plurality of nationally imagined Europes, as the member states imagine the EU through their own lenses of national identity and purposes. And this in turn makes it very hard to have a common sense of identity akin to that of a nation-state. But instead of a sense of nationhood, perhaps this composite identity based on overlapping understandings of the EU is what constitutes "region-hood."

The EU's indeterminate sovereignty, combined with the vagueness of its boundaries and the uncertainty of its identity, for a long time allowed it to be whatever the beholder wished—less of a threat to national sovereignty and identity for those who feared a superstate and more of a promise for those who hoped for a federal Europe with supranational sovereignty and identity. But today this inconclusiveness no longer calms fears or inspires hope.

On the contrary, the EU's very existence only adds to national identity crises, which are themselves very different from one member state to the next. Thus, in the United Kingdom the identity crisis centers on devolution, the nature of "Britishness," and the unraveling of the very idea of union as increasing numbers of Scots favor independence. In France, the crisis focuses on the nature of republican citizenship and *laïcité* (secularism), in particular with regard to the headscarf issue. In the Netherlands, the very image of the country as a tolerant society is in question, first raised in Pim Fortuyn's election campaign, when he argued for intolerance of the allegedly intolerant (read Muslim immigrants) in order to maintain a tolerant society. In Germany, the questions of identity divide the former East from the West not only with regard to postwar collective memories but also in coming to terms with the Nazi past. In Poland, the question of identity splits nationalist conservative Catholics, represented by the Kaczyński twins leading the country, from center-left secularists and former dissidents. In Belgium, the dissolution of the country itself is under debate, as increasing numbers of the Flemish favor cutting the French loose.

The problems posed by the EU for national identities are played out very differently in these different countries. But they also tend to divide Eastern from Western Europe. Thus, whereas in the East, the elites are skeptical and the mass publics are largely pro-European, in the West, the elites tend to be highly pro-European and the public is increasingly skeptical.

Economy

In addition to these "regional state" characteristics, the EU also has a highly differentiated economy. Unlike the more integrated economies of most advanced industrial nation-states and despite increasing EU-led monetary and market integration, the EU member states continue to be highly differentiated in their types of capitalisms and welfare states. This makes for very different public responses to the challenges of both globalization and Europeanization.

The member states are characterized by at least three varieties of capitalism: liberal market economies, exemplified by Britain, where arms'-length business interrelationships and radically decentralized labor relations are arbitrated by a hands-off state; coordinated market economies, exemplified by Germany, where network-based business relationships and cooperative, corporatist labor relations are facilitated by an "enabling" state;[10] and state-influenced market economies, exemplified by France and Italy, where informally networked business relationships, whether forged through state training (France) or family ties (Italy), and unstable labor relations, whether radically decentralized (France) or corporatist (Italy), are enhanced or hindered by an "influencing" state.[11]

The member states also fall into different families of welfare states, of which there are also at least three: the Scandinavian social-democratic systems, in which the high level of benefits and services represents a challenge for sustainability; the liberal Anglo-Saxon systems, in which the low level of benefits and services increases the risk of poverty; and the conservative continental social systems, in which the reasonably high level of benefits and low level of services is linked to higher unemployment and lower labor force participation rates.[12] But despite these continuing differences in member states' capitalisms and welfare states, globalization and Europeanization have both been major forces for change. Together they have promoted liberalization, deregulation, and privatization across varieties of capitalism and rationalization across families of welfare states.

For EU member states, and in particular those who belong to the euro zone, Europeanization has arguably been an even greater force for change than globalization. This is because while Europeanization has acted as a conduit for globalization, by pressing for greater openness in capital and product markets, it has also served as a shield against it, by reducing macroeconomic exposure to the vagaries of the financial markets through the single currency and enhancing microeconomic economies of scale through the single market. As a result, Europeanization has produced both convergence *and* divergence, as common monetary and market policies have brought national regulatory regimes closer together while facilitating the development of truly European firms, even as national politicoeconomic and socioeconomic regimes continue to differ.[13]

The EU's growing predominance in the economic arena has become increasingly politically contentious in recent years, albeit for different reasons on different sides of the political spectrum. Britain has pushed for greater economic liberalization while complaining about the increasing juridification. France has increasingly resisted liberalization, worried about globalization in general and about Europeanization's threat to public services in particular. Germany has been reasonably content with the current level of liberalization but has been concerned about the incursions on the "social market economy" from Competition Directorate decisions. And whereas Italy has also accepted liberalization, it simply has not implemented much of the legislation. Public perceptions, moreover, run the gamut from fears on the right that open markets and enlargement bring in immigrants who take jobs and increase unemployment to concerns on the left that the EU threatens the welfare state, whether through the euro or the "home-country rules" of the original services directive (now much revised).

Governance and Democracy

The EU's regional state also consists of a compound governance system and a fragmented democracy. Unlike most national governmental systems, the EU's governance system is not only more "multilevel" because it includes EU, national, and regional levels.[14] It is also more "multicentered" as a result of the geographical dispersion of its governing activities. And it is more "multiform,"[15] as a result of the differing institutional designs of its member states. These designs form a continuum from more "simple" polities where governing activity tends to be channeled through a single authority as a result of unitary states, statist policymaking processes, and majoritarian representation systems, as in France or Britain, to "compound" polities where governing activity is more dispersed across multiple authorities as a result of federal or regionalized states, corporatist processes, and/or proportional representation, as in Germany and Italy. By comparison, the EU can be seen as more "compound" than any nation-state, given its own even greater dispersion of governing activity.

Moreover, the EU is unlike nation-states' mature democracies, which have a full range of democratic legitimizing mechanisms—including political participation *by* the people, citizen representation *of* the people, effective government *for* the people, and, adding a preposition to Abraham Lincoln's famous dictum, interest consultation *with* the people. Instead, the EU has a fragmented democracy in which legitimacy is split between governing effectiveness *for* the people and interest consultation *with* the people at the EU level and political participation *by* the people and citizen representation *of* the people at the national level. For Fritz Scharpf, this kind of fragmentation is key to understanding the democratic deficit, in which "output democracy" through effective governance cannot make up for the lack of "input democracy" through political participation.[16] Only a few scholars see little problem with this fragmentation, including Giandomenico Majone, who defends the EU as providing "output democracy" through effective regulatory governance, and Andrew Moravcsik, who sees it as no worse than national democracies, given its checks and balances and delegated authorities.[17]

However, though the EU may be no worse than national democracies with regard to the structural bases for democracy, given its institutional balancing of powers, or even the procedural bases, given its openness to interest consultation, it is a lot worse than national democracies when it comes to the representative bases for democracy. This is because it lacks the direct connection with the electorate that makes it possible for citizens to express their views about national policies directly, by voting, and that forces national elected political leaders to respond or be voted out of office. Admittedly, the EU's attempts to remedy this democratic deficit by increasing accountability and transparency or by bringing in more civil society do a lot to improve effective governing *for* and interest consultation *with* the people. But they do nothing to solve the problem of political participation *by* and citizen representation *of* the people. It should come as no surprise, therefore, that once national electorates finally had a chance to vote directly with regard to the EU, in the cases of the French and Dutch referenda on the Constitutional Treaty, that they would not answer the question asked regarding EU institutional reform but would rather respond to the whole slew of issues related to sovereignty, *finalité*, identity, and economics.

THE IMPACT ON NATIONAL POLITICS

EU policies related to questions of sovereignty, boundaries, identity, and economics all represent the substantive issues that can make for problems in national politics with regard to the EU. The complexity of the EU's governance system, together with the split-level nature of its democracy, by contrast, represent the institutional design or polity issues that also make for problems in national politics and representative democracy more generally. This is particularly true because while EU-level decisionmaking is characterized by *policy without politics*, because it carries on making policies without much politics, national decisionmaking consists of *politics without policy*, because national politics continues, but without much sway over EU policies.

The EU's "Policy without Politics"

Representative democracy has been in a crisis for quite a while now, and not just in the EU.[18] Europeanization is not responsible for this condition, although it further contributes to the crisis in its member states in ways not found in traditional nation-states. This is because the EU's member states, as part of a regional state, do not have the same flexibility in responding to citizen concerns as in a traditional nation-state. Whereas concerns related to questions of sovereignty, boundaries, identity, and the economy can all be dealt with directly by nation-state governments, for better or worse, EU member state governments have to seek common policies in the EU with regard to more and more of these issues, for better or worse. And whereas the citizens of nation-states can make their approval or disapproval of national government policies clear directly, by voting the government in or out, the citizens of the EU member states cannot do so with regard to EU-related policies, because they cannot "vote the scoundrels out." Instead, they tend to hold national politicians accountable for policies for which they are not fully responsible, over which they often have little control, and to which they may not even be politically committed.

The special problem of the EU, then, is related to the institutional realities of EU politics and its impact on national politics. EU politics has little in common with national politics because it lacks a directly elected president, a strong legislature, and vigorous political parties and partisan competition. At the EU level, national partisan politics has been marginalized, as party differences and left-right political contestation have been submerged by the general quest for consensus and compromise.[19] Most important, however, EU politics is not really politics at all in any traditional sense of party and partisanship, for it is mostly about interests, whether the politics of national interests in the Council, the politics of public interest in the European Parliament, or the politics of organized interests in the Commission. The upshot is that the EU consists largely of *policy without politics*.

National "Politics without Policy"

EU-level *policy without politics* makes for national *politics without policy*, as increasing numbers of policies are removed from the national political arena to be transferred to the EU, leaving national citizens with little direct input on the EU-related policies that affect them, and only national politicians to hold to account for them.[20] This has a variety of destabilizing effects on national politics: direct, indirect, and collateral.

The direct effects resulting from the lack of EU politics are responsible for the increasing divisiveness of national party politics in the European Parliament and national elections, whether over EU policies or the very fact of integration. But these effects are for the moment very weak, given the lack of the kind of strong, partisan party politics at the EU level that is found at the national level.[21] Nonetheless, European Parliament elections have already complicated national electoral politics by acting as referenda on government performance[22] and by adding another source of cleavage to national party politics.[23]

The indirect effects are of much greater concern for national politics than the direct effects, and follow from the Europeanization of national policies that, already depoliticized at the EU level, are further depoliticized at the national level because they have been taken out of the national political arena. This is depoliticizing to the extent that it reduces political parties' policy options, policy instruments, and policy repertoire, which in turn hollows out party competition and devalues national electoral competition.[24] What is more, it impoverishes national political debate because once these Europeanized policy sectors are taken off the national political agenda, they are no longer the focus of national leaders' communicative discourse.

The collateral effects from the direct and indirect effects are even more serious, with EU-related depoliticization serving to demobilize some voters and radicalize others while pushing yet others into alternative forms of participation. On the one hand, citizens may turn away from traditional representative politics—demoralized by the lack of national politics and consequently demobilized electorally. This can be seen in the lower rates of participation in national as well as EU voting.[25] On the other hand, instead of being demobilized, citizens may be mobilized to vote for the political extremes. The rise in populist extremist parties on the right in particular are testimony to this, whether new third-party movements in majoritarian systems such as the extreme-right National Front in France,[26] or flash parties in multiparty systems such as Pim Fortuyn's radical-right party in the Netherlands.

Rather than becoming demobilized or radicalized with regard to voting, however, citizens may instead turn to interest-based politics or to other forms of non-party-based activism, whether conventional interest group politics, advocacy politics, or social movements, whether focused on influencing the policy process or the legal system via appeal through the national courts to the European Court of Justice. This is not necessarily a bad thing, given that participation *by* the people through voting is a blunt-edged instrument, little able to parse through the complicated questions arising from decisions that have become more and more technical. But these may still not be very satisfying correctives for citizens focused on participatory democracy *by* the people. Other correctives, such as direct democracy, in particular through referenda, engender other problems. These include voter fatigue as a result of the proliferation of elections, resulting in less rather than more participation.[27] Moreover, on EU referenda, one inevitably gets national answers to European questions.

Although politics is a large part of the problem for democracy in Europe today, in particular as political parties on the left as well as the right become politicized along integration/sovereignty lines, and as voters become demobilized or radicalized on EU-related issues, politics can also be part of the solution. But politics can play this constructive role only if national leaders can come up with new legitimating ideas and discourse for Europe and new ways of bringing politics back into EU policymaking.

The Failures of Political Leaders' Discourse

The current problems with regard to the impact of the EU are at least partly due to the failure of national politicians to communicate and deliberate with national publics about the polity issues, that is, the EU-related changes to national practices as they relate to questions of sovereignty, boundaries, identity, and democracy. And they have been made worse by the fact that when political leaders have talked about the changes to national policies, in particular economic ones, the discourse has been mainly one of shifting the blame for unpopular policies—claiming that "the EU made us do it"—while taking the credit for popular policies, often without even mentioning the role of the EU.

Part of the communicative problem is built into the very nature of the EU. It is a natural by-product of the thinness of the European public sphere, given the lack of a substantial EU-level representative politics and the paucity of EU-level leaders able to speak directly to a European public, given the lack of a common language, of a truly European media, or even of a fully European public opinion. This is why the reforms proposed in the Constitutional Treaty for a foreign minister and a nonrotating president were viewed as an improvement, as a way to provide a single voice through which to speak to EU policies. Other suggestions, dropped from the final treaty draft, could have done more, such as making the EU a truly deliberative sphere by lifting the veil of secrecy from the Council, and having public debates in the Council by national leaders speaking as Europeans to European issues. This would also have made it more difficult for them to say one thing in meetings with EU leaders and another to national publics. By the same token, however, such discourse "in the shadow of transparency" would also make it more difficult for the Council to reach any agreements at all! The EU has been built on bargains made behind closed doors, based on compromises that members might have second thoughts about agreeing to, were they to have to legitimate them after the fact in public debate. And of course, if the EU were to suffer from paralysis as a result, the greater deliberative democracy would be an exercise in frustration, and a bigger turn-off to European citizens than even the current system.

For the moment, in any event, the communicative discourse necessarily comes largely by way of national leaders speaking to national publics in national languages reported by national media to form national public opinion. And the problem here, as noted above, is that national leaders have rarely informed the public about the EU-related changes in national practices, let alone sought to reconceptualize national ideas about democracy in light of the new practices. Their silence on the polity issues regarding sovereignty, boundaries, identity, and democracy, together with their blame shifting or credit taking on the policy issues, especially on the economy, have largely left the field open to the political extremes. And all this makes for serious problems not just for the EU but also for national democracy.

We can think about this problem in terms of the building blocks of identity, and how this relates to the ways in which different member states have engaged with the EU over time. Such engagement is not just a question of *being*, that is, the result of differences in history, culture, and politics, as reflected in deeply rooted national conceptions of citizenship with different understandings of sovereignty, political rights, and identity. It is also a question of *doing*, involving how member states have engaged in Europe—for example, France as leader through much of the EU's history, Germany as willing partner, Italy as enthusiastic follower, and Britain as awkward partner. But such engagement is equally a question of *saying*, which affects how actors perceive what they are *doing* and transforms their *being*.[28]

To legitimize engaging in Europe, French leaders' communicative discourse beginning with Charles de Gaulle has emphasized the country's leadership in Europe, with all that has brought in gains not only in economic interests but also in identity, through *grandeur*, thereby enabling them to ignore any losses to "Republican state" sovereignty. The British pro-EU discourse, by contrast, since Harold Macmillan has consistently focused on the gains in economic interest while remaining silent on the losses to parliamentary sovereignty and the "historically established rights of Englishmen"—the concern of the Euroskeptics. The German and Italian discourses have been much less concerned with questions of sovereignty and rights than of identity. And here, while German discourse since Konrad Adenauer has portrayed EU membership as enhancing a German-as-European national identity, out of a troubled past *being* into an economically prosperous *doing*, Italian discourse since Alcide de Gasperi has presented an Italian-as-European identity as a source of national pride, with the EU itself as the rescuer of the nation-state.

The problem today is that these long-standing discourses no longer *say* what these countries have been *doing* or what they have *become*. French leaders' dilemma is that while they continue to evoke the original vision of French leadership in Europe, as good for the economy and identity, the public sees that France no longer leads Europe, is in crisis over its national identity, and increasingly blames EU neoliberalism for its economic difficulties. The British, by contrast, struggle with their lack of any vision of Britain in Europe, because the discourse of economic interest does not respond to growing concerns about sovereignty and identity. Worse, the idea of British separateness in Europe could very well lead to the reality of British separation from Europe in the event of a referendum on Britain "in or out of Europe." The Germans, moreover, need to update their vision of "German-as-European" in light of the changes related to unification and fading memories of World War II, especially because they increasingly question the benefits of membership and worry about the EU's impact on the social market economy. The Italians, finally, need to concern themselves not so much with their vision of Italy in Europe as with their implementation of European rules in Italy, for their pride in being European is likely to suffer if they do not do more to bring the country into conformity with EU law.

CONCLUSION: CAN WE SOLVE THE DEMOCRATIC DEFICIT?

For democracy in the EU to cease being a problem, national leaders and publics need to talk and think more clearly about who they are and where they are going, together in the EU as well as individually within each member state. They require not just new narratives about the EU—beyond peace and prosperity—but also new narratives about what being in Europe means to national democracy. For the EU, a new narrative already exists with regard to its role in the world—that of a "normative power" engaged in multilateralism, respectful of the rule of law, and promoting democracy through its "power of attraction." But at the national level, the EU member states certainly require new narratives that must come from the inside, by rethinking their national understandings of democracy and reevaluating their national visions of Europe. Only once they do this will it be possible for them to think about producing a real constitutional settlement for the European Union.

Ideas and discourse alone, however, are not enough to solve the problems for politics in the EU. This also requires institutional remedies. At the EU level, implementing any number of the democratizing reforms contained in the Constitutional Treaty would certainly be steps in the right direction, such as closer relations with national parliaments, citizens' right to petition, a greater role for the ombudsman, more opportunities for civil society involvement, and the constitutionalization of the Charter of Fundamental Human Rights. Beyond this, creating "big issues" forums for deliberations might also help, or having the Commission outline the political implications of policy choices to add political considerations to the Council as well as the European Parliament's deliberations about the issues.[29] But can the EU be further politicized, say, by giving the Parliament more power along with the right to elect the Commission president?[30] The problem with this question is that introducing partisan politics into the EU's *policy without politics* could very well undermine what the EU does well, that is, governing *for* and *with* the people.

At the national level, democratizing reforms are also in order, given that the EU has altered the traditional workings of all national democracies. For all member states, because more and more decisions are made at the EU level, national governments need to find new ways to bring the citizens back in. And they need to do this not only with regard to the EU level of governance, by helping citizens to organize themselves in ways that would enable them to gain access and influence in Brussels. They also need to do it at the national level, by bringing them into national decisionmaking processes focused on the EU. They may even need to rethink the organization of national democracy itself—in particular in simple polities, where the concentration of authority has become an increasing impediment to citizens' involvement in the decisions that most affect their lives. For any of this to happen, however, national leaders will need to recognize the problem and begin to speak about it with national publics. Will it happen? Hope springs eternal.

Notes

1. See Jan Zielonka, *Europe as Empire* (Oxford: Oxford University Press, 2006); and Stefan Collignon, *Vive la République Européenne* (Paris: Editions de la Martinière, 2004). Also see Glyn Morgan, *The Idea of a European Superstate* (Princeton, N.J.: Princeton University Press, 2005).

2. Vivien A. Schmidt, *Democracy in Europe: The EU and National Polities* (Oxford: Oxford University Press, 2006).

3. Robert O. Keohane and Stanley Hoffmann, eds., *The New European Community: Decision-Making and Institutional Change* (Boulder, Colo.: Westview Press, 1991), introduction.

4. Jolyon Howorth, *Security and Defence Policy in the European Union* (Basingstoke, U.K.: Palgrave Macmillan, 2007), 60.

5. Kenneth Dyson, "Still Elusive Union? Paradoxes of Power in Economic and Monetary Union," paper presented at University American College Skopje conference "Reflections on European Integration: 50 Years of the Treaty of Rome," Foreign and Commonwealth Office, London, March 22–24, 2007.

6. Stefano Bartolini, *Re-Structuring Europe: Centre Formation, System Building and Political Structuring between the Nation State and the European Union* (Oxford: Oxford University Press, 2005), 375.

7. Maurizio Ferrera, *The Boundaries of Welfare: European Integration and the New Spatial Politics of Social Protection* (Oxford: Oxford University Press, 2005).

8. Jolyon Howorth, "Being and Doing in Europe since 1945: Contrasting Dichotomies of Identity and Efficiency," in *Why Europe?* ed. J. Andrews (Basingstoke, U.K.: Palgrave Macmillan, 2000), 85–96.

9. See Jürgen Habermas, *Between Facts and Norms: Contributions to a Discourse Theory* (Cambridge: Polity Press, 1996), 495; and Furio Cerutti, "A Political Identity of the Europeans?" *Thesis Eleven* 13, no. 4 (2003): 26–45.

10. Peter Hall and David Soskice, *Varieties of Capitalism* (Oxford: Oxford University Press, 2000).

11. Vivien A. Schmidt, *The Futures of European Capitalism* (Oxford: Oxford University Press, 2002), 102–154.

12. Gosta Esping-Andersen, *Three Worlds of Welfare State Capitalism* (Cambridge: Polity Press, 1990). Frtiz W. Scharpf and Vivien A. Schmidt, *Welfare and Work in the Open Economy* (Oxford: Oxford University Press, 2000).

13. Schmidt, *Futures of European Capitalism*, chap. 1.

14. Gary Marks and Liesbet Hooghe, *Multi-Level Governance and European Integration* (Lanham, Md.: Rowman & Littlefield, 2001).

15. Kalypso Nicolaides, "The Federal Vision beyond the Nation-State," in *The Federal Vision*, ed. Kalypso Nicolaides and Robert Howse (Oxford: Oxford University Press, 2001), 439–482.

16. Fritz W. Scharpf, *Governing in Europe* (Oxford: Oxford University Press, 1999).

17. Giandomenico Majone, "Europe's Democratic Deficit," *European Law Journal* 4, no. 1 (1998): 5; Andrew Moravcsik, "Reassessing Legitimacy in the European Union," *Journal of Common Market Studies* 40, no. 4 (November 2002): 603–624.

18. Russell Dalton, *Democratic Challenges, Democratic Choices: The Decline in Political Support in Advanced Industrial Democracies* (Oxford: Oxford University Press, 2003).

19. Robert Ladrech, ed., "The Europeanization of Party Politics," Special Issue, *Party Politics* 8, no. 4 (2002): 387–503.

20. See Schmidt, *Democracy in Europe*, 155–218. Also see Peter Mair, "Political Parties and Party Systems," in *Europeanization: New Research Agendas*, ed. Paolo Graziano and Maarten Vink (Basingstoke, U.K.: Palgrave Macmillan, 2007).

21. Peter Mair, "Popular Party Democracy and the Construction of the European Union Political System," paper presented at the workshop "Sustainability and the European Union," European Consortium for Political Research joint session, Uppsala, April 2004; C. Van der Eijk, and M. Franklin, "Potential for Contestation on European Matters at National Elections in Europe," in *European Integration and Political Conflict*, ed. Gary Marks and Marco R. Steenbergen (Cambridge: Cambridge University Press, 2004).

22. Peter Mair, "The Limited Impact of Europe on National Party Systems," in *Europeanised Politics? European Integration and National Political Systems*, ed. Klaus Goetz and Simon Hix (London: Frank Cass, 2001); Matthew Gabel, "European Integration, Voters, and National Politics" in *Contentious European: Protest and Politics in an Emerging Polity*, ed. Doug Imig and Sidney Tarrow (Lanham, Md.: Rowman & Littlefield, 2001).

23. Matthew Gabel and Christopher J. Anderson, "The Structure of Citizen Attitudes and the European Political Space," *Comparative Political Studies* 35 (2002): 893–913; Liesbet Hooghe and Gary Marks, "The Making of a Polity: The Struggle over European Integration," in *Continuity and Change in Contemporary Capitalism*, ed. Herbert Kitschelt, Peter Lange, Gary Marks, and John Stephens (Cambridge: Cambridge University Press, 1999), 70–97.

24. Mair, "Popular Party Democracy."

25. Pierre Bréchon, "Des valeurs politiques entre pérennité et changement," *Futuribles* 277 (2002): 92–128; the citation here is on page 103.

26. N. Mayer, *Ces Français qui votent FN* (Paris: Flammarion, 1999).

27. Russell Dalton and Mark Gray, "Expanding the Electoral Marketplace" in *Democracy Transformed? Expanding Political Opportunities in Advanced Industrial Democracies*, ed. Bruce Cain, Russell Dalton, and Susan E. Scarrow (Oxford: Oxford University Press, 2003).

28. Vivien A. Schmidt, "Adapting to Europe: Is It Harder for Britain?" *British Journal of Politics and International Relations* 8 (2006): 15–33; Vivien A. Schmidt, "Trapped by their Ideas: French Elites' Discourses of European Integration and Globalization," *Journal of European Public Policy* 14, no. 4 (forthcoming); Sergio Fabbrini, ed., *L'Europeizzazione dell'Italia: L'impatto dell'Unione Europea sulle istituzioni e le politische italiane* (Rome: Laterza, 2003).

29. Paul Magnette, "European Governance and Civic Participation: Beyond Elitist Citizenship?" *Political Studies* 51 (2003): 144–160.

30. Simon Hix, *The Political System of the European Union* (Basingstoke, U.K.: Palgrave Macmillan, 2005).

CHAPTER FIVE

THE EUROPEAN UNION

A POWER IN THE WORLD—NOT (YET) A WORLD POWER?

Jolyon Howorth

The distinction implicit in the title of this chapter is more than just a play on words. Since the end of the Cold War, the European Union has emerged as a major player on the international stage. It is the largest trading bloc in the world, the unit with the largest gross domestic product in the world (having overtaken the United States in 2005), and the market with the biggest portfolio of interregional trade in the world. The euro, whatever its structural or political weaknesses, has established itself as the alternative global reserve currency to the dollar. The European Commission can prevent purely internal U.S. mergers and acquisitions and can even bring a giant like Microsoft to heel. When the EU trade commissioner speaks to China, or in the framework of the World Trade Organization, he speaks with a single European voice that commands respect. The EU and its member states contribute over 55 percent of the aid and development monies given to the global South. The EU is increasingly seen as the most successful and complete example of a regional regime or regional state,[1] and it is regarded as a model to be emulated by the growing ranks of similar regimes: the Association of Southeast Asian Nations, the African Union, the Union of South American Nations, and the like. In terms of soft power, the EU attracted over 300 million overseas tourists in 2004, compared with 50 million for the United States and 40 million for China. In the same year, more than 375,000 asylum seekers applied to EU countries for admission (as opposed to 50,000 for the United States), and 4 EU countries alone admitted as many as 163,000.

Finally, since 2003 the EU has emerged as a key player in international crisis management, deploying some 20 civilian and military intervention missions to 16 different countries on three continents. The EU is a power in the world. Not only does it successfully promote and defend its own collective interests but, as we shall see, it also increasingly exercises a normative influence over the nature and pattern of international relations.

Yet the EU cannot be considered a world power in its own right. It lacks both the political and constitutional unity of a major nation-state. It does not enjoy "sovereignty" in the traditional Westphalian sense, either internally or externally. Its ambitions, both internal and external, are constrained by an ongoing tension between the Union itself and its member states. It has no seat at the United Nations or, with the exception of the World Trade Organization, direct presence in any of the major intergovernmental organizations (International Monetary Fund, Organization for Cooperation and Development in Europe, World Bank, Organization for Security and Cooperation in Europe).[2] It does not boast a standing army or the capacity to project military force in ways that could affect the global balance of power. In purely geopolitical terms, Europe has a built-in disadvantage. The smallest of the main continents, it covers just 6.5 percent of the Earth's land surface, yet it contains (*excluding* the Commonwealth of Independent States member countries) no fewer than 44 nation-states. Contrast that with Asia, which covers almost 30 percent of the global land surface and contains 41 nation-states; North America, with 13 percent and just 2 states; South America, with a further 13 percent and 20 states; or Australia, with 4 percent belonging to a single nation. Europe has by far the highest ratio of separate political units to surface area. In the globalized world of the twenty-first century, this is not a recipe for maximum international impact. In short, the EU is not a "world power" in the way that this term might depict the United States today or the Concert of Powers in the eighteenth and nineteenth centuries.

The truth, however, is that the EU does not aspire to be a power of the traditional type. Its origins and ethos suggest ways of doing international relations differently, with an emphasis on transcending sovereignty, promoting international law and international institutions, preferring multilateralism and diplomacy to unilateralism and coercion, and prioritizing legitimacy over naked power. Until the very turn of the century, it set its face resolutely against the adoption of any form of hard power and basked in its well-deserved reputation as a purely "civilian power."[3] During the Cold War, security and defense issues were dealt with exclusively via NATO—period. When, in the context of the Balkan wars of the early 1990s, the European Union sought to increase its military capacity for crisis management, this was initially attempted via the Atlantic Alliance, through the mechanisms involved in European Security and Defense Identity.[4] The security ambitions of the EU were laid out in the 1992 Petersberg Tasks (humanitarian responses, peacekeeping and peacemaking); political decisionmaking was to be managed via the Western European Union; and military capacity assured by borrowing assets from NATO, a process referred to as "Berlin-Plus."[5]

Alas, this creative set of arrangements proved grossly inadequate to the task. Within a decade, the Petersberg Tasks were revealed to be far too limited in scope to deal with the new challenges of the twenty-first century, the Western European Union proved to be a body too weak and incoherent to formulate and manage security policy, and the process of borrowing assets from NATO ended up being a mere stopgap while the EU decided on its own autonomous requirements for military capacity.

In December 1998, the Franco-British Declaration of Saint-Malo crossed a series of Rubicons in European security policy. By stating that the EU needed to "play its full role on the international stage," it expressed a new proactivism in international affairs. By deciding to bestow upon the EU directly new institutional capacity for decisionmaking in security and defense policy, it broke with 40 years of a strictly civilian policy agenda. By openly espousing the project of developing autonomous military capacity, it enshrined the EU's ambition to become a security actor in its own right. By suggesting that such ambitions would contribute "to the vitality of a modernised Atlantic Alliance," it acknowledged that NATO was being recast—implicitly in ways that were not yet entirely clear. The Saint-Malo process rapidly gave birth to a new EU policy area: the European Security and Defense Policy (ESDP).[6] The innovative aspects of the ESDP, which we examine below in depth, are (1) the emergence of a new range of Brussels-based institutions facilitating consensus seeking and coherent policymaking; (2) the development of EU military and civilian intervention capacity appropriate for the challenges of the twenty-first century; (3) an emerging European strategic culture; (4) a growing portfolio of overseas missions delivering the concrete reality of this new policy area; and (5) a new form of synergy between the United States and the EU, and between NATO and the ESDP. In all these aspects, the ESDP can be perceived as both forming a partnership with the United States and offering an alternative vision of international relations.

INSTITUTIONS AND DECISIONMAKING

Before the launch of the ESDP, in addition to the long-standing *national* institutions of foreign and security policymaking in each member state, there were already no fewer than nine specifically EU bodies with an input into EU decisionmaking in this policy area.[7] Saint-Malo, with its call for "appropriate structures," instead of leading to the rationalization of these bodies, merely layered on several new ones, of which three had already established themselves as crucial: the Political and Security Committee (see below), the EU Military Committee, and the EU Military Staff—all of which are roughly modeled on their NATO equivalents.

The very complexity of this institutional nexus poses a problem in international relations. Traditionally, all international actors, and especially powerful actors, have developed a hierarchical relationship between policymaking institutions and central leadership. The former may offer divergent and even at times contradictory advice; but the leader—usually the head of state or government—arbitrates, decides, and leads. Nowhere is this process clearer than in countries such as the United States, France, and the United Kingdom. Over the centuries, this has been the sine qua non of the international impact of great powers. And yet the EU is, in a very real sense, *leaderless*.[8] It is, in many ways, the exact opposite of a great power such as the United States. Ultimate decisionmaking power rests in the hands of the intergovernmental European Council, represented by its heads of state and government. The EU is hugely constrained by the requirement that its security (and even more so its defense) policies be the object of unanimous agreement among 27 sovereign entities. In this sense, it is almost inevitably lacking in strategic thrust or "heroic" objectives. U.S. analysts who, detecting intentions from outcomes, have sensed in the ESDP an attempt to balance against the United States have seriously misunderstood the processes involved in security and defense policymaking in the EU.[9]

And yet, decisions are made, policy is made, and over the last few years the ESDP has gone from strength to strength. One of the key institutional drivers of this process has been the Political and Security Committee (PSC), a central Brussels-based body comprising one ambassador from each of the 27 member states, plus a representative from the European Commission, which meets at least twice weekly. According to the defunct Constitutional Treaty, the PSC "monitors the international situation in the areas covered by the [Common Foreign and Security Policy] and contributes to the definition of policies by delivering opinions to the Council . . . or on its own initiative."[10] It also monitors the implementation of agreed-on policies. Moreover, it exercises, under the responsibility of the Council and of the high representative of the Union for foreign affairs and security policy, "the political control and strategic direction of crisis management operations." PSC ambassadors are appointed by their respective member states to represent the interests of those states in forging a common foreign and security policy. Yet interviews with the members of the PSC reveal a unanimous desire to achieve consensus. All members of the committee value its "clublike" atmosphere and stress that a significant measure of socialization ensures that the dominant mode of interaction is consensus seeking rather than bargaining around fixed national positions.

The reality of the ESDP shows that a viable consensus normally emerges in the PSC. The degree of socialization that functions in the committee is a major factor in generating compromise. The members know one another extremely well. Their average tenure is about three years. When, for example, the French ambassador lays out her country's position on, say, the EU mission in Afghanistan, the others know immediately how to read that position, how to react to it, and how to work with it to achieve consensus. Though the ambassadors are involved in a constant *European learning process* through daily interaction with their peers, they also perform a didactic function with respect to their national capitals, communicating the sense of collective European opinion in the PSC and suggesting how national positions can be modified to achieve collective results. Thus, although the PSC ambassadors remain under the direct control of their respective Ministry of Foreign Affairs, their capacity to influence thinking and opinion both at home and in Brussels is considerable. They are involved in a constant, albeit inchoate, process of generating a specifically European strategic culture, which amounts to much more than the lowest common denominator of the EU's member states.[11] A crucial aspect of that emerging strategic culture is the acquisition of appropriate civilian and military capacity.

CIVILIAN AND MILITARY CAPACITY

When the acronym ESDP was first coined, it generated furious controversy over the alleged inappropriateness of the EU's acquisition of military instruments. Academics deplored the demise of the EU as a "civilian power."[12] U.S. officials feared that the EU would emerge as a serious military competitor for Washington. Journalists and commentators, usually of the Euroskeptic variety, had a field day attacking the dangers (or deriding the pretensions) of the "European army." The designation by the Helsinki European Council in December 1999 of a "Headline Goal" of EU forces comprising 60,000 troops, 100 warships, and 400 aircraft was taken as evidence that the ESDP was little more than traditional European militarism disguised in a peacekeeping skin. Moreover, the fact that the EU's early overseas interventions were dominated by military missions (in the Balkans and in Africa) appeared to confirm this martial interpretation of the ESDP's true colors. Such an impression, however understandable, was misguided.

The EU has no expeditionary ambitions of the traditional type, and it would be politically impossible to imagine circumstances in which all 27 member states might support an EU military invasion of a sovereign state. The overseas operations undertaken by the ESDP are limited to crisis management, even though article III-309 of the defunct Constitutional Treaty broadened the original Petersberg Tasks to include "joint disarmament operations, *humanitarian and rescue tasks*, military advice and assistance tasks, conflict prevention and *peacekeeping tasks, tasks of combat forces undertaken for crisis management, including peacemaking* and postconflict stabilization" and added, for good measure, the need to "contribute to the fight against terrorism."[13] All EU military missions to date have fallen squarely under these categories and, despite the reference to the fight against terrorism, it is clear that the EU collectively sees that struggle in essentially nonmilitary terms.[14]

Moreover, almost all overseas missions have been undertaken within the terms of reference of an explicit UN mandate. The development of collective EU military capacity is slow and somewhat ill focused, reflecting some difficulty among the member states in deciding precisely what sort of military actor the Union seeks to become.[15] Politically, the EU is well aware that "victory" is assured less by the application of military force than by how that force is applied. The use of military force is thus "increasingly constrained by legal and policy considerations based on general international law and the law of armed conflict."[16]

Current planning assumptions for the next 20 years, formulated by the European Defence Agency, involve concentration on four strategic "enablers": synergy, agility, selectivity, and sustainability. All these features will take EU forces further down the same road as that already taken by the U.S. military. But the EU is unlikely to embrace full-scale network-centric warfare. At most, it will seek to develop network-enabled capacity, allowing it to "plug in" to advances—mainly led by the United States—in information technology. Yet, to stay abreast of this burgeoning technology will require vast networks of highly trained researchers working transnationally to combine expertise in an ever wider range of technological developments. It will also require considerable resource inputs, which currently appear to be beyond the political tolerance of an EU likely to be subjected to a massive demand for resources in other sectors. These major decisions on the *nature* of the EU's future armed forces are already generating intense political debate across its member states.

In any case, the ESDP is predicated on the belief that success cannot be measured in terms of initial military inputs but of eventual political outcomes. These will require close attention to the finer points of nation building—the promotion of human rights, the rule of law, security-sector reform, and good governance. It is in this area of civilian crisis management that the EU has seen the most spectacular developments. Some have mocked the EU's soft power and argued that, without hard power to back it up, little can be achieved. The reverse is probably true. As we have seen in the Western Balkans, in the Middle East, and in Afghanistan, without the complementary deployment of *civilian* instruments of crisis management, the application of naked military power can often lead to failure.

Civilian crisis management is a concept that has only recently entered the political lexicon. It refers to the entire range of nonmilitary instruments that are called for in crisis situations—whether preconflict or postconflict. Police forces, state-building capacity, specially trained judges, lawyers, civil administrators, customs officials, civil protection, and disaster relief agents, demobilization and reintegration specialists, security-sector reform instruments—all these and other capacities are subsumed under the generic title of civilian crisis management. It covers a much broader range of instruments than the military component of the ESDP and involves a much greater degree of institutional flexibility, for it calls on agencies from all three of the "pillars" of the 1992 Treaty on the European Union. This is at least as important a component of the ESDP as the strictly military element, and many would argue that it is ultimately more important. Yet its emergence has gone largely unheralded. The EU's achievement in assembling all these instruments has been remarkable.[17] It is in this area that the demand is heaviest, and in many ways the ESDP's greatest challenge is in being able to cope with the constant requests, from all around the world, for its services in civilian crisis management.

Although all ESDP missions have combined both military and civilian instruments, the large majority of them have been predominantly civilian rather than military. For this reason, the EU Council of Ministers, in June 2007, agreed on a new chain of command for such missions, based on the establishment of a Civilian Planning and Conduct Capability within the Council Secretariat. This unprecedented body, the civilian equivalent of a military planning headquarters, will be headed by a civilian operation commander who, under the political control and strategic direction of the PSC and the overall authority of the high representative of the Union for foreign affairs and security policy, will be responsible for the planning and conduct of civilian ESDP missions.[18] As we shall see below, the most ambitious of these missions have been those prepared in 2007 for Afghanistan and Kosovo.

AN EMBRYONIC EU STRATEGIC CULTURE?

The European Union's forays into overseas operations suggest the gradual emergence of a distinctive EU strategic culture. It is too soon to say with any certainty whether something that could be identified as a single, or at least a distinctive, European security strategy or strategic culture is actually taking shape. Something is happening, but we are uncertain as to what. As François Heisbourg remarked, quoting Samuel Johnson's comment on the dog that walked on its hind legs: "It is not done well, but you are surprised it is done at all."[19] Realists and those who believe that strategy can only be devised by nation-states remain unconvinced that the EU will ever get its collective security act together. However, a number of important recent studies allow us to see more clearly into the outlines of such a development. Bastian Giegerich and Christoph Meyer illustrate the best and the most imaginative of the recent constructivist analyses of strategic culture.[20]

Although each of their approaches, despite some overlap, is methodologically distinct, and although they focus to some extent on different countries, their conclusions are comparable and complementary. Giegerich studied the impact of EU-level security policy on the strategic cultures of eight EU countries (Austria, France, Germany, Britain, Denmark, Ireland, Spain, and Sweden) and found that adaptation of those national cultures to an emerging European strategic culture was "gradual and limited but driven by constant interaction and the emergence of collective norms."[21] Meyer compared the evolution of both public and elite opinion in four countries (Germany, France, Britain, and Poland) through an analysis of changing threat perceptions, mediatized crisis learning, and institutional socialization and found "areas of shared consensus and convergence, particularly regarding a more activist interpretation of goals regarding humanitarian intervention, an increasing support for the role of the EU as a military actor, and a growing concern over domestic and international authorization." He also charts convergence on threat perception (with the rapid demise of any sense of territorial threat), and even on democracy promotion as a desirable norm. Both scholars stress that the process of convergence is limited and slow (this being a value that is both highly personal and relative) and that the challenges to the emergence of a genuinely trans-EU strategic culture remain strong. But both nevertheless detect clear signs of convergence.

The document that encapsulates in policy terms many of these ideas is, of course, the December 2003 European Security Strategy, *A Secure Europe in a Better World*, which reflects three key concepts that have informed the overall normative approach of the ESDP.[22] The first is that of "comprehensive security." Security, in this concept, is seen as indivisible (I cannot be secure if my neighbor remains insecure). To this extent, it is conceptually the opposite of defense (my security derives from my neighbor's weakness and insecurity). The comprehensive approach addresses basic human rights and fundamental freedoms and economic and environmental cooperation as well as peace and stability. All these are closely linked, as noted by Sven Biscop, to the second key concept, that of global public goods, which emerged out of debates within the UN—physical security and stability; enforceable legal order; open and inclusive economic order; general well-being; and health, education, and a clean environment.[23] Third, the notion of comprehensive security is increasingly linked to the new theories of human security, which is defined as "freedom for individuals from basic insecurities caused by gross human rights violations."[24]

Two key features of the security strategy are stressed: that "the first line of defence will often be abroad," via conflict *prevention*; and that none of the new threats is purely military or manageable through purely military means. The strategic objectives rest on two main pillars: *building security in the European region*, and creating a viable new international order. The former entails developing, through a comprehensive neighborhood policy, a "ring of friends from the Caucasus to the Balkans and around the Mediterranean." The former is almost overtly post-Westphalian in flavor. The EU document is strong in its assertion of a commitment to upholding and developing international law and in recognizing the UN as the main source of international legitimacy. Things are happening in Europe: Past divisions are being transcended; societies, nations, and cultures are being reconstructed through intercultural interaction; the international system is perceived as being reconfigured around a small number of poles; and the task of the future is to contribute collectively toward the vast universal challenge of tackling the root causes of poverty, inequality, exclusion, and dismissal.[25]

In this sense, it is indeed possible to detect elements of trans-European convergence on strategic-cultural norms. Thus, the decision made by the German Cabinet in October 2006 to accept that German armed forces can, and indeed must, participate in crisis management missions to right humanitarian wrongs and to correct gross imbalances in power relations—not between states but between rulers and peoples—marked a major shift in German security culture. There is, of course, a long way to go. In particular, leaders have made little effort to explain the ESDP properly to their citizens—to present it as a *European* project and not as a vital *national* add-on to what would otherwise be a hopelessly inefficient European mess. But the signs are incontrovertible that a strategic culture of a very different sort is developing in the European Union and, equally significantly, that this development is widely welcomed around the world as a new and unprecedented "vector for stability in international relations."[26]

OVERSEAS MISSIONS: THE EU AS GLOBAL ACTOR?

Since January 2003, barely four years after Saint-Malo, the EU has undertaken almost 20 overseas missions in sixteen different countries and on three continents. These have ranged from small-scale rule of law missions in countries like Georgia and Iraq to significant military interventions in Bosnia-Herzegovina, Congo, and Chad; from border control missions involving Moldova/Ukraine or Palestine/Egypt to police missions in Afghanistan, Congo, Kosovo, and Macedonia; and from a peace-monitoring mission in Aceh to security-sector reform and military assistance missions in Sudan/Darfur and Congo.

Are these missions transforming the EU into a world power? In the traditional sense, the answer is clearly in the negative. The total number of troops deployed on the five or six predominantly military missions barely tops 12,000; the total personnel deployed on the mainly civilian missions has been fewer than 2,000. Most of the operations were short-term interventions lasting from 4 to 18 months. None of them fundamentally altered power relations either between or within the states involved. And although the EU presence has been felt as far away as Indonesia, Afghanistan, and Congo, the vast majority of the effort has been directed to the EU's neighborhood—the Balkans, Black Sea, Southern Caucasus, and Mediterranean. The countries affected by those operations all now have borders with EU member states.[27] The impact of the ESDP's activism has overwhelmingly been to help stabilize its periphery.

Yet, seen from a different perspective, these missions have helped to showcase the EU as a global actor of a new and different type: one that is able to deploy a vast range of appropriate instruments in the cause of nation building and state building, postconflict reconstruction, judicial reform and policing, and peacekeeping and peacemaking. In the twenty-first-century world, interstate conflict is becoming a rare phenomenon. The *demand* for intervention forces comes overwhelmingly from vulnerable, internally conflict-prone, crisis-ridden, or failing states—where civilian populations invariably bear the brunt of political chaos. The value added that the EU can offer is both practical and "normatively correct." For example, when the government of Indonesia, in conjunction with its long-term insurgent adversary, the Free Aceh Movement, were seeking an international body with the capacity and the legitimacy to supervise the implementation of the peace agreement that put an end to 30 years of civil war, some of the more obvious candidates (United Nations, Association of Southeast Asian Nations) were ruled out for political reasons. The EU was seen as the ideal partner in what proved to be a smooth and consensual transition from war to peace. Over the past 2 years, the number of countries soliciting EU assistance in monitoring and mediating potential crises has grown constantly, and the Council Secretariat in Brussels, which handles these requests, has been forced to recognize that the EU's supply of appropriate resources is vastly outstripped by global demand. There has even been talk of a "reverse Berlin-Plus" process whereby the EU might be called upon to lend crisis management assets to NATO, which is sorely lacking in such instruments. In this sense, the ESDP not only *can* but *should* be seen as blazing a new trail to the entire business of international relations, one consistent with its underlying ethos and with the postmodern strategic culture informing this ethos.

In support of its growing involvement in overseas missions, the EU, rapidly digesting the lessons of its early missions, has been developing specialized capacity across a huge range of instruments. In the military field, fifteen "battle-groups"—units of 1,500 troops trained for combat in jungle, desert, or mountain conditions—have been created, often involving forces from a range of countries (e.g., Poland, Germany, Slovakia, Latvia, Lithuania), and even including one non-EU member state (e.g., Sweden, Finland, Norway, Estonia, Ireland). An EU "reservoir" of specially trained officials—judges, prosecutors, administrators, penitentiary officers, civil protection officers, and human rights monitors—is taking shape, ready to deploy in short order to crisis zones. Several thousand police officers from across all member states are being prepared for overseas deployments. And, as we saw above, a special Civilian Planning and Conduct Capability has now been devised to ensure forward planning and the operational coordination of these increasingly numerous and often highly sensitive missions. This civilian headquarter will operate in tight coordination with the Civil-Military Planning Cell (otherwise known as the EU Operations Centre), which has been developed alongside the EU Military Staff in preparation for the day when the EU will need to assume the detailed planning of a substantial military mission which, for one reason or another, cannot be handled either by NATO planners at Headquarters or by one of the national permanent joint headquarters fielded by the United Kingdom, France, Germany, Italy, or Greece. This EU Ops Centre has been the subject of furious quarrels between the predominantly Europeanist members of the EU and those Atlanticist states that evaluate every development in terms of its likely impact on the transatlantic relationship. The very notion of the EU's possessing autonomous capacity for strategic and operational planning has been seen in some national capitals as undermining NATO and as destructive of the EU-U.S. partnership. Yet the facility was activated for the first time in June 2007 in the context of a military exercise focusing on the key military aspects of crisis management. This tension between purely European developments in the crisis management field and the ongoing participation of almost all EU member states in NATO has been one of the most contentious aspects of the ESDP story. It is to this tension that we must now turn.

THE ESDP AND TRANSATLANTIC RELATIONS

The presence, in the Saint-Malo Declaration of 1998, of the ominous-sounding word "autonomous" immediately sparked a fierce debate between protagonists and adversaries of the ESDP on both sides of the Atlantic. In Robert Hunter's question, was the ESDP going to be NATO's "companion" or its "competitor?" Though some saw the dichotomy as a zero-sum game (interpreted either positively or negatively), others—probably the majority of commentators and analysts—insisted that there was no incompatibility between the ESDP and NATO. Much of the early discussion was based on two significant misperceptions or false assumptions. The first was that transatlantic relations in general and NATO in particular, without the seismic tremors from the birth of the ESDP, had clear and harmonious new objectives in the post–Cold War world. The second was that the ESDP was destined to emerge as an actor of the same type as NATO itself. Neither of these propositions had much foundation. Even before the end of the Cold War, it was obvious to many analysts that the EU as a whole could not continue indefinitely to avoid any responsibility for its own security and that, once the existential security threat posed by the USSR was removed, European member states would not have the same incentive to align themselves automatically with Uncle Sam. Transatlantic relations, in other words, were bound to become more complex as the United States shifted its geostrategic focus from Europe to Asia and the Gulf, and as the EU, through the single market project and its consequences, matured as a single international actor. Moreover, whereas NATO was a military alliance designed to fight a major war with the Soviet Union, the ESDP emerged, in large part, as a response to the EU's perceived need to be able to deploy a range of crisis management tools to the Balkans and other neighboring regions.

Transatlantic tensions over the ESDP have evolved constantly. Whereas initially, many Americans feared defection and growing rivalry from the EU, and whereas subsequently, in the context of the Iraq war, loyalty to Washington could be projected as the litmus test between "old" and "new" Europe, by the middle years of George W. Bush's second term (2006–2007) most nonacademic observers had concluded not only that there was no objective tension between the ESDP and NATO but also that the latter was in fact fortunate to have the former as a partner in the complex business of bringing stability to the world's crisis zones.[28] Indeed, it would not be an exaggeration to suggest that, between 1998 and 2008, the "problem/solution" relationship was turned on its head. Initially, NATO was the solution and the ESDP was the problem; subsequently, it seemed almost the other way around. This was all the more so in that the sorts of operations for which NATO was optimally configured, and on which it was politically united, became increasingly rare, whereas those for which the ESDP was preparing were emerging as a new type of international relations norm. It is not insignificant that, since the dawn of the twenty-first century, the only country that has seen a NATO deployment has been Afghanistan, the focus of NATO's one and only invocation of article 5; whereas, as we have seen, the ESDP has been deploying all around the planet, engaging in missions that, by any objective criteria, also promote and secure the interests both of the Alliance in general and of transatlantic relations more generally.

If there is an ongoing tension, it derives from a fundamental shift in what I have called the "Euro-Atlantic security dilemma."[29] The post-1945 challenge was to build up Europe's own military capacity while retaining the U.S. commitment to European security. On the one hand, Britain feared that if Europe demonstrated genuine ability to take care of itself militarily, the United States would revert to isolationism. On the other hand, France expressed confidence that the United States would take more seriously allies who took themselves seriously. London and Paris invariably adopted positions on European security that were driven by their path-dependent policy preferences with regard to the Euro-Atlantic security dilemma. This remained true in the early years of the ESDP. And yet, in the post–Cold War world, the former defining issue of U.S. commitment to Europe increasingly lacked salience. U.S. solidarity was needed in the Balkans, pending the buildup of European capacity, but even before 1989 the United States had shifted its strategic focus. Via the "out-of-area or out-of-business" debate of the 1990s, NATO gradually ceased to be an alliance designed to deliver U.S. commitment to European security and gradually became an alliance geared to delivering European support for American global strategy.[30] The debate within Europe was no longer about how to ensure a continued U.S. security guarantee but how to respond to U.S. global strategy. In the United States, the debate was all about leadership: how to encourage the Europeans to secure their own continent without undermining U.S. leadership of the Atlantic Alliance. These debates were massively stimulated by the wars in the Balkans, particularly Kosovo; by the rise of the ESDP; and, above all, by the consequences of the September 11, 2001, terrorist attacks.

Relations between the ESDP and NATO remain, at one level, important to the future directions of both bodies. The ESDP needs NATO to provide access both to military instruments and to planning facilities and to help the EU acquire an autonomous military capacity. NATO needs the ESDP because a coordinated and muscular European capacity is of greater use to the Alliance than a disparate and uncoordinated one and because the EU has developed instruments of nation building and postconflict reconstruction that NATO lacks and needs. Nevertheless, they remain distinct organizations, with different objectives and working methods and somewhat different memberships. As long as suspicions abound as to one another's ultimate strategic purpose, tensions will persist. The United States is bound to remain wary of a new kid on the block aiming at "security autonomy." Washington is accustomed to an EU that talks above its weight while punching below it. It has had difficulty coming to terms with a different balance between rhetoric and reality. Some EU member states, for their part, will remain cautious about an organization that is transforming itself into a type of global police officer. The EU collectively will continue to insist on multilateral procedures, on appropriate dialogue, and on respect for the primacy and overarching legitimacy of the United Nations. The EU-U.S. political relationship remains, for both parties, a first-order priority. But the military relationship, so central during the Cold War, has become a second-order priority. Therein lies the major problem for transatlantic relations generally and for ESDP-NATO relations in particular.

CONCLUSION

The emergence of the EU as an international actor of a new type has given rise to many misunderstandings and crossed wires, both within Europe and across the Atlantic. The ESDP, it must be stressed, is still only a few years old. Its footprint is evolving slowly. There is little point in speculating, in 2007, what sort of an actor it will have become by 2025 or 2050. There is no question but that the European Union will continue to refine its current mix of civilian and military instruments designed to deliver international crisis management. The extent to which this defines the EU as a world power will depend less on its own activism and more on the acceptance by the other major global actors of a new set of practices and rules for international relations reflecting a postmodern and post-Westphalian normative framework.[31] This will be the defining challenge for international relations in the twenty-first century. The EU is well placed to play a leading role in this process of norm redefinition. It is generating a new form of discourse in international relations. The question is: Who is listening?

Notes

1. Vivien Schmidt has coined the expression "regional state" to refer to the phenomenon of EU integration. See Vivien Schmidt, *Democracy in Europe: The EU and National Polities* (Oxford: Oxford University Press, 2006), 8–45.

2. The EU is a member of the World Trade Organization in its own right, as is each of its 27 member states. The European Commission alone speaks for the EU at almost all World Trade Organization meetings. The acquisition of "legal personality" via the Lisbon Treaty signed in December 2007 would allow it to engage, alongside its member states, with other intergovernmental organizations as a single actor.

3. Mario Telo, *Europe: A Civilian Power* (London: Palgrave, 2006).

4. On the European Security and Defense Identity, see Robert Hunter, *The European Security and Defense Policy: NATO's Companion—or Competi-*

tor? (Santa Monica, Calif.: RAND, 2000); Jolyon Howorth and John Keeler, eds., *Defending Europe: The EU, NATO and the Quest for European Autonomy* (London: Palgrave, 2003), chap. 1.

5. This is so called because although the political principles were agreed on at a NATO foreign ministers' meeting in Berlin in June 1996, the practical details required a further six years to hammer out (hence the phrase "Berlin-Plus").

6. Jolyon Howorth, *Security and Defence Policy in the European Union* (London: Palgrave, 2007).

7. Namely: European Council, General Affairs Council, Committee of Permanent Representatives, Political Committee, Council Secretariat, rotating EU presidency, European Commission, European Parliament, and high representative for the Common Foreign and Security Policy.

8. Anand Menon, "Security Policy: The Logic of Leaderlessness," in *Leaderless Europe*, ed. Jack Hayward (Oxford: Oxford University Press, 2007).

9. Jolyon Howorth and Anand Menon, "Complexity and International Institutions: Why the European Union Isn't Balancing the United States," forthcoming in *International Security*.

10. Article III-307.

11. Interviews with all 28 ambassadors to the Political and Security Committee, Brussels, January–September 2007.

12. See Karen E. Smith, "The End of Civilian Power EU: A Welcome Demise or Cause for Concern?" *International Spectator* 35, no. 2 (2000): 11–28.

13. Items in italics were thus in the original (1992) Petersberg Tasks.

14. The EU counterterrorism strategy of December 2005 outlines four approaches: "prevent, protect, pursue, respond," none of which involves any explicit military instruments; see http://register.consilium.eu.int/pdf/en/05/st14/st14469-re04.en05.pdf.

15. Jolyon Howorth, "The Transformation of Europe's Military Capability 1989-2005," in *Service to Country: Personnel Policy and the Transformation of Western Militaries*, ed. Curtis L. Gilroy and Cindy Williams (Cambridge, Mass.: MIT Press, 2006), 37–63.

16. European Defence Agency, *An Initial Long-Term Vision for European Defence Capability and Capacity Needs*, October 2006; http://www.eda.europa.eu/genericitem.aspx?area=Organisation&id=146.

17. Agnieszka Nowak, *Civilian Crisis Management the EU Way*, Chaillot Paper 90 (Paris: EU Institute of Strategic Studies, 2006).

18. For details, see the *ESDP Newsletter*, no. 4, July 2007, 6.

19. François Heisbourg, "The 'European Security Strategy' Is Not a Security Strategy," in *A European Way of War* (London: Centre for European Reform, 2004), 28.

20. Bastian Giegerich, *European Security and Strategic Culture: National Responses to the EU's Security and Defence Policy* (Baden Baden: Nomos, 2006); Christoph O. Meyer, *The Quest for a European Strategic Culture: Changing Norms on Security and Defence in the European Union* (London: Palgrave, 2006).

21. Giegerich, *European Security and Strategic Culture*, 195.

22. European Council, *A Secure Europe in a Better World* (Brussels: European Union, 2003); http://ue.eu.int/uedocs/cmsUpload/78367.pdf.

23. Sven Biscop, *The European Security Strategy: A Global Agenda for Positive Power* (Aldershot, U.K.: Ashgate, 2005).

24. Mary Kaldor and Marlies Glasius, eds., *A Human Security Doctrine for Europe* (London: Routledge, 2006).

25. See Martin Ortega, *Building the Future: The EU's Contribution to Global Governance*, Chaillot Paper 100 (Paris: EU Institute of Strategic Studies, 2007).

26. Martin Ortega, ed., *Global Views on the European Union*, Chaillot Paper 72 (Paris: EU Institute of Strategic Studies, 2004), 120.

27. Some of them (Cyprus and Palestine, Romania/Bulgaria, and Georgia) are maritime borders.

28. U.S. academic analysis, influenced by realism, tends to see the ESDP as a case of balancing against American power. See *International Security* 30, no. 1 (Summer 2005); and Howorth and Menon, "Complexity and International Institutions."

29. Jolyon Howorth, "The Euro-Atlantic Security Dilemma: France, Britain and the ESDP," *Journal of Transatlantic Studies* 3, no. 1 (2005): 39–54.

30. David C. Gompert and F. Stephen Larrabee, *America and Europe: A Partnership for a New Era* (Cambridge: Cambridge University Press, 1997).

31. Robert Cooper, *The Breaking of Nations: Order and Chaos in the Twenty-First Century* (New York: Atlantic Monthly Press, 2003).

PART FOUR

The State of the Alliance

CHAPTER SIX

_____

NATO

SURVIVING 9/11

Hans Binnendijk and Richard L. Kugler

What is the state of NATO today? Though NATO may not be performing as well as its supporters wish, it is doing better than its critics have expected when stock is taken of the complex new missions and difficult strategic environment the Atlantic Alliance is facing. Certainly NATO is doing better than during 2002 and 2003, one of the most troubled periods in its nearly six decades of existence. Shortly after the terrorist attacks on the United States of September 11, 2001, NATO declared an article 5 emergency, the first time it had ever invoked its collective defense clause. Yet when the United States invaded Afghanistan two months later, it turned aside offers for participation by European forces because they lacked the precision strike capabilities for the combat missions being pursued. Having been left standing on the sidelines and watching events in Afghanistan, the NATO allies came away embarrassed. In the fall of 2002, the Prague Summit was a success; for example, it launched the creation of the NATO Response Force (NRF) and Allied Command Transformation. Then, however, came the damaging debate over the impending invasion of Iraq, which split the Alliance, polarizing the United States and Britain against Germany and France in a bitter feud, and further damaging NATO's reputation and self-confidence.

Now, in 2007, the anger over Iraq has been replaced by a more forthcoming dialogue over transatlantic security policy, and NATO is taking steps to improve European military forces for power projection missions. Moreover, NATO is operating military forces in Kosovo and Afghanistan, two places where the stakes are high, the risks are serious and increasing, and success is essential. Overall, NATO is surviving the disruptions and strains that flowed in the aftermath of 9/11, and it is grappling with new challenges. But it is far from functioning perfectly, and it faces internal and external troubles that, if unresolved, could threaten its future effectiveness and relevance.

If NATO's glass today is only half full, where should it be headed tomorrow? An old slogan holds that NATO works better in practice than in theory. In the years ahead, as discussed below, NATO will need to make important improvements to both its practices and its theory in several areas. These improvements do not need to be made overnight, but NATO's members cannot afford to dawdle in pursuing them. An appropriate, necessary target for achieving them, or at least making significant progress on them, is the Berlin Summit of 2009, which will follow the Bucharest Summit of 2008. NATO thus has a two-year window in which to act, which is not a lot of time for a large, often-cumbersome alliance that typically moves slowly when big changes are in the works. A sense of commitment and timeliness is needed.

NATO'S PERFORMANCE OF ITS STRATEGIC MISSIONS, PAST AND PRESENT

The stage can be set for analyzing NATO's contemporary agenda by briefly recalling its historical performance over the past six decades, including its efforts to blend theory and practice. During its first four decades, from the late 1940s to the late 1980s, NATO's main mission focused on waging the Cold War and contending with the bipolar international system of that era. NATO entered the Cold War as a newly created alliance in weak shape facing an imposing Soviet military threat at the borders of its European members. Initially, NATO established an integrated military command and adopted two new strategic policies to guide its efforts: containment and deterrence. Both strategic policies suited the enduring requirements of that era, but NATO lacked the military power in Europe to carry them out. Had war broken out at its birth, NATO's forces would have been defeated quickly and easily. In this setting, containment and deterrence were not assured, and victory in the Cold War seemed within the grasp of the Soviet Union.

Building Stronger Cold War Defenses

To remedy its military weakness, NATO set about building a viable defense posture in the early 1950s. Its initial effort, embodied in the Lisbon defense goals, called for very large conventional forces in northern, central, and southern Europe. But these goals proved unaffordable in light of the European nations' efforts to focus their money on economic recovery. In response, NATO adopted a military strategy of massive retaliation, which called for relatively inexpensive nuclear forces to form the backbone of its deterrent posture. The effort initially was successful, but by the late 1950s massive retaliation was rapidly losing its viability because the Soviet Union was building a nuclear posture of its own. The weakening of massive retaliation threw NATO into a prolonged, agonizing debate about how to respond. In 1967, NATO finally reached agreement on a new strategy of forward defense and flexible response, which called for a combination of nuclear deterrence and stronger conventional defenses. Thereafter, NATO began the slow process of improving its conventional forces through a combination of U.S. and European efforts.

The 1970s and 1980s witnessed a growing arms race in Central Europe, in which NATO's force modernization steadily gained momentum in ways that transformed the military balance there.[1] By the late 1980s, the effort had proved successful enough to deny the Soviet Union unquestioned military supremacy in Europe. Not only was NATO now more secure but the Soviet Union found itself facing bankruptcy partly because it had invested far too much money in building military power. Shortly thereafter, the Soviet Union—its economy weak, its political system ineffective, and its ideology discredited—threw in the towel.

NATO played an instrumental role in winning the Cold War because it found a way to successfully blend theory and practice. NATO started weak and improved only slowly, but its steady pace had a strong cumulative effect, thereby earning the Alliance a letter grade of "A" at the end of the contest. The act of creating this permanent peacetime Alliance was a new feature of international politics, and it required its members to accept some losses of sovereignty and to negotiate with each other to find common ground. NATO's members embraced alliance partnership because it was a viable way to combine their scarce resources and thereby defend themselves at affordable cost. Equally important, NATO was able to craft a "transatlantic bargain" that assigned roles and missions to each of its members. The United States made major military contributions to NATO's security, but so did such important members as Britain, Germany, and France, as well as a host of smaller countries. NATO's integrated command played the vital role of combining these national military contributions to form multinational postures that ably defended all three regions. NATO succeeded because it formed an Alliance-wide consensus behind strategic policies that had strong substantive content, and it then implemented these policies well enough—despite some continuing blemishes, shortfalls, and risks—to meet the demanding security requirements of the day. Achieving this positive outcome was not easy; it required enormous strategic labor, high defense spending, patience, and persistence. Yet the success achieved made this sustained commitment well worthwhile.

Enlarging NATO after the Cold War

When the Cold War abruptly ended, bipolarity was replaced by a new, amorphous international system that endured until 9/11. Although Europe's borders no longer faced a major military threat, NATO's members decided to keep the alliance alive and functioning. They did so partly because they judged that the new era held unknown dangers, and because they wanted to preserve the practice of close transatlantic collaboration that NATO brought. The Cold War had taught them the valuable lesson that Alliance membership could not only save money but also could enhance the political and military power of members far beyond what any of them could achieve individually. Their decision was embodied in the new NATO strategic concept, which focused on multiregional operations in Europe and the creation of a multinational corps, that was adopted at the Rome Summit of 1990.

Within a few years, a new main mission confronted the Alliance: enlarging into Eastern Europe. Enlargement, its advocates said, was needed not only to remedy a security vacuum but also to help support the pursuit of democracy and capitalism in Eastern Europe, and to unify all of Europe in common institutions. At first, Partnerships for Peace (PFP) enabled interested countries to pursue collaborative relations with NATO's military forces. With PFP under way, NATO's members turned to the idea of formally admitting new members into the Alliance—a process that began in 1999 when Poland, the Czech Republic, and Hungary were admitted. In 2002, seven additional countries gained membership: the Baltic states of Estonia, Latvia, and Lithuania, plus Slovenia, Slovakia, Romania, and Bulgaria. Within the short span of only three years, NATO had grown from 16 members to 26, leaving the Alliance in charge of the security affairs of most of Europe, even as additional countries, in the Balkans and elsewhere, remain eager for membership.[2]

This enlargement process, which has not yet fully run its course, worked effectively because NATO planned it well in both theory and practice—effectively enough thus far to earn a grade of "A-." Although controversial at first, NATO's enlargement became feasible because the United States worked cooperatively with Britain, Germany, and France, thereby forming a close transatlantic partnership that, history shows, is needed to make NATO act with vision and power. The dual process of NATO and European Union enlargement has been animated by the vision of making Europe whole and free. Within only a few years, this effort has transformed Europe from being a cockpit of global calamity to becoming a poster child for unity, peace, and progress. Yet this effort is not yet complete, and thorny issues remain regarding the admission of Turkey to the EU, Ukraine's relationship with NATO and the EU, continued progress in Eastern Europe, and political stability in the Balkans.

Performing New Missions

Even as NATO has successfully enlarged in Europe, it has been compelled to address the growing need to pursue a whole set of complex new strategic missions that arise from menacing events in regions beyond its traditional geopolitical perimeters. Although the terrorist attacks of 9/11 were the signature event that announced the arrival of a new and turbulent international system, the need for NATO's expeditionary missions in distant areas emerged a decade earlier. In 1990–1991, the United States led a large United Nations–authorized coalition to eject Iraq from Kuwait. The Desert Storm campaign was a success, but it also exposed a large and growing difference between impressive U.S. capabilities for power projection and, Britain and France aside, the paltry capabilities of most European countries, including Germany, which had spent the past decades focusing on defending their borders.

In late 1995, NATO was called upon to send large peacekeeping forces to Bosnia, where they remained for several years. Then, in 1999

NATO was compelled to wage war in order to eject Serbian forces from Kosovo. Its military campaign took the form of air bombardment led by U.S. forces, which flew about 75 percent of the combat missions. But when Serbia finally capitulated and withdrew its forces, NATO was called upon to send large ground forces to maintain the peace for future years. The events in Bosnia and Kosovo showed that NATO forces could project power for enduring peacekeeping missions, but the Kosovo war again called into question the capacity of European members swiftly to project sizable forces for demanding combat missions.[3]

The events following 9/11 graphically illuminated not only the emergence of a dangerous new international system but also NATO's imperative need to become more proficient at expeditionary operations for a wide spectrum of missions, ranging from peacekeeping, to combat, to lengthy stabilization and reconstruction efforts. Thus, six years after 9/11, NATO is leading a large International Security Assistance Force of about 40,000 troops—including over 20,000 European troops—in Afghanistan, a country whose future stability is far from ensured. In addition, NATO is performing support missions for the U.S.-led coalition in Iraq even as it deals with both Kosovo and Afghanistan. What the future holds for demands upon NATO to perform expeditionary missions is to be seen; much will depend upon the outcomes in Afghanistan and Iraq as well as events elsewhere (including Darfur). But if present trends are a valid indicator, requirements for these missions are likely to remain high, and they could increase.

The growing array of complex new missions facing NATO is not limited to expeditionary operations. Indeed, terrorism and the mounting threat of weapons of mass destruction (WMD) proliferation are compelling the Alliance to devote growing attention to new forms of transatlantic homeland defense missions. In addition to defending against terrorist attacks aimed at European and American targets, NATO is now concerned about guarding sea approaches to alliance ports (Operation Active Endeavor), addressing future requirements for ballistic missile defense (BMD), and being prepared for civil emergencies and consequence management missions. Likewise, it faces the prospect of dealing with energy security and potential cyberattacks on its information networks as well as those of its members.[4] All these new missions are unfamiliar to NATO, and the Alliance is not yet well endowed—politically or militarily—to perform them. Nor does NATO have a legacy of successful experience in similar areas to draw upon for inspiration or guidance.

In handling these new missions and their preparedness requirements, NATO's performance has been spotty—earning a letter grade of "C" and even lower in some specific areas, but with a final grade of "Incomplete" because the process of change is still unfolding. The good news is that NATO is not failing in some holistic sense, and it has been showing signs of improving in several arenas. Seen in historical perspective, however, such a slow start is not necessarily surprising. So it was during the Cold War, too, when NATO gradually gained momentum only over a period of many years. The same pattern of a slow initial response followed by more vigorous performance also applies to NATO enlargement, which had to overcome early misgivings and was accepted only begrudgingly. The same may apply today, but the accelerating pace of events in the post-9/11 world suggests that the Alliance may not have as much time as it did in past years. At a minimum, NATO cannot afford the luxury of acting in leisurely ways—the risks and dangers are too great for such a response.

THE POLITICAL ENVIRONMENT FOR COMPLEX NEW MISSIONS

Beyond question, NATO's ability to perform its complex new missions—for both homeland defense and power projection—is rendered more difficult and demanding by the political environment in which it is operating. This is the case both within the Alliance and outside its borders, across a rapidly globalizing world of promise and peril. Dealing with this political environment, which is unlike anything experienced during the Cold War or its immediate aftermath, will be anything but easy, and it will require considerable skill upon the part of NATO and its members.

Strained Transatlantic Relations

Today's political environment is characterized by unusual stress and uncertainty within the alliance itself. Transatlantic relations, which traditionally have provided the glue that holds NATO together, continue to suffer from the aftershocks of not only the invasion of Iraq but also other areas of U.S.-European policy disputes, for example, global warming, arms control, the International Criminal Court, and global trade policies. Relations between the governments of the United States and its European allies have been restored to a relatively even keel, but public opinion remains more volatile.

Within the United States, public anger toward Germany and France has receded, but there is widespread uncertainty about Europe's reliability for difficult global security missions in the years ahead. In Congress and elsewhere, perceptions of low European defense spending, unfair burden sharing, and sluggish strategic responses have rankled critics of NATO.[5] The key reality is that the United States is a European power by strategic choice, not by geography. It will remain a NATO leader only if its own legitimate vital interests continue to be served by this role. Isolated policy disputes seem unlikely to fracture American public support for this role; many such disputes have occurred over NATO's long history, and the United States has never been seriously tempted to abandon NATO or Europe in response. But this support conceivably could erode if the United States were to be marginalized in Europe and/or if Europe were seen as withdrawing into a self-protective shell, thereby leaving the United States to handle a dangerous world without Europe by its side. The upshot is that European governments will need to take American domestic politics and public opinion into account in their handling of transatlantic relations. The key is to ensure that NATO works effectively not only for Europe but also for the United States.

Across Europe, public support for the United States and NATO is an even bigger problem. Numerous public opinion polls have documented an alarming decline in public support for the United States. Although such support has increased somewhat since the nadir of 2002–2003, it remains disturbingly low; in January 2007, a BBC poll found that fully 57 percent of British people view U.S. influence in the world in negative terms, and only 33 percent see it as positive. In Germany, the negative figure was 77 percent; and in France, 69 percent. In March 2007, another poll revealed majorities in Britain, France, Germany, and Spain as viewing the United States as the greatest threat to world peace. Still another poll found that support for NATO as essential to European security had declined from 69 percent in 2002 to 55 percent in 2006. Reflective of this declining support for NATO, recent polls show that 60 to 84 percent of Europeans—depending on the country—judge that the EU should be doing more in security affairs.[6]

Low public opinion polls of this sort do not necessarily reflect the attitudes and policies of most European governments, but they create a climate of opinion that governments will be hard pressed to brush aside if they persist. Regardless of their direct impact on policy, they reflect the decline of America's stock among its closest friends, on a continent that heavily owes its security and freedom to strong American support over the past decades. As such, they are a problem not only for European governments but for the U.S. government as well.

Admittedly, too much can be made of such public sentiments. To a degree, they reflect transient anger at the George W. Bush administration and its allegedly muscular, unilateralist conduct. Even so, low polls may ultimately prove enduring. After all, Europe is no longer militarily threatened in ways that were the case during the Cold War, and the importance its public opinion attaches to U.S. security guarantees and to NATO have naturally suffered. Moreover, with the United States a truly global power, and with Europe mostly focused on its own demanding continental affairs, differing priorities come to be reflected in public opinion. Diplomatic frictions are cause for further trouble. For example, the United States continues to be wary that European efforts to employ the EU for military purposes will come at the expense of NATO. Meanwhile, Europeans continue to be wary of the U.S. effort to promote democracy in the Middle East and elsewhere, and have reacted distrustfully to such U.S. initiatives as ongoing efforts to install a BMD site in Europe. Such frictions make it harder for U.S. and European governments to work together, which in turn gives rise to adverse public opinion.

Also important, the United States and Europe are often seen—on both sides of the Atlantic—as being on two different cultural wavelengths. Whereas the United States is seen as highly religious, ultracapitalist, and increasingly influenced by Hispanic and Asian immigrants, Europe is seen as secular, partly socialist, and increasingly influenced by Islamic immigrants. A few years ago, these disparate societal and cultural trends, coupled with differing attitudes toward security policies, led one American writer to claim that while the United States is from Mars, Europe is from Venus.[7] Both metaphors are highly exaggerated; the United States is not warlike or imperialist, and Europe—which maintains 2.4 million troops under arms compared to only 1.4 million in the United States—is not pacifist. In any case, the United States and Europe share many cultural bonds and increasingly interlocking economies as well as mutual support for democracy, capitalism, and multilateral collaboration. At a fundamental level, nonetheless, the United States and Europe are undeniably two different strategic entities with similar but separate interests. As history shows, cooperation between them does not come automatically and should not be taken for granted. In coming years, it will have to be nourished and advanced by wise diplomacy and collaborative policies on both sides of the Atlantic—policies that advance the interests and priorities of both the United States and Europe.

Worsening Relations with Russia

If future transatlantic relations seem hopeful, the same cannot be said for relations with Russia. A decade ago, many observers judged that Russia was on the path to becoming a full-fledged democracy in close partnership with the United States and Europe. Under President Vladimir Putin, however, Russia has been taking a different course, and its rapidly improving economy, powered by sales of oil and natural gas, is giving it a capacity to act more boldly in world affairs. Russia's political system still holds elections for the presidency and other offices, but it cannot be called a true democracy. A better description is that it currently is suspended somewhere between quasi-democracy and authoritarian capitalism, with the trends pointed in the latter direction. A hallmark of Putin's leadership has been the centralization of political and economic power in the Kremlin, enhanced control by the security bureaucracies, and the stifling of dissent, freedom of the press, and other democratic institutions.

Meanwhile, Putin's foreign policy has been marked by a growing assertion of Russian geopolitical interests, often through the use of bullying and coercion: threats to cut off energy supplies (to Ukraine and Belarus, for example), the assassination of dissidents at home or even Russian defectors abroad (like Litvinenko), and an alleged cyberattack on Estonia's information networks. Russia also still maintains its controversial military presence in Chechnya, Georgia, and Moldova, and it otherwise shows signs of intimidating its vulnerable neighbors in former Soviet territories. In the Balkans, it supports Serbia and is hostile to Kosovo independence; and in the Persian Gulf, it grudgingly supports relatively weak sanctions aimed at derailing Iran's quest for nuclear weapons. Meanwhile, Putin and his aides, complaining about U.S. and NATO policies, have threatened to withdraw from the Conventional Forces in Europe (CFE) Treaty, to scuttle the Intermediate Nuclear Forces (INF) Treaty, and to target with nuclear weapons those NATO countries hosting BMD systems, even as they paradoxically offered to cooperate with NATO in establishing missile defenses against threats from the south—by allowing NATO to use a Russian radar system in Azerbaijan for early warning of missile attacks.

These trends in Russian foreign policy reflect more than passing emotions in need of psychotherapy. Nor is it enough to suggest a new millennial ideology or a resort to imperialism. Rather, Russia seems to be propelled by a statist mentality—that is, by a hardheaded willingness to assert traditional interests and to reestablish Russia as an important player on the world scene, with a zone of control around its borders and a renewed capacity to drive wedges between the United States and Europe, and within Europe itself. On the whole, a foreign policy that seems reminiscent of the Russian tsars and some aspects of Soviet leadership is overreaching, but it may nonetheless continue beyond Putin's tenure.

Although such a foreign policy could put Russia on a collision course with NATO, a new Cold War does not seem in the offing. One key reason is that while Russia will remain a nuclear power, it no longer has the conventional forces to carry out big offensive military campaigns. Yet it will possess other instruments of leverage—including economic power—to influence its vulnerable neighbors. If so, such pressure tactics would make it necessary for the United States and its allies to take steps for the protection of NATO's new members, as well as other nearby countries that aspire to embrace democracy and to join Western institutions. In this setting, there would be new and worrisome risks; the challenge for the United States, Europe, and NATO will be to carry out their obligations to friends and allies while employing a firm but forthcoming diplomacy toward Russia that avoids a contentious and conflictual Cold Peace.

Wise diplomacy can be used to help defuse further military tensions in NATO-Russian relations. Though the Russian government is sensitive about potential threats around its borders, none of NATO's defense plans pose such threats. This certainly is the case for NATO's interest in installing BMD radar sites and a small force of 10 missile interceptors in Eastern Europe. Intended to defend against future threats from the south, this BMD capability would not be nearly large enough or oriented to pose a menace to Russia's intercontinental ballistic missile force and its overall nuclear deterrence posture. Nor do other NATO military activities—like establishing limited training sites in Eastern Europe and pursuing cooperative relations with PFP partners—create legitimate reasons for Russia to deploy intermediate-range ballistic missiles aimed at Europe or to reconstitute a large army capable of major offensive campaigns. For Russia to scuttle the CFE and INF treaties would not only elevate tensions with NATO but also damage Russia's own interests by polarizing NATO and Europe against Russia. Given these realities, a "dual-track" diplomacy that would not trade away NATO's BMD deployments but would establish and institutionalize a process of consultation and cooperation on the full range of defense issues between Russia and NATO would lessen reciprocal complaints and threats of reprisals. There are too many dangers from the south to permit the luxury of geopolitical and military competition between NATO and Russia, but the diplomatic challenge is to convince the Russian government to view its security priorities in terms that encourage cooperation, and for NATO to approach cooperation in terms that are sensitive to legitimate Russian concerns.

Turmoil in the Middle East

Although the potential troubles facing relations with Russia are worrisome, they pale by comparison with the troubles arising in the Middle East and the so-called southern arc of instability. Thus far, most of this vast region has not benefited from globalization but has instead remained mired in sluggish economic growth, with ineffective governance, growing populations, and unstable societies. In this setting, militant Islamic fundamentalism has taken hold in ways that pose a growing menace not only to existing monarchies but also to hopes for spreading democracy and market economies there. Islamic fundamentalism, in turn, has become a religious breeding ground for terrorism. In past decades, terrorism was mostly viewed as confined to the Middle East and as a reaction to the Israeli-Palestinian conflict. But because globalization is empowering nonstate actors to operate on the world stage, al Qaeda and other terrorist groups now have the capacity to inflict damage across great distances. Despite multilateral efforts to combat it, the threat of terrorism does not seem likely to recede anytime soon, and it may grow and become even more dangerous. The prospect of terrorists armed with WMD is especially frightening and real enough to be taken seriously.[8]

Terrorism is far from the only danger arising from the Middle East and surrounding regions. One danger is another Israeli-Arab war, which would further poison relations across the Middle East. Another danger is that the U.S.-led intervention in Iraq could fail in ways that spill over into a regional war, thus giving rise to ascending violence and turmoil in that country and elsewhere. The same applies to Afghanistan. Defeat in both countries could seriously damage U.S. and European influence across the entire zone. Another danger is that various Arab monarchies—for example, Egypt, Jordan, and Saudi Arabia—might fall victim to domestic unrest and be replaced by fundamentalist Islamic regimes. Yet another danger is that of failed states at multiple places across the Middle East and adjoining regions (like Pakistan), thus giving rise to rampant ethnic and religious violence. Yet another danger is interstate conflict and war in a geostrategic zone known for its mutual hatreds and lack of multilateral cooperation—for example, an Indian-Pakistani war between two nuclear powers. But with Iran seemingly dedicated to the goal of acquiring nuclear weapons and delivery systems that can reach distant areas, the gravest danger may well be accelerating WMD proliferation. The possession of such weapons could lead Iran to exert coercive political pressures on its neighbors while striving to become a Persian Gulf hegemon; nor can its use of its nuclear weapons against Israel, or turning them over to terrorists, be ruled out. Iran's acquisition of nuclear weapons could motivate other countries to seek them in turn, thus creating a highly unstable zone of proliferation and hair-trigger nuclear force postures among countries animated by fear and suspicion toward each other.[9]

All these dangers are real, and they are not mutually exclusive. The most fearsome scenario is that of a region composed of multiple fundamentalist Islamic regimes, failed states, many terrorist groups, rampant violence, and numerous nuclear powers. Conversely, optimistic scenarios of greater peace, democracy, and prosperity can be imagined, but though they may be plausible, the odds today do not favor them anytime soon. Nor will they transpire until strong strategic barriers are established to prevent dangerous trends from further engulfing the Greater Middle East and adjoining regions.

What are the implications for U.S.-European interests and policies? Although enhanced homeland defenses can help lessen vulnerabilities to terrorism and WMD attack, globalization makes it impossible for the United States and Europe to wall themselves off against dangers emanating from the Greater Middle East. Nor can the United States and Europe aspire quickly to transform this heterogeneous, chaotic region in the ways that enlargement worked in Eastern Europe. The setbacks encountered in Iraq have shown that the conditions for stable democracy may not exist there and perhaps in other countries as well. U.S. and European involvement in the Greater Middle East thus is necessary, but it must be guided by achievable goals, multilateral instruments that can attain their purposes, and traditional diplomacy that employs the art of the possible while not losing sight of ultimate visions.

How will NATO be affected? Afghanistan and the training of Iraq's military aside, NATO currently is involved in the Greater Middle East only peripherally, mainly through limited but growing efforts to establish constructive relations with militaries there (e.g., the Mediterranean Dialogue and the Istanbul Cooperation Initiative). Though some observers judge that NATO should continue to maintain a low profile there, strategic trends seem pointed in the direction of expanding NATO involvements. Indeed, a growing number of NATO missions in peace, crisis, and war seem possible if the need arises and the United States and Europe can establish the necessary consensus. Such missions could be undertaken by the integrated command, or in support of either ad hoc U.S.-European coalitions or the EU.

The need for military preparedness does not imply that resort to military force should be a regular feature in the Middle East and Persian Gulf; indeed, the experience in Iraq raises a cautionary flag in this regard. Depending upon the outcome in Iraq, the future U.S.-European peacetime military presence there may need to be small with low visibility, backed by an over-the-horizon capacity for swift interventions, which should be launched only when essential and when the path to military and political success can be clearly established. Conversely, Iranian deployment of nuclear weapons and delivery systems could require military action against that country—a difficult act that could fail and/or divide NATO—or at least mandate the presence of sizable U.S. and European forces aimed at creating a deterrence umbrella over friends and allies. Though future contingencies cannot be predicted, NATO will need to be prepared for the full spectrum of missions, while working with other institutions to embed military power in a comprehensive political approach to the region.

The Need to Look Both Inward and Outward

In summary, emerging trends in the political environment dictate that NATO will need to look both inward and outward in the years ahead. It will need to look inward to maintain its cohesion and public support while attending to homeland defense and the security requirements of a unifying Europe. But NATO's fate will also be heavily determined by its capacity to look outward, and to prepare and act accordingly. Some observers proclaim that NATO should become a fully global alliance, with involvements as far away as Asia. Regardless of how this ambitious vision is appraised, NATO will need to become a multiregion alliance whose strategic horizon extends well eastward and southward from Europe. It will need to deal effectively with a resurgent Russia and with other big powers, such as China and India, that are intent on influencing the future global security order. In addition, it will need to contribute importantly to U.S. and European efforts in the Greater Middle East and adjoining regions. These security challenges—which have been acknowledged by NATO's Riga Summit Declaration of November 2006—will not be mastered easily, for they create complexities and demands that rival or exceed those of the Cold War. The agenda of creating appropriate theories and practices for handling these challenges and their associated missions is daunting, but not beyond NATO's capacity if it takes full advantage of its time-tested political and military assets.

NATO'S DEFENSE AND SECURITY AGENDA

The past three NATO Summits at Prague (2002), Istanbul (2004), and Riga (2006) all issued fine-sounding communiqués calling for a dynamic Alliance focused on strategic affairs. Yet, despite tangible improvements, NATO is being questioned for not moving fast and boldly enough. To chart the Alliance's future course, the Bucharest Summit of 2008 is a benchmark, but it is likely to be devoted mainly to enlargement. While a minisummit may be held in the spring of 2009 for NATO's 60th anniversary, strategic issues are most likely to be addressed the following November during a Summit in Berlin that will mark the 20th anniversary of the fall of the Berlin Wall. Four separate but interrelated areas should dominate the agenda: first, to accelerate improvements in NATO's military forces and capabilities for new-era missions and homeland defense; second, to carry out effectively NATO operations in Afghanistan and Kosovo; third, to pursue closer cooperation between the United States and the EU, as well as with other institutions, in order to build a better capacity for pursuing comprehensive approaches to new missions and strategic priorities; and fourth, to forge the needed consensus behind a new NATO strategic concept that provides an updated policy and strategy for guiding the Alliance.

Improved Capabilities

Then–NATO secretary-general George Robertson often chanted the mantra "capabilities, capabilities, capabilities." This mantra reflected his focus on strengthening NATO with new military capabilities for new missions. Owing heavily to his leadership, the Prague Summit of 2002 launched NATO on the course of transformation, crafted a Prague Capabilities Commitment to help chart NATO's force goals, called for the creation of the NRF to execute high-technology strike missions and to serve as a model for transformation, and created the new Allied Command Transformation (ACT) to help close the widening gap between U.S. and European forces for expeditionary missions. The Istanbul Summit of 2004 urged continuation of these important changes, and the Riga Summit of 2006 took the unusual step of using its communiqué, plus the accompanying *Comprehensive Political Guidance (CPG)*, to spell out in considerable detail how NATO forces and capabilities needed to improve.[10]

The Riga Summit called for concrete steps in such disparate areas as flexible forces for the full spectrum of missions, better Special Operations Forces (SOF), better stabilization and reconstruction (S&R) assets, higher readiness, improved information networking, better command structures, improved intelligence, better precision strike systems, improved WMD defense assets, better standardization and interoperability, better airlift for strategic mobility, and improved logistic support for sustaining operations in distant areas. In calling for better forces for expeditionary missions, NATO did not have purely small contingencies in mind. The *CPG* called for a capacity to launch and sustain concurrent major joint operations and smaller operations, including at strategic distance. To this end, it called for 40 percent of NATO's ground forces to be structured, prepared, and equipped for deployable operations, and for 8 percent to be ready to undertake such actions at any single time. NATO did not publicly specify exactly what these percentages mean for force goals, but a reasonable estimate is that they translate into preparing 20 to 25 of NATO's divisions (or their equivalent in brigades) for deployability, and making 4 to 5 divisions ready for such missions at any time. The *CPG* also calls for commensurate contributions from air and naval forces. Forty percent of these assets would equate to about 1,200 tactical combat aircraft and 250 naval warships.[11]

How do current European and NATO defense plans and programs stack up in relation to these ambitious standards for improved deployability, modernization, and transformation? Overall, NATO's progress has been faster than many critics realize, but slower than wanted by NATO's military authorities and the U.S. government. Moreover, the track record varies considerably among NATO's members. Britain and France have made substantial progress toward reforming their forces for expeditionary missions and acquiring transformational assets, and they plan further progress in the years ahead. In recent years, Germany and the Netherlands have also embarked upon this process of change, as have a few other countries. Elsewhere across Europe, progress has been slower and less visionary—a product of low defense budgets and scarce investment funds, a problem that plagues nearly every European country to one degree or another.

Even so, new combat aircraft and ships, modern munitions, unmanned aerial vehicle reconnaissance assets, information networks, and other technologies are being acquired slowly but steadily—with Europe's wealthiest countries leading the pace and the less wealthy countries trailing behind. Hope for accelerating progress in the near term comes from the fact that significant improvements in combat capability can come from low-cost, high-leverage changes to training, doctrine, critical enabling assets, and force structures. Such improvements can be combined together to elevate European forces that, in many cases, already possess modern platforms and do not need expensive new weapons for some time. Barring a major increase in European defense spending, 5 to 10 more years will be needed before longer-term modernization programs have their full impact. During this extended period, such new assets as the Joint Strike Fighter, the Eurofighter, the Network Enabled Capability, and the Ground Surveillance Monitor system—as well as other new weapon systems—will be arriving. But in the intervening years, European military capabilities will be improving, as will the capacity to perform new missions and to operate with U.S. military forces.

Apart from calling for higher European defense spending, much can be done to help meet these sound military goals by the time of the November 2009 summit in Berlin. For one, NATO's interest in defense transformation must be maintained by political and military leaders in its member states. In the United States, fatigue with Iraq and abnormally high defense budgets have combined with disillusion over the Pentagon's focus on futurist technologies to begin giving transformation a bad name. But properly interpreted, transformation does not have to be fixated on one technological and operational agenda. Instead, it should be seen as a process aimed at preparing military forces for new missions. If the new missions now include counterinsurgency and S&R operations, then transformation should be broadened to focus on them. Regardless, the disillusions with transformation apply to the United States, not to Europe and NATO, where this term is focused not on high technology but on the strategic basics of power projection and expeditionary operations. NATO and the Europeans need to remain focused on transformation as it applies to them.

High-level leadership in this arena can help preserve a supportive atmosphere in Europe and the United States regardless of the travails in Iraq. NATO can help by breathing more energetic life into the ACT, which has suffered from being disconnected from both SHAPE headquarters (the headquarters of Allied Command Operations, or ACO) as well as from the U.S. Joint Forces Command (JFCOM). Currently a U.S. military officer heads both JFCOM and ACT; eliminating such dual hatting and putting a European officer in charge of ACT would improve this arrangement. Regardless of command practices, ACT needs to become better connected to both ACO and JFCOM and to be given a well-focused NATO and European transformation agenda to pursue.

Another near-term priority is to ensure that the NRF continues succeeding. The NRF achieved full operational capability in the fall of 2006, but continuing labor power shortages—the NRF totals about 25,000 military personnel from all components—will need to be overcome with such steps as elongating its six-month period of rotational duty, reducing its size, dropping its forced entry mission, or establishing a tiered readiness system. For example, a longer period of rotational duty might provide a more-capable force while reducing cumulative labor power requirements continuously to populate one on-duty NRF while another is training to assume future duty within six months. Care must be taken, however, to prevent the NRF from losing its sharp military edge and its usability for swift strike missions. Common funding of the NRF is a priority to help ensure that its contributing members do not bear the full burden of its expenses. Also important, the NRF will not retain the enthusiasm of European militaries if it is perpetually kept at high readiness but never used. Giving the NRF a tour of duty in Afghanistan could contribute to its prowess, help demonstrate its strategic utility, and enhance NATO's effectiveness.

Faster progress on creating better NATO forces and capabilities for SOF and S&R missions also makes sense. The 2006 Riga Summit called for establishing an SOF Coordination Center but failed to identify its final location. Establishing this facility is a near-term priority; an equal priority is assembling the related multinational forces of several hundred U.S. and European troops, and creating common doctrine and capabilities so that they can be used for future missions in the near term. Similarly, the Riga Summit mentioned the need for better S&R capabilities, but it took no steps to establish a command structure or coordination center or to specify the size and characteristics of the forces that may be needed. Although some European militaries prefer to remain exclusively focused on combat missions, other militaries have expressed interest in the S&R mission, and have the labor power to contribute importantly. Because the S&R mission could be increasingly demanding, NATO needs to play a leadership role in identifying requirements, establishing force goals, and coordinating the training and equipping of units.

NATO also can intensify its focus on preparing High Readiness Forces (HRF) for expeditionary missions. Whether the configuration of ground forces envisioned by the *CPG* is optimal is not clear, however; the 4 or 5 HRF divisions sought by the *CPG* may not be enough to satisfy NATO's elevated sense of requirements in this arena, and a total of 6 to 8 divisions would better meet the needs of NATO's military commanders. Meanwhile, the large pool of 20 to 25 mobilizable divisions called for by the *CPG* runs the risk of diluting NATO's ability to properly focus its energies for force improvement. A pool this sizable is mainly intended to provide a rotational base for long-term sustainment in distant areas, but a requirement for this many divisions seems improbable. For expeditionary missions, NATO might be better served by a bigger ready posture of 6 to 8 divisions and a smaller total pool of 12 to 15 divisions.

Regardless of the numbers chosen, NATO's near-term priority should be to focus intently on making at least four divisions, as well as commensurate air and naval forces, truly ready for swift deployment and a wide spectrum of expeditionary missions. Improvements in such key areas as information networks, strategic mobility, and multinational logistics are especially needed if NATO's Allied Rapid Reaction Corps, or one of its other five deployable multinational corps headquarters, is to deploy with a full complement of troops and engage in high-intensity combat in distant areas. Ideally, information networks should extend at least down to the brigade or battalion level and should be sufficiently comprehensive to permit regular joint operations with air and naval forces. Strategic transport is a long-standing NATO deficiency that needs remedial solutions. A 15-nation consortium has been established to acquire a few big C-17 transports, NATO has created an airlift management organization, and it will await the eventual procurement of the A-400M transport. Even so, NATO's airlift capacity will not come close anytime soon to the capacity to lift a large force of four well-armed divisions, which could weigh over 500,000 tons. Reliance upon improved multinational sealift is the only solution to this problem. NATO needs to enhance its capacity swiftly to mobilize commercial ships capable of carrying military cargoes; fortunately, progress in this arena is being made. Likewise, integrated multinational logistics assets are necessary for expeditionary missions in order to trim support needs, accelerate deployment rates, and help produce greater combat effectiveness.

Finally, NATO can accelerate its preparations for new homeland defense missions, which are bringing article 5 back to life as an important factor in the Alliance's strategic calculus. Continued progress on analyzing how BMDs against southern threats can best be established is a high priority, for such threats could materialize in the coming years. Missile defenses are needed for both NATO military forces and for continental Europe as well as for the United States. The challenge is to assemble a proper combination of command, control, and communications facilities; radar sites; and layered missile deployments that will best provide protection at affordable cost. An equal challenge will be to forge a consensus among European countries and to respond to Russia's concerns. Defense against terrorism is mostly the responsibility of member countries and their law enforcement agencies. But in addition to guarding sea approaches to ports, NATO can play a contributing role in civil emergencies and consequence management. In addition, NATO clearly will need to work closely with member governments, the EU, and other institutions to become better prepared to help ensure energy security and to defend against cyberattacks on information networks, which have the potential to damage not only NATO military forces but also European civilian infrastructures.[12]

Effective Operations

In today's setting, Lord Robertson's mantra of NATO's capabilities has been supplemented by another mantra, that of Secretary-General Jaap de Hoop Scheffer: "operations, operations, operations." This mantra reflects the dramatic growth of NATO's external operations, and their compelling importance for its interests and effectiveness, as well as for global security and stability. Until and beyond 2009, its operations in Afghanistan and Kosovo will rightfully claim a great deal of its attention. The Riga Summit Declaration proclaimed Afghanistan to be NATO's top priority, but failure is a worrisome possibility. NATO's mission there, through the UN-authorized International Security Assistance Force (ISAF), is to contribute to peace and stability, and to support the Afghan government in its efforts to provide security and S&R (table 6.1). ISAF operates alongside U.S. forces for Operation Enduring Freedom, which pursues combat missions against the Taliban and al Qaeda. ISAF grew during 2006–2007 from 10,000 personnel to 40,000, and the number of Provincial Reconstruction Teams (PRTs) grew from 9 to 25, with additional PRTs under consideration.[13] Surface appearances might suggest a combined military presence of 55,000 troops—counting ISAF and Operation Enduring Freedom—should be enough to pacify the country. But Afghanistan is a big country, with a population larger than Iraq's, where 160,000 U.S. and allied troops have not succeeded in their pacification missions. Similar to the situation in Iraq, Afghanistan's government and military forces have not yet been highly effective. To date, 40,000 members of the Afghan National Army and more than 60,000 members of the Afghan National Police have been trained, but both institutions will not reach full size and effectiveness for several more years. The result has been to leave U.S. and NATO military forces stretched thin, in the face of grueling opposition by the Taliban aimed at wearing down the willingness of their governments to stay the course.

Table 6.1. International Security Assistance Force Troops in
Afghanistan, May 2007

Country	Troops (thousands)
United States	17.0
United Kingdom	6.7
Germany	3.0
Canada	2.5
Netherlands	2.2
Italy	2.0
Turkey	1.2
Poland	1.1
France	1.0
Others	5.0

Source: International Security Assistance Force data.

A further complication is that when NATO first assumed command of ISAF, several European contingents there (e.g., German forces) operated under national mandates and caveats limiting their deployment to relatively peaceful areas of Afghanistan and prohibiting their use in major combat operations. These restrictions have been loosened somewhat, and ISAF forces and PRTs have been allowed to spread out farther over the countryside, including into dangerous areas. The result has been greater participation by European forces in combat with the Taliban, but a related rise in European casualties—plus embarrassing involvements in firefights that have killed innocent Afghan citizens and the prospect that military actions might spread into northwestern Pakistan against Taliban strongholds—have increased public and political opposition in several countries, like Germany, Italy, and Canada.

Improvements to U.S. and NATO force operations can enhance the effectiveness of combat, S&R, and training missions there, and as Afghan forces develop greater competence, they can gradually assume security burdens and responsibilities. At issue, nonetheless, is whether European and American resolve will wither before the Afghan government can take over, thus compelling major troop withdrawals and exposing the country to gains, and perhaps reconquest, by the Taliban.

With intervention in Afghanistan often equated across Europe with intervention in Iraq, distaste for the latter gives rise to lukewarm support for the former, despite the differing motives and consequences of these two interventions. Afghanistan was invaded because it was a locus of international terrorism and the launch pad for 9/11; Iraq's invasion aimed at removing the Saddam Hussein regime and its alleged WMD. The United States and NATO cannot afford to let remote Afghanistan again become a safe haven for al Qaeda and other terrorist groups. If anything, ISAF should have more troops at its disposal, and its presence should be extended another three to five years, while needed help from the UN, the World Bank, the EU, and other international institutions is also increased.

In Kosovo, the UN-authorized Kosovo Force's (KFOR's) prospects are brighter than ISAF's, its missions are less demanding, and its operations are more mature. KFOR's mission is to provide a climate of security and stability, and to work with other institutions to help build a democratic government there. The Riga Summit proclaimed its support for the efforts of UN special envoy Martti Ahtisaari to conclude the process successfully. Meanwhile, NATO improved its military operations by reducing national caveats on force usage and by adopting a task-force approach. Notwithstanding such progress, conditions in Kosovo still have the capacity to deteriorate rapidly into a powder keg unless Kosovo's independence from Serbia is successfully negotiated to the mutual satisfaction of all the parties involved, including Russia. Pending such an outcome, Kosovo might declare independence on its own, and thereby trigger renewed internal violence plus a military confrontation with Serbia. In the coming period, therefore, even though NATO's activities in Kosovo will be mainly focused on diplomacy, and though the EU may acquire a growing leadership role, KFOR's continuing military presence there will be needed to prevent all sides from resorting to violence.

Enhanced Cooperation and a Comprehensive Approach

In today's setting, a new mantra might properly be added to NATO's strategic agenda: "cooperation, cooperation, cooperation." One reason is that enhancing multilateral cooperation within NATO will be key to determining its capacity to succeed in its complex new missions. In addition, enhanced cooperation within NATO and with other institutions, including the EU, will be critical to carrying out the Riga

Summit's call for a comprehensive approach to addressing security and development challenges. The idea behind a comprehensive approach is not only to enhance NATO's effectiveness for complex missions but also to harness multiple instruments—political, diplomatic, economic, and military—that must be employed effectively to achieve common strategic goals. A comprehensive approach is needed to provide better, more effective options than reliance upon improvised, ad hoc approaches to each operation—approaches that often fail to work when they are cobbled together at the last moment. In 2006 at Riga, NATO's leaders called for the prompt creation of practical proposals that could help advance this agenda.

When developing these proposals, close cooperation between the United States and its European NATO allies is a must. The United States can contribute to this agenda by reaffirming its military commitment to the Alliance. As part of its global military reposturing, the U.S. military presence in Europe is being reduced from 150,000 personnel to about 65,000, cutting the U.S. Army presence from four heavy brigades in Germany and an airmobile brigade in Italy to only a single Stryker brigade in Germany plus the airmobile unit in Italy, thus leaving a single Army Stryker brigade to fulfill core interoperability and training missions—and leaving perhaps two or three Army brigades in Central Europe. This condition creates the misimpression that the United States views Europe as a launch pad for operations elsewhere and is downplaying its commitment to NATO's multilateralism. Regardless of future troop levels, regularly committing units to the NRF and assuming command of one of NATO's six deployable corps would help correct that view.

Steps also can be taken to enhance the cooperation of European members with each other, with NATO, and with the United States. French president Nicolas Sarkozy's stance creates an opportunity to further strengthen France's already important role in NATO and to enhance U.S.-European cooperation as well as NATO's cohesion and effectiveness. France's military forces are among NATO's best for power projection, and they are participating in the NRF, the Eurocorps, ISAF, and other Alliance military activities. If common agreement can be found, a more preeminent role for France in NATO's command structure makes sense. For example, France could be given leadership of the NATO command in Lisbon and/or leadership positions in ACT and ACO.

The goal of strengthening France's role in NATO should not be seen in isolation. Britain will need to continue playing its traditional leadership role in close partnership with the United States, and Germany will need to continue emerging from its earlier reluctance to play a strong role in carrying out new NATO missions. Similar contributing roles are required by other long-standing Alliance members—as is the case, for example, with Denmark's leadership in helping NATO forge a comprehensive approach. Cooperative outreach to NATO's new members and PFP partners also makes sense. Already Poland has been contributing importantly to ISAF and coalition operations in Iraq, and some other new members have been similarly active. New members could be encouraged to focus on specialized roles and missions in areas where they possess usable assets and competencies. Similarly, PFP partners, which include such wealthy, advanced countries as Sweden and Finland, should be able to respond to NATO's invitation to contribute to the NRF. Enhanced PFP cooperation with Ukraine and Georgia also is important to help bring greater stability and security to them and their regions.

A closer, more collaborative relationship between NATO and the EU is also paramount so that both institutions can better perform their important strategic roles. The Riga Summit Declaration pointed out that a cooperative dialogue is already taking place between NATO and the EU at high levels and in such places as the Balkans and Africa. Nonetheless, critics argue that the ideological distance between the two institutions remains wide and that their professional bureaucracies often still view each other in competitive terms. Enduring competition between them can only be self-defeating for both bodies, and it is unnecessary, for they play complementary roles that must be harmonized. NATO remains Europe's premier defense alliance and repository of multilateral military capabilities and close ties to the U.S. military. The EU provides an institution to harness Europe's considerable political, diplomatic, and economic power not only for unifying the continent but also for pursuing stable security affairs elsewhere. These two potent but interdependent institutions need to work closely together, not view each other as rivals or fail to cooperate closely.

In recent years, the EU has been pursuing a common security and defense policy (the European Security and Defense Policy, or ESDP), and it has been striving to enhance its military prowess by establishing a rapid reaction force as well as 15 battalion-sized battle groups that can be deployed outside Europe. The Berlin-Plus accord provides a vehicle for the EU to draw upon NATO military assets for support when both bodies so agree. The time when the EU's military strength will be sufficient to greatly lessen Europe's dependence upon NATO, however, lies in the distant future. In the years ahead, NATO needs to support sensible EU military programs while discouraging any unnecessary duplication that would waste scarce defense resources. To the extent of the politically possible, EU military forces and capabilities should draw closer to NATO in an effort to create complementary roles and missions that serve both bodies. For example, some EU battle groups could be assigned to the NRF, and some of the EU's constabulary forces could be made available for NATO's S&R missions.

Another practical idea of strategic import is to pursue enhanced military cooperation with friends and allies in distant regions. Though few observers support NATO enlargement as far away as Asia, cooperative activities with such countries as Australia, Japan, South Korea, and India can enhance the scope of potential multilateral actions with them when the need arises—as has been the case in Iraq and Afghanistan. NATO-sponsored activities, for example, could take the form of common training, exercises, and joint planning. In addition to strengthening NATO's capacity, such activities could help encourage greater military and defense cooperation in unstable regions where multilateralism is badly needed. This is the case in Asia, but it also holds true for such regions as the Caucasus, South Central Asia, the Greater Middle East, and Africa. The Riga Summit Declaration did not embrace the idea of global partnerships for NATO, partly because of some members' opposition, but in the coming years, this idea could become an important contributor to NATO's comprehensive approach and its need to pursue multiple demanding security missions.

As agreed by NATO's members, a comprehensive approach also requires that it work collaboratively with multiple international institutions, which include the UN, the World Bank and International Monetary Fund, and nongovernmental organizations, as well as local actors in distant regions. This directive does not imply that NATO should start performing civilian functions, but it does mean that in many cases, military and civilian functions must be blended together so that both perform effectively on behalf of common strategic goals. Such collaboration is especially needed in regions that require both security and development, and where one cannot be pursued without making progress in the other. The need to work with diverse actors, in turn, means that NATO must develop the institutional capacities to perform this task. Progress has already been made in the Balkans and Afghanistan, but more will be needed in the coming years.

Achieving closer cooperation between NATO and multiple other institutions is vital, but it will not be achieved easily or quickly. Regardless of institutional arrangements, a comprehensive approach aimed at fusing military and civilian instruments can work only if it is guided by sound policies that are implemented effectively. As Iraq has shown, success does not always follow promptly in the wake of a significant application of military and economic resources. The key to success is to become skilled at "effects-based approaches" to planning and operations. This technique requires careful appraisals of the relationships between ends and means, and between complex actions and complicated consequences. The idea is to blend diverse instruments to ensure that they achieve not only their immediate military goals but also their enduring political, economic, and strategic goals. It requires not only adequate resources and instruments but also intellectual acuity in applying them so that they work effectively in achieving their desired results. This form of strategic effects-based approaches has been taking hold within the U.S. military and interagency community and at NATO Headquarters as well. It needs to continue being adopted and nourished.

A New Strategic Concept

The idea of writing a new NATO strategic concept is never popular at NATO Headquarters and among member governments because it entails intense multilateral negotiations and can trigger divisive debates over strategic fundamentals. Yet history shows that NATO needs a relevant strategic concept to help unite its members in common causes and to provide a future sense of direction and purpose. The strategic concepts of 1967, 1990, and 1999 were all hard to negotiate; but once they were adopted, they played important roles in preserving NATO's cohesion and advancing its strategic effectiveness. The current strategic concept was written for the Washington Summit of 1999, and it has become outdated because of the major changes that have arisen since then. As a result, NATO is left relying upon summits and ministerial sessions to issue communiqués that craft new strategic directions. So it was with the *Comprehensive Political Guidance*, which was originally intended to help craft new political guidance; when it emerged, however, it mainly focused on the technical details of NATO military plans and programs, and it did not address in any detail new strategic priorities and relationships. Instead, it merely reaffirmed the 1999 strategic concept's directive that NATO should remain a collective defense alliance under article 5 and should also be prepared to carry out non–article 5 crisis response operations.

A new strategic concept is needed, and it should be ready for adoption at the Berlin Summit of 2009. The new document should reaffirm the centrality of close transatlantic relations between the United States and Europe and should provide a new sense of roles, missions, defense requirements and force goals, burden sharing, authorities and responsibilities, and Alliance decisionmaking procedures. A key goal should be a new transatlantic bargain that serves the United States and Europe, and that cements their enduring strategic partnership on terms that can be strongly supported on both sides of the Alliance. The new strategic concept should identify the continuing importance of old collective defense missions, but it should also cover such new missions as missile defense, defense against terrorism, cyberdefense, and energy security. Equally important, it should articulate the growing importance of new NATO missions inside and outside Europe, and it should provide a common policy and strategy for dealing with Russia, the Balkans, the Greater Middle East, and other endangered regions. It should also provide clear guidance on working with the EU and other international institutions as part of a comprehensive approach. NATO's recent success in promoting internal dialogue, adopting new policies, and pursuing new practices may make writing a new strategic concept easier than is realized in some quarters. If necessary, perhaps NATO can begin soon by forming a team of outside experts from the United States and Europe that can prepare an unofficial report, which in turn can serve as a basis for drafting the new strategic concept.

CONCLUSION

NATO faces a future that is full of challenges and troubles but also provides opportunities—if the Alliance is up to the task. A stronger transatlantic alliance that performs well in theory and practice, and that can perform new missions adeptly, is needed for Europe, adjoining regions, and globally. The United States must contribute to this endeavor, and so must European members. Although the United States and Europe total only about 15 percent of the world's population, they possess nearly 50 percent of its economic wealth, and they can muster substantial political and military power. Yet they must stand together, for if they fall apart, they will both surely fail. NATO is their main instrument for standing together in the critical realm of security and defense affairs, and it can be an alliance that reaches out to cooperate with other institutions and actors in the pursuit of comprehensive policies that require multiple instruments. But NATO cannot be an alliance in stasis. It must remain an alliance constantly in motion, with new strategic priorities and capacities in mind. Fulfilling this mandate frames the strategic agenda ahead—for the Berlin Summit and long afterward.

Notes

1. For details on U.S. and NATO defense modernization programs during the Cold War, see Richard L. Kugler, *Commitment to Purpose: How Alliance Partnership Won the Cold War* (Santa Monica, Calif.: RAND, 1993).

2. For analysis of the politics and policies of NATO enlargement, see Ronald D. Asmus, *Opening NATO's Door: How the Alliance Remade Itself for a New Era* (New York: Columbia University Press, 2002).

3. For a portrayal of NATO's actions during the Kosovo War, see Wesley K. Clark, *Waging Modern War: Bosnia, Kosovo, and the Future of Combat* (New York: PublicAffairs, 2001).

4. Energy security issues especially arise because Europe relies heavily upon the Persian Gulf for oil and upon Russia for oil and gas. Cyberthreats are worrisome because so-called Botnets can be used for denial-of-service attacks aimed at flooding, and therefore temporarily crippling, multiple information networks, both civil and military.

5. Whereas U.S. peacetime defense spending (wartime missions aside) consumes about 4 percent of gross domestic product, European defense spending totals only about 2 percent of GDP. The difference is especially manifested in bigger U.S. investment budgets for research, development, testing, and evaluation (RDT&E) and for procurement, which determine the rate of force modernization.

6. See BBC World Service Poll, "World View of U.S. Role Goes From Bad to Worse," January 23, 2007; *Financial Times* / Harris Interactive Poll, "Except for Spain, Majorities or Pluralities in Five European Countries Believe Life Has Become Worse Since Joining the EU," March 19, 2007; German

Marshall Fund and Compagnia di São Paolo, "Transatlantic Trends, Key Findings 2006," June 2006.

7. See Robert Kagan, *Of Paradise and Power: America and Europe in the New World Order* (New York: Vintage Books, 2004).

8. For an analysis of contemporary writings about global security trends, see Hans Binnendijk and Richard Kugler, *Seeing the Elephant: The U.S. Role in Global Security* (Washington, D.C.: Potomac Books, 2006).

9. For a historical analysis of Western policies toward Iran, see Kenneth Pollack, *The Persian Puzzle: The Conflict between Iran and America* (New York: Random House, 2004).

10. See NATO, *Riga Summit Declaration* (Brussels: NATO Headquarters, 2006); and NATO, *Comprehensive Political Guidance of the Riga Summit* (Brussels: NATO Headquarters, 2006).

11. European members of NATO field a total of about 70 division-equivalents, 3,100 tactical combat aircraft, and 600 naval ships. Of these ground forces, not all are committed to NATO and some are maintained at a low level of readiness that makes them unavailable for potential deployment missions. For some years, NATO's premier force for such missions has been the Allied Rapid Reaction Corps, which is capable of commanding 4 to 5 divisions. A pool of 20 to 25 potentially deployable divisions is large enough to provide all members with an opportunity to contribute meaningfully, with national forces ranging from 2 divisions to single brigades. For details on NATO/European forces, see International Institute for Strategic Studies, *The Military Balance, 2006–2007* (London: International Institute for Strategic Studies, 2006).

12. For analysis, see *CTNSP/INSS Special Report: Transatlantic Homeland Defenses* (Washington, D.C.: National Defense University Press, 2006).

13. See NATO, *Final Communiqué: Meeting of the North Atlantic Council Defense Ministers Session* (Brussels: NATO Headquarters, 2007).

CHAPTER SEVEN

NATO AT 60

A VIEW FROM EUROPE

Benoît d'Aboville

The North Atlantic Treaty Organization has not only survived its original purpose, which had to do with the collective defense of Europe against the threat of the Soviet Union and, eventually, its Warsaw Pact allies. In the much more complex post–Cold War security environment, NATO has come to embrace new and increasingly ambitious goals and missions—to an extent that now leads some to fear an overly ambitious agenda. This chapter seeks to ascertain whether these goals and missions can be sustained in the years ahead without a deep evolution of the Alliance itself, and, assuming its sustainability, a related transformation of transatlantic relations.

A VERY ADAPTABLE ALLIANCE

Over the years, NATO has repeatedly demonstrated its capacity to respond to ongoing changes in the geopolitical conditions it has faced, showing remarkable institutional adaptability and political resiliency. However, the challenges for the future are daunting: How can the Alliance stay efficient while the gap between U.S. and European military capacities continues to grow? What are the limits of the "open door" approach to NATO enlargement, if any? Can NATO retain both political legitimacy and domestic support for expeditionary missions—and if so, how? Will the main purpose of the Alliance remain centered on the defense of the European continent, and what would be the price of NATO "going global" to its cohesion?

During and since the Cold War, the evolution of NATO has not been the result of grand designs, notwithstanding many strenuous, and occasionally divisive, attempts to develop and implement long-term "strategic concepts." Instead, what usually mattered most for the allies, and best moved the organization to adapt its structures, were the immediate consequences of geopolitical changes and the need to face the new challenges they raised. So it was, for example, with the achievement of nuclear parity by the Soviet Union, which led to a strategy of flexible response; and so it was, too, with such NATO-defining moments as the deployment of Intermediate Nuclear Forces, the end of the Warsaw Pact, the calls for NATO enlargement to its former members, the Balkan wars and, most recently, the shock of the September 11, 2001, terrorist attacks and the war in Iraq.[1]

Throughout, NATO's ability to adapt and transform has always been underpinned by the continuing strength of the transatlantic partnership. Though the partnership has covered vital economic and political dimensions that have gone beyond the security guarantee that defined the transatlantic relationship at its birth, defense has remained its most convincing raison d'être—the essence of Europe's commitment to a formalized relationship with the United States, and, for Washington, the political-military framework of choice for its involvement with and in Europe.

Admittedly, such premises have often been questioned on both sides of the Atlantic. In Europe especially, there have been recurring doubts about the continued centrality of the Alliance for Washington, where each generational change of American elites has been viewed as further evidence that U.S. priorities were shifting to Asia. After the Cold War, therefore, and especially after 9/11, an open U.S. interest in "coalitions" whose composition would respond to the nature of the "missions" to be undertaken appeared to confirm such European apprehensions of a U.S. drift.[2] With the strategic interests of the United States now defined by growing concerns about the Middle East and Asia, where they might no longer be necessarily consonant with those of the European NATO allies, the institutional framework of the Alliance might no longer be America's security institution of choice. Instead, NATO risked becoming a mere "toolbox" that would be especially usable for its senior partner—a condition that reflected neither the initial U.S. postwar aspirations nor Europe's post–Cold War expectations. Thus, an Alliance that had often been unsure of itself and of its post–Cold War relevance forgot that those discussions about the centrality of NATO were not new and predated the George W. Bush administration, which, however, gave them an official status that was truly unprecedented, in tone as well as in substance.

"If American military operations abroad are executed entirely by "unilateral force," wrote Irving Kristol nearly three decades ago, "a corresponding unilateral foreign policy will emerge. From having been the centerpiece of American foreign policy, NATO will become an afterthought and then a mere memory. Not that the United States will ever repudiate a very keen interest in the defense of Western Europe. But the European partners in NATO will discover the partnership to have been dissolved, and that they are now allies of convenience-client states...And unless they increase their own defense expenditures, ... they could end up as allies of inconvenience."[3] After the Cold War, this warning appeared about to be confirmed. The Gulf War first, and the wars in Bosnia and, especially, Kosovo next, led many in the Pentagon not only to reject the "war by the committee" allegedly waged by NATO in Kosovo—by exaggerating the downside of the necessary aspects of political accommodation between allies—but also to point to the growing lack of interoperability and deployment capacities of the European armed forces (with possibly the exception, at that time, of the British forces).

The idea still lingers that NATO could somehow stand in the way of the exercise of American power and therefore affect the execution of U.S. policies. Yet, six years after 9/11, the failure of the U.S. strategy in Iraq has shown that unilateralism carries a heavy price, and that even for a peerless power like the United States the allies can have political, if not military, value. How—meaning in what structure—the support of such allies should be sought by Washington in the future is not clear: through NATO, with mission-based coalitions, on the basis of strategic bilateral partnerships, or by training and equipping local partners. There are many available options, and all of them are likely to remain on the table for some time to come. But in Europe at least, it is now believed that NATO is back as an obvious choice, even if not necessarily (or always) the first.

The approach pursued by the United States in Iraq—the so-called coalition of the willing—can hardly be viewed as a model for the future. Politically, such a coalition added little to the international legitimacy of the operation, but its impact proved to be highly negative at the domestic level of the concerned states. Militarily, the 33 "willing" countries, soon to be reduced to 25, contributed less than 8 percent of the troops deployed in Iraq in 2007, at a cost for U.S. taxpayers of $3.5 billion (with 66 percent of these funds going to Poland, which is nevertheless complaining about the lack of financial gains provided by its "willingness," and 20 percent going to Jordan for safeguarding the Iraqi borders).[4] As Julian Lindley-French notes, "For the Americans, the Alliance is a tool to project American security through American leadership. All that matters therefore is the necessary military capacity and capabilities to do the job. For most Western Europeans, the Alliance is the forum for influencing American policy and thereafter agreeing strategy. For Central and Eastern Europe the Alliance guarantees their territorial integrity. Today the Alliance stands on the cusp between strategic collective security and collective defence and, in an ideal world, the three camps could be fashioned into a useful strategic tool."[5]

The fact that NATO's first order of business should remain the military security and collective defense of its members is not in question. However, the nature of military operations has changed, and these changes raise a series of new challenges. Adding to these challenges is the idea of a "Global NATO" that would literally "reinvent the West," because the Alliance would not only be extended to likeminded states but also assume the civilian and military challenges of stabilization and reconstruction (S&R) to map a plan for a renewed, or even recast, alliance. More clarity is needed to explain the consequences of such decisions for NATO's military requirements and, in institutional terms, about the forging of new relationships with the United Nations, the European Union, and other regional organizations.

THE CHALLENGE OF NATO'S OPEN DOOR

In November 2006, before the Riga Summit, the NATO secretary-general publicly asked for a "Global NATO" as a goal that might be "overdue" because NATO already risked being "overstretched." In so doing, the secretary-general was reasserting the Alliance's commitment to an "open door policy" to candidate countries in Europe, but he was also advocating the development of political partnerships outside the continent, including in Asia. These twin processes will remain at the heart of NATO discussions about what the Alliance should become in the next 10 years. The first aspect of these discussions—the continuation of NATO's enlargement in Europe—does not raise as many difficulties as a so-called evolution, some would say "drift," toward a "Global NATO," which could modify the very nature and purpose of the Alliance.

The 2006 NATO summit made no formal decision on either of these issues. With regard to further enlargement, there was merely agreement to review the matter at the next summit, expected to be held in 2008, even though the 26 Alliance members confirmed the importance of the Membership Accession Plan, and the so-called intensified dialogue with Ukraine and Georgia. As to an expansion of new formal partnerships outside Europe and the Mediterranean, the issue of a "more political and expanded network of partnership for NATO" was also merely left on the table, with further discussions expected to be held at the next summit in 2008, or even at the 2009 anniversary summit.[6]

The reluctance shown in Riga came from different quarters. The so-called new NATO members were concerned about a weakening of the article 5 guarantee in a diluted global alliance whose collective defense organization would be transformed into a club of contributors for expeditionary missions. Their domestic audiences had been "sold" on the idea of joining NATO because membership would not only consecrate their "return" into the Europe to which they had always belonged but would also provide protection against their Russian neighbor in the East. Keeping stability and security on the European continent was the original purpose of the Alliance, and it remains the number one priority for most of its current members, especially in the former Warsaw Pact countries in Central and Southeastern Europe and the formerly Soviet Baltic states. Anything that appears to weaken the original NATO security guarantee is and will be questioned by those countries. Criticism of a Global NATO also comes from European members that fear a more political alliance that would provide an alibi for weakened military priorities; at a time when Afghanistan is clearly the dominant issue for NATO and its future, a "Global NATO" is seen as an untimely distraction from the true priorities of the Alliance.

Finally, and most generally, a majority of NATO members wonder what such an evolution of NATO ambitions and structures would entail for the present Alliance. No one will dispute that NATO is as much about article 5 (collective defense) as it is about article 4 (political consultation), but those consultations are not supposed to be a kind of permanent diplomatic review of the state of the world (or, as the French would put it, *"un café du commerce mondial"*). Instead, all NATO members should focus on how, when, and under which procedures the allies will be able to match their military and political commitments with their resources.

For the 26 NATO allies, coping with present military needs is already a challenge. To try to broaden the role of the Alliance to the full spectrum of security threats likely to arise in a rapidly changing strategic context is an open-ended quest. With whom and how will NATO work—against whom, and for what? The threat may be considered as global, and it can be expected to take many forms. But given the work already done by other international organizations, including the EU, what added value could the Alliance bring in areas like climate change, pandemics, immigration, or even terrorism (which is mainly about police and intelligence)?

After the end of the Cold War and the fall of the Berlin Wall, NATO was especially sensitive to the criticism of "being no longer relevant."[7] For several years, the "relevance question" was the other side of the coin of NATO's success against the Warsaw Pact—a constant nagging point of debate within and outside the Alliance. This institutional complex of being somehow sidelined by history may explain why the NATO bureaucracies seemingly attempted to snatch every new theme or problem wherever it was thought they could assert a proprietary role, without considering what is being done by other institutions elsewhere.

Enlarging its membership to the new democracies in order to reach the goal of a "Europe whole and free" was NATO's historic first answer to the "relevance question." Together with EU enlargement, NATO enlargement helped to stabilize Eastern and Central Europe and proved to be a considerable success. Within NATO, it did not affect the way NATO business was conducted: The table of the North Atlantic Council was enlarged, and the discussions could (and did) take a little longer, but the chemistry between members was not substantially altered. As the need for consensus remained the constitutional rule of the Alliance, attempts to speak of a NATO "majority" and "minority," or of "old Europe" versus "new Europe," as during the Iraq discussions, were without much or lasting effect. "Cherry picking" between allies was considered within the Alliance as a dangerous challenge to the very nature of the organization, a challenge that could readily backfire against any member.

In theory at least, article 10 of the Washington Treaty keeps an "open door policy" on enlargement—seemingly an open-ended invitation to all countries in Europe to join NATO. In practice, however, this is not and never was the case, and membership always had and still has a political price. Thus, the first wave of post–Cold War enlargement to three Central European countries (the Czech Republic, Hungary, and Poland) was politically associated with the establishment of a special relationship with Russia, namely, the NATO Russia Council. That set the stage for the Prague Summit, in the fall of 2002, which endorsed a second wave of enlargement (and the fifth since NATO's inception in 1949) by bringing in the three Baltic states (Estonia, Latvia, and Lithuania) plus Rumania and Bulgaria, as well as Slovakia and Slovenia.

However, for the next applicants for NATO membership, in the Balkans and the Caucasus region, the situation appears more complicated. First, though applications for membership are considered on the individual merits and performance of each state, measured through the Membership Accession Plan, the stability of the region is also taken into account, if not formally at least politically. Would it be possible, then, to dissociate Croatia and Macedonia from their Balkan neighbors, or Albania from the evolution of the Kosovo issue, or Georgia from the problem of Caucasus stability? With regard to Ukraine, an internal consensus on NATO membership in all parts of the country is still missing, and more stability in its complex relationship with Russia may still be needed.

During the past 10 years, acceding to NATO and gaining membership in the EU moved on nearly parallel tracks, even if the two processes were fundamentally distinct. The fact that the process of EU enlargement is now likely to pause, at least until the procedures of internal governance are adapted to a wider Union, may have an effect on NATO enlargement, either because NATO membership will appear as a useful stopgap measure for concerned countries, or because new forms of partnership will emerge on both sides.

AN EXPEDITIONARY NATO

During the years since 9/11, priority has been given to another role for the Alliance: going beyond the NATO area to address the global security threat faced by its members. Thus, shortly after the attacks on U.S. territory, NATO invoked article 5 as a sign of solidarity with the United States, but military operations in Afghanistan were nonetheless launched without NATO participation for obvious and deliberate reasons: A direct attack on the United States demanded, at least initially, a response that would be visibly American. Only subsequently did NATO become involved in Afghanistan, at first through its discreet support of the Dutch-German contingent within the Operation Enduring Freedom (OEF) coalition, in the form of headquarters support. At first, the International Security Assistance Force (ISAF) was restricted to Kabul and the North, but it was then expanded to the West and eventually, after three years, it took over the whole country, but not without discussions about the division of responsibilities between the OEF and ISAF chains of command. As a result, both missions have remained active in the theater.

After the Balkans, in the much more difficult environment found in Afghanistan, NATO was therefore confronted with the complexity of modern peacekeeping: fighting the Taliban, but also trying to provide stability throughout the country; and supporting the authority of the Afghan central government but without substituting for it. The role of the allied contingents toward drug trafficking (through the support of the Afghan police and armed forces), the problems of training the Afghan National Army, and the issue of the civil military actions implemented through the various national Provincial Reconstruction Teams have been the staple of all NATO discussions ever since. Inside the Alliance, the issue of so-called caveats and parallel chains of command has also raised many questions from the United States and among the other NATO members. Declared or undeclared caveats can make the job more difficult for commanders, but in an alliance of sovereign democratic nations, whose hands are tied by legal and constitutional rules, caveats appear to be unavoidable. In fact, no ally is devoid of some caveats.

At the same time, NATO increased its patrols in the Mediterranean and embarked on some humanitarian operations for political reasons. Though NATO did not participate in the tsunami relief operations, which affected an area deemed to be the responsibility of the U.S. Pacific Command, the Alliance, using the NATO Response Force, nevertheless helped earthquake victims in Pakistan a few months later, with the aim of bolstering NATO's image in one of Afghanistan's neighbors.

The fact that NATO helped the United States after Hurricane Katrina inflicted considerable damage on Louisiana and Mississippi—with such measures as the ferrying of some parcels by the NATO Response Force—remained unnoticed by Americans and was of marginal utility compared with other forms of bilateral aid. Pressed to act on Darfur but limited by the refusal of Sudan and the African Union to see NATO involvement on the ground, the Alliance, in parallel with the EU, helped to ferry African Union contingents within the UN framework and provide, again in parallel with the EU, some technical assistance to the African Union headquarters in Addis Ababa.

However, all these actions have been more a product of seizing political opportunities to change the image of NATO than a new strategic orientation of the Alliance. It is therefore somewhat exaggerated to proclaim that "with little fanfare—and even less notice," NATO has gone global, and that "created to protect post-war Western Europe from the Soviet Union, the alliance is now seeking to bring stability to other parts of the world."[8] This may well be an ambition for NATO's future, but it is far from the reality of NATO's present condition.

THE MILITARY IMPERATIVE AND ITS DISTRACTIONS

Because the allies' forces are presently overcommitted and overstretched, causing widespread reluctance to add "boots on the ground," there has been a temptation to look in two new directions. The first such direction would reassign roles within the Alliance between those members that are willing and able to conduct "high-intensity" military operations and others who prefer to give priority to their S&R role, even if that could be an invitation to an open-ended commitment without an explicit exit strategy.

Recent operations have shown, however, that there is an ambiguous and fluctuating dividing line between high-intensity missions and stabilization tasks. Increasingly, this distinction is being challenged and raising difficulties for some members that must respond to the specific demands of their parliament and public opinion not to engage in combat operations. Several factors are at play in this blurring of the S&R role: the quick, almost instantaneous reversibility of any security situation on the ground (as NATO discovered during the Kosovo riots of 2004), the increasingly sophisticated weaponry of opponents, and the changing nature of war itself. It is no longer sufficient to win the entry battle to stabilize the crisis. More and more, the urban context of warfare does not allow for a clear break between military combatants and other actors in the fighting, as Iraq has amply demonstrated.

For outside contributors and smaller Alliance members to specialize in the civilian aspects of peacemaking, either because they lack relevant military capacities or because of the political attractiveness of this approach in domestic politics, would therefore be dangerous for the Alliance and for its overall military efficiency in any theater. It would also lead to a split-level NATO, with a few members doing the high-end military jobs and the others doing the softer tasks. On a midterm perspective, it would ultimately encourage the drift of the Alliance toward a de facto abandonment of hard military tasks or to placing that onus on only a few members.

It is therefore not surprising that there is no agreement for NATO to invest civilian tools in S&R. Military leaders do not want responsibility for such a task because it would divert them from their core mission. Many NATO members also point to the fact that S&R would be conducted at the expense of both the Alliance's military identity and its political solidarity. And in any case, all members recognize that there are other organizations that already have the means and competencies for S&R and, like the EU, are willing to invest in the broad range of instruments needed for such missions (from providing administrators, judges, and police to funding and even managing reconstruction programs).

A second alternative to further deployment on the ground is to offer new political incentives for contributions by countries outside the institutional limits of NATO membership. Based on an unspoken pessimistic assumption about what the current NATO members are able and willing to bring, such an approach would risk becoming a self-fulfilling prophecy: The more the Alliance develops into a consortium of standing "clubs of contributors," drawn from various non-NATO circles, the less the solidarity principle within the Alliance will have a positive effect on the behavior of its members.

Offering a new form of institutional partnership to non-NATO contributing countries in Afghanistan—like New Zealand, Australia, and Japan—has been presented as an encouragement for those countries to provide more money, troops, and technical assistance. Nothing, however, is said about political counterparts, which might take the form of the contributors' own security needs; because those needs might be distinct from core NATO security concerns, they would add further to the current members' security burdens. The same applies for some neutral European countries that also have forces in Afghanistan. In fact, those countries have already been involved indirectly in the decisionmaking process to the degree that military decisions, including the Operation Plan, are discussed with them. Why go further, then, and institutionalize new procedures, like a new status of "semi-external members," when the present procedures are satisfactory?

Prospects of "semi-external membership" also raise delicate questions. At which levels of contribution should a country be upgraded and considered a party to the decisionmaking process? What about the enshrined role of North Atlantic Council as the top forum for NATO decisions if it is superseded by the contributors' committees? How will financial issues be delineated, especially at a time when there are difficult discussions about where to limit the collective funding? Finally, and no less important, also at issue would be the public perception of such an evolution of the Alliance: If the allies, as well as non-allies, are put at the same level as mere partners of an ad hoc coalition, the perception that NATO is more and more a toolbox for expeditionary purposes will be reinforced, thereby making the Alliance tied to the ups and down of public opinion toward those external operations.

Beyond looking for new military contributions, another ambition exists at the political level: making NATO "global" to turn it into a new political instrument, and in fact "reinventing the West." Turning NATO into a "new alliance of democracies" is not without some problems of its own, however. To be sure, all members of the Alliance cherish its values and are ready to defend them; this is already written into the NATO Charter. But they also respect the diversity of cultures and opinions, because that principle is at the core of democracy. NATO should not be an instrument of a "crusade" designed to sell its values as universal values applicable to and desirable for all. Moreover, a "Global NATO" extended to Japan, South Korea, Australia, and India will raise questions of inclusiveness. Where else? In Asia, what about Pakistan— or Indonesia? Outside Asia, where else? Some other possible members of the new Global NATO might include Argentina and Brazil, not to mention, predictably enough, Israel.[9] Bringing all the Asian countries already in a "strategic relationship" with the United States also into an association with NATO would give the feeling of a new anti-China coalition, aimed at balancing the geopolitical rise of Beijing in the emerging new multipolarity. Would there be echoes, in another form, of the SEATO Pact of the 1950s? Where will the new boundaries of the members' collective security commitments be; for example, what about Taiwan relative to China, and South Korea relative to North Korea? Clearly, the Alliance has no taste for a scenario that would appear to assert a Global NATO as a competing political alternative to the UN, which would surely be weakened even if it might not be defeated.

RELATIONS WITH THE UN AND THE EU

Last but not least, we must consider the relationship between an expeditionary NATO and both the UN and the EU, to which 21 alliance members now belong. Beyond the UN's legitimizing role and the coordination of various international institutions and donors that it brings, one should recognize that for many peacekeeping operations, the UN is best placed to do the job.[10] For the UN, working with regional organizations and NATO is not too difficult on a case-by-case basis. Already the UN has sent around the world more than three times the number of troops deployed by NATO. The military role and quality of these peacekeepers differ widely, but in recent years the UN has become a political framework that cannot be ignored by the Alliance. The rise of new emerging global powers in coming years will make it even more important.

There is therefore nothing shameful for the Alliance to recognize that the UN is sometimes better positioned to act than NATO. Lebanon was a case in point. In Darfur, under the principle that "African crises are for Africans to solve," many African countries have explicitly rejected a larger and visible role for NATO on the ground. In Haiti, the Congo, or even in the Balkans, the EU has proven to be more able than NATO to act locally—for reasons that vary from one area to the next. Between NATO and the EU, the goal should therefore be effective political cooperation and a sharing of the military roles, with particular emphasis on stabilization.

It is now widely acknowledged that there are almost never decisive military solutions to a crisis; working for a political outcome is always necessary and presupposes a wide array of types of cooperation between international financial institutions, various regional organizations, and all donors, including the EU. NATO has neither the capacity nor even the will to coordinate those different programs.

The Berlin-Plus agreement and the establishment of an EU cell in NATO's SHAPE Headquarters provides enough of an instrument. The Balkan experience has shown that such an instrument works quite well, provided that there is a political spirit of cooperation. There is no need to imagine a complicated structure for a global political dialogue that already exists at a transatlantic level and includes the EU. It is therefore highly exaggerated to speak about "a frozen relationship" between the two organizations. Beyond the "problem" of Turkey, which is circumstantial, there are all sorts of compelling reasons for NATO and the EU to act together and in a complementary manner.

The key difficulties are not operational but (still) political. The prerequisite for a smooth relationship between the EU and NATO remains the recognition of their equal status and responsibility in managing the transatlantic relationship, including at the defense and security level. The EU exists now as an international actor and therefore expects to be recognized as a global interlocutor by the United States—"a power in the world"—without any fear that NATO might be accordingly undermined.[11] Consequently, in the new triangular relationship between the EU, NATO, and the United States, NATO should not pretend to be at the apex and have an exclusive hold on the security dimension.

On a very practical level, the EU cannot become NATO's subordinate "civilian agency," providing funds and a convenient exit strategy at the mere asking of NATO—a kind of reverse Berlin-Plus. As a matter of credibility and efficiency, the EU should be able to autonomously decide on and manage its own contributions. If not, one wonders on what basis the EU could invest resources and political capital in a theater where its role would be constructed as subordinate.

In fact, the Berlin-Plus agreement already states that NATO accepts that the EU can either act independently when it so decides for reasons of its own or cooperate with NATO, in which case the necessary interoperability procedures are accordingly set up. But for the EU to act, the institutional tools to implement and conduct a military-diplomatic action should also be available, including the required EU staff, both political and military, in Brussels. In sum, pragmatism, rather than theology or political maneuvering for institutional primacy, should remain the cardinal rule of the relationship between NATO and the EU. As with the EU, the next years for NATO suggest a very simple, and yet vitally significant, observation: Its members have a good Alliance, whose future credibility hangs on the way its involvement in Afghanistan turns. There need not be conflict with the EU, whose relationship with NATO should in turn be willing and positive. It is therefore imperative for NATO to concentrate on doing the right job and not change its nature into a global political "talking forum"—even for good causes like democracy or the defense and promotion of "our values." In that case, the price, instead of the enhanced NATO that is wanted or even the present NATO, would be the Organization for Security and Cooperation in Europe "in uniform," an outcome not sought by anyone.

Notes

1. Benoît d'Aboville, "Où va l'OTAN aujourd'hui?" *Commentaire* 29, no. 115 (Autumn 2006): 577–588.

2. See Donald Rumsfeld, "Defense Secretary's Annual Report to the President and the Congress," August 15, 2002: "Wars are best fought by coalitions of the willing—but they should not be fought by committee... .The mission must determine the coalition. The coalition must not determine the mission."

3. Irving Kristol, "Does NATO Exist?" in *NATO, the Next Thirty Years: The Changing Political, Economic and Military Setting*, ed. Kenneth A. Myers (Boulder, Colo.: Westview Press, 1980), 370–371.

4. "Stabilizing and Rebuilding Iraq: Coalition Support and International Donor Commitments," statement of Joseph A. Christoff, director of international affairs and trade, U.S. Government Accountability Office, May 9, 2007.

5. Julian Lindley-French, "NATO's Tipping Point? The Search for Alliance Strategic Consensus," working paper for CSIS NATO/EU-NATO Working Group, September 15, 2006.

6. Riga Summit Declaration, issued by the Heads of State and Government participating in the meeting of the North Atlantic Council in Riga, November 29, 2006.

7. See, e.g., Richard Lugar, "NATO: Out of Area or Out of Business?" remarks at Open Forum, U.S. Department of State, August 2, 1993.

8. Ivo Daalder and James Goldgeier, "Global NATO," *Foreign Affairs* 85, no. 5 (September–October 2006): 105.

9. Ronald D Asmus and Bruce P. Jackson, "Does Israel Belong in the EU and NATO?" *Policy Review* 129 (February–March 2005): 47–56.

10. James Dobbins, "The UN's Role in Nation-Building: From the Belgian Congo to Iraq," *Survival* 46, no. 4 (Winter 2004–2005): 81–102.

11. See chapter 5 in this volume by Jolyon Howorth.

PART FIVE

The State of the Partnership

CHAPTER EIGHT

NATO AND THE EU

TERMS OF ENGAGEMENT OR ESTRANGEMENT?

Julian Lindley-French

"**O**perational commitments across three continents demonstrate clearly how NATO is safeguarding the security of its member states, defending our common values and projecting stability," observed Jaap de Hoop Scheffer, the NATO secretary-general, in mid-July 2006. "But our operations are not the only means we have to achieve these goals. Because the best way to safeguard our values is by nourishing them—by upholding values at home, and advocating them abroad. By believing in the power of open, democratic systems and liberal economic systems. By helping other countries to open up their societies too."[1] Later in the year, Javier Solana, the high representative for the European Union's Common Foreign and Security Policy, spoke along similar lines: "The idealism behind the EU's foundation is vital to defining who and what we are today. And it helps to appreciate the value of the European Union as a force for good in the world. We have carefully built a zone of peace, democracy and the rule of law of more than 500 million people. Now we have to extend that zone further. And to answer the call for Europe to act. To promote peace and protect the vulnerable. That is the aim of the Common Foreign and Security Policy."[2]

With NATO and the EU thus committed to similar objectives, with almost the same mission, it is a paradoxical irony that the strategic partnership between these institutions has failed—with dangerous consequences for the security of their members on both sides of the Atlantic. This chapter examines the causes of this failure and what it says about the ability of Europeans and North Americans to together engage complexity with credibility. The conclusions are succinct. First, American security can only be achieved through partnership. Second, American strategic leadership remains vital, even though events since the terrorist attacks of September 11, 2001, have raised serious questions about the United States' ability to lead. Third, Europeans cannot hide from strategic change: Europe is now a strategic actor with global responsibilities, and Europeans must prepare for a global security role, including effective coercive military action. It is therefore all the more surprising that while the world is changing fast, much of the security thinking in America and Europe seems locked in the 1990s, often with 1980s capabilities, structures, and mentalities that are more reflective of inner tensions over leadership and accountability than the need to generate effective security in a dangerous world.

There has been some progress over the years. The EU-NATO Declaration on European Security and Defense Policy (ESDP) was issued in December 2002, and in March 2003 the Berlin-Plus agreement gave the EU access to NATO assets and capabilities for some EU-led operations. The EU and NATO have also cooperated to promote better collaboration over crisis management operations. In March 2003, the Comprehensive Framework for EU-NATO Permanent Relations was concluded, and that same month NATO's Operation Allied Harmony was replaced by the EU's Operation Concordia in the Former Yugoslav Republic of Macedonia. For six days in November 2003, the first joint NATO-EU crisis management exercise was held. In early December 2004, NATO's Stabilization Force in Bosnia handed over to EU Force (EUFOR), which has remained in Bosnia ever since. However, given the changes taking place in the security environment, such progress is far too little, far too late. Much in the NATO-EU relationship will depend, therefore, on the political and strategic trajectory of the West over the next few years, on the generation or otherwise of strategic consensus, and on the accommodation, if any, that can be found between two very different organizations.

THE NATO-EU STANDOFF

Regretfully, the NATO-EU relationship—or rather the NATO-versus-EU standoff—is too often antagonistic, which implies competition over hierarchy, strategic method, and political philosophy. This is not a recent phenomenon, and it transcends any specific U.S. administration or government in Europe. Indeed, it is a standoff that has been in the making since 1950, when the Schumann Declaration set Europe and North America on different political tracks. That the crisis in that relationship has come to the fore today is partly due to the very different ways that many Americans and most Europeans see the world, but it is equally a function of the different political underpinnings of the two organizations. NATO and its founding document, the 1949 North Atlantic Treaty, is a classical military-security alliance between nation-states, with a clear leader around which it is organized. The European Union and its latest iteration, the 2007 Lisbon Treaty, continues to reveal a hybrid beast, part interstate alliance, part supranational institution. Much of the tension in the relationship is thus the result of very different treaties and legal personalities.

It is at the junction of power, political philosophy, institutional form, and legal identity where many of the problems in what should be the West's pivotal institutional relationship are to be found. As a result, the NATO-EU relationship faces several basic problems. First, there is no natural center of gravity between American grand strategy and European strategy (such as it exists). Indeed, the strategic dilemma is also fast becoming a Euro-Euro problem as the very concept of strategy is replaced in Europe by the supremacy of bureaucracy. Second, transformation within NATO, based as it is on a fundamentally American power and military-strategic concept, is leading Europeans committed to following America's lead inexorably toward a capability/capacity crunch. Limited European defense efforts (particularly budgets) are being forced to make uncomfortable choices between high-end capability and not-so-high-end capacity, both of which are needed by Europeans but only one of which can be afforded.

However, much of the tension in the relationship is a function of what might be called the struggle for the inner-Western space, primarily, though not exclusively, between France and the United States. Unfortunately, the struggle for the inner-European space that so complicates relations between NATO and the EU necessarily creates in other European states an almost obsessive disregard for what is taking place elsewhere in the world. However, it is the implicit and explicit Franco-American struggle that has done the most damage to an effective working relationship between the two institutions. With the election of President Nicolas Sarkozy in France in May 2007, and prior to the election of a new U.S. president in November 2008, there are signs of a softening of battle lines. Sarkozy's assurance that "American friends …can rely on our friendship" and that "France will always be next to them when they need us" is to be welcomed. But many in Washington will recall similar assurances in the past.[3] The plain fact is that such is the debilitating impact of what is now a 60-year-old bilateral struggle over who has "the biggest idea in the West" that much of the dysfunction in the NATO-EU relationship can be ascribed to it. The other allies are frankly mightily leery of what has become a dispute that above all others prevents the establishment of a proper and relevant working strategic concept. Although much of the struggle is fought through a series of proxy wars as both Paris and Washington hide behind the tactical intransigence of the likes of Malta and Cyprus in the EU and Turkey in NATO, the problem is fundamentally of French and American making, and until a new strategic settlement is reached between the two it is difficult to see how the political environment can be created for a more effective NATO-EU relationship.

This strategic impasse has reinforced what is an overt tendency on the part of many Europeans to recognize only as much threat as they can afford. This in turn has reinforced the overbureaucratization of security that reinforces paralysis in the NATO-EU relationship. Ultimately, it is this strategy vacuum and the crisis in consensus it generates that prevents NATO and the EU from having enough strategic self-confidence, as institutions, to establish an effective working relationship in which they could calmly carry out the strategic missions assigned to them by political masters, and, thereafter, establish an appropriate mix of task sharing and a division of labor generated by the circumstances of the day. Indeed, because the institutions themselves are too often called upon to make strategy in an effort to expand their competence, which is not their place, *strategy* is replaced with *bureaucracy*. By definition, bureaucracies are antistrategic because they are instruments of a self-perpetuating process. Consequently, in the absence of strategy, new metaphors for bureaucracy appear, each often with its own language of "action," "guidance," "goal," and/or "approach."

Thus, a very real danger exists that NATO's much-vaunted Concerted Planning and Action of Civil and Military Activities in International Operations, otherwise known as the Comprehensive Approach, will simply become another exercise in bureaucracy protecting and extending itself at the expense of the cost-effective security so necessary today.

That is precisely what has happened to Headline Goal 2010 within the EU. Indeed, the bureaucratic approach to security not only reduces its effectiveness but also exaggerates both the time and money needed to prepare for a strategic security future. This problem is magnified at the NATO-EU level because in the absence of strategy bureaucracies not only compete but tend to emphasize differences to justify their competence, resulting in excessive delay and cost. Part of the problem is that it is very hard for alliances to work effectively together because they add an extra layer of complexity to what is normally an already exceedingly complex set of interstate and bureaucratic relations. Consequently, the center of gravity moves away from effectiveness at the teeth end, to the preservation of status at the tail end. Only strong political leadership can overcome that. That is why the search for a real NATO Strategic Concept by 2009 will be vital not just for NATO but also for the European Union.

NATO AND THE EU: COPING WITH ESTRANGEMENT

The state of NATO-EU relations is thus to be profoundly regretted whatever is said on a fairly regular basis by the overly optimistic but sterile and cynical statements of institutional political correctness to which the two organizations are prone. In January 2007, de Hoop Scheffer was right to call for a "new chapter" in NATO's relations with the EU, based on improved cooperation in Kosovo, a concerted approach in Afghanistan, the harmonization of military transformations, a comprehensive dialogue about future security challenges, and the enlargement processes of the two organizations.[4] Pointedly, however, in that same speech the NATO secretary-general chose to recall that the NATO-EU strategic partnership is considered in some parts a "frozen conflict"—a point of view that can hardly be construed as optimistic.

Placing the institutional cart before the strategic horse is a dangerous mistake. When engaging complexity, the options afforded by multiple political and security identities are priceless. NATO and the EU as strategic security tools give their members that flexibility. The EU could not do what NATO is doing in Afghanistan. It cannot of itself (or as yet) provide a Treaty of Washington–type article 5. Equally, what Europeans are doing in Lebanon could not be done by NATO, even if it is not strictly an EU operation. It is inconceivable that the July 2007 Anglo-French initiative in Darfur could lead to a NATO-led operation due to the sensibilities in the region about an overt American, and, by extension, NATO presence, even if it is also unlikely to involve an overt EU presence. Moreover, EU action in Bosnia communicates a whole different message or strategic narrative to all parties to the conflict about style, method, and engagement than, say, NATO action in Kosovo. That is precisely how it should be. *Vive la différence* should be the NATO-EU mantra because such contrasts in approach and emphasis are mutually reinforcing strengths, not weaknesses. It is therefore a profound shame that the Iraq legacy and the political tensions underpinning the NATO-EU relationship continue, and seemingly will continue, to prevent a real, pragmatic, and effective working relationship.

Tinkering with the NATO-EU Permanent Arrangements, or adjusting the Berlin-Plus process to give the EU access to NATO's assets and capabilities, will not resolve the tensions in this estranged relationship. Behind such tensions is the urgent need for modernization, made long overdue by the closed minds of too many Americans and the closed purses of too many Europeans. Too often, Americans put the travails of the transatlantic relationship down to European vacillation and weakness; but much of the responsibility for the failed relationship is in Washington, not Brussels. The United States is entering a period of profound political weakness. Not only has the war in Iraq become particularly unpopular; so has the war in Afghanistan, as the gap between American grand strategy and intended consequence has grown daily. Indeed, it does Washington no credit talking about the British "defeat" in southern Iraq when what passes for policy in Washington has done so much to undermine the British. Had decisionmakers in the United States listened more carefully to their British counterparts in preinvasion and early postinvasion days about how best to achieve stability in such places, they might have been less responsive to those suggesting that Iraq was ripe for democracy. It is in the gap between pragmatism and idealism that the Iraq policy has failed. Thus, it is self-evident that the United States is unsure as to its future direction, where it should focus its leadership, and how it should generate the effect that such leadership requires. Put simply, it would be unreasonable in the extreme for the United States to expect its allies to follow unquestioningly what now passes for strategy.

For all its failings, American strategic leadership remains nonetheless vital in a world awash with uncertainty and instability, and all but the most hardened Europsychotics must accept that. However, the old assumptions upon which the transatlantic relationship was founded are no longer valid, and it is insufficient in such a complex political environment to trot out tired mantras about shared values and interests. Having said that, both sides must work harder at the cerebral underpinnings of a relationship that is still vital. First and foremost, the United States must be clear about which Europe it wants. The paradox is that the strong Europe over which political Washington often seems conflicted would be clearly in the U.S. interest. Indeed, a truly strategic Europe would provide a modernized transatlantic relationship with strategic options for not just Europeans but also North Americans. The problem is that such a Europe would also reduce America's power to lead. This dichotomy is what would be hard to reconcile.

Unfortunately, the collision point of a strategically defensive America and a strategically pretentious Europe is the NATO-EU nonstrategic partnership. It is therefore to be regretted that the failure of so many Europeans to invest adequately in their own security as the down payment on a meaningful transatlantic relationship has led progressively to the bypassing of both NATO and the EU. Such are the political and security weaknesses of both institutions that Mikhail Gorbachev's so-called Sinatra doctrine, by which Warsaw Pact members were invited to "do it their way," seems equally applicable to members of both NATO and the EU. That is precisely what the United States, the United Kingdom, and France are increasingly doing—outside both institutions.

Consequently, the transatlantic relationship is fast becoming a relationship in which resentful American leadership is matched by resentful European "followership." Certainly, the current NATO-EU relationship demonstrates just how far both North Americans and Europeans are from a mature relationship between partners committed to an active policy of engagement. Thus, until a basic political Rubicon is crossed in the transatlantic relationship, it is hard to see how the NATO-EU strategic partnership can be anything other than a dangerous contradiction in terms.

Unfortunately, it is a mark of the strategic inversion from which both NATO and the EU suffer that so much political energy is lost dealing with the membership asymmetry of the two organizations. Much of that energy is necessarily focused on Turkey, and the victory of the AK Party in the Turkish elections held in July 2007 once again reinforced the importance of Ankara as a member of the West—one that is pivotal to the engagement of North Americans and Europeans with much of the Muslim world. Those in Europe who say that Turkey can never be European underestimate Turkey's importance to European society and security, while those in the United States who insist on Turkey's membership in the EU fail to understand how difficult it is to join the Union if a society does not feel itself European. Much of the NATO-EU strategic partnership in the near future will depend upon how well they can both treat Turkey with sensitivity.

A NEW EU-NATO STRATEGIC AGENDA

In today's strategic environment, the concept of "hard" and "soft" power is anachronistic—all that matters is effect, and, to that end, effects-based operations and planning as part of a total security package. That basic premise should be the starting point for a true NATO-EU strategic partnership.

Effectiveness requires staying power, as well as fighting power, and the cost to those that stay over time could well become greater than to those that fight to force initial entry. Contemporary security policy is often about difficult choices in places like Afghanistan. Withdrawal is not an option, because unmolested strategic crime and systemic terrorism will chase the West back to its own back streets. Thus, pulling out of Afghanistan would greatly exacerbate "blowback"—not least because in an age when the democratization of mass destruction is palpable, the dark side of globalization means that anyone can get anything given time, determination and money, and freedom from the pressure of positive power. Thus, the only "option" is to stay and make the benefits of legality outweigh what are, by Western standards, the benefits of illegality across the broad spectrum of criminal effect. Yet achieving this would require applying economic, financial, and security tools as a single package above and beyond what has been thus far committed to Afghanistan. Indeed, the mess in Afghanistan puts the factional game playing between NATO and the EU into stark relief. The price is being paid daily by young North Americans, Europeans, and others on behalf of a strategy without purpose, underpinned by institutions without a clue, and let down by governments too often financially absent without leave.

Nonetheless, given the change that the world is experiencing, the sheer economic power of the West means that it is doomed to retain the leadership mantle. It is another paradox of this strange strategic age that there is as yet no Newtonian balance between growth and decline; the East might be emerging, but the West is not declining. By 2020, China and India together may represent 30 percent of world gross domestic product, but even on the basis of the most pessimistic assumptions, North America and Western Europe, which collectively represent now some 60 percent of global GDP, will still be the world's dominant economic, political, and strategic grouping. This makes the West's halfhearted attempts in Afghanistan at first glance so puzzling. In pursuit of success, the West has invested nothing like the resources it could, and the dysfunctional NATO-EU relationship plays no small part in this fundamental failure. There is more to this failure than the lingering discord over Iraq, which admittedly continues to pollute the mission in Afghanistan. Nor is it enough to evoke the collective weakness or absence of European strategic vision, and vain attempts to convince Europeans to follow American grand strategy with meager European resources. More to the point, the fact is that the West is profoundly split over the balance to be struck between projection and protection. Thus, what passes for "strategy" has become focused on sustaining the delusion of millions (particularly in Europe) that they are not engaged in a war, thereby breaking the link between the provision of security and its cost. With governments thus on an extended strategic vacation, the short term takes precedence over the long term. In short, the problem is an absence of leadership.

That is why the essential link has been broken between much of Western society and the young men and women who act on its behalf in Afghanistan. It is why one sees the emergence of military ghettoes across the West full of soldiers and their families under the most intense pressure detached from a society that understands little of what they do and seemingly cares even less. Above all, it is why the pointless institutionalism of the West's security effort must be brought to an end through a pragmatic program promoting NATO-EU strategic synergy.

Harmonizing Strategic Concepts

According to the 2006 *NATO Handbook*, "NATO's essential and enduring purpose, set out in the Washington Treaty, is to safeguard the freedom and security of all its members by political and military means."[5] Again, a significant parallel can be found with the EU, whose Berlin Declaration of March 2007 evoked "major challenges which do not stop at national borders. The European Union is our response to these challenges…. We will fight terrorism, organized crime and illegal immigration together…. We are committed to the peaceful resolution of conflicts in the world and to ensuring that people do not become the victims of war, terrorism and violence."[6]

Like all alliances, both NATO and the EU (which, in security terms, is in reality an interstate alliance) are founded on an essentially simple contract: The less powerful enjoy the security of the most powerful in return for a share of their responsibilities. In today's world, this means sharing risk. In the "good old days" of the Cold War, it was much easier to apportion risk and response due to the military nature of confrontation. "Bean counting" was the name of the game, and "security" was linked intrinsically to the numbers of ships, submarines, tanks, missiles, and warheads possessed by each side in the ongoing conflict. But in today's complex security environment, it has become trickier to identify a balance because of the number and nature of actors involved in the complex multipolarity created by the dark side of globalization. Necessarily, the containment of insecurity is a function of generic security (as opposed to purely military) capabilities and capacities.

The future roles and missions of both NATO and the EU will depend, therefore, on the outcome of the search for an elusive strategic consensus. According, again, to the 2006 *NATO Handbook*, "at the institutional level, international organizations including the United Nations, the European Union, and the Organization for Security and Cooperation in Europe are recognizing the need to meet threats such as terrorism square on, with all the resources available, and to coordinate this effort rather than to rely on the resources of any single organization."[7] What should this mean in practice, however? Lessons from Afghanistan and Iraq apply. First, armed forces stabilize; they do not reconstruct. Second, reconstruction in complex environments takes place not after but during conflict, precisely because reconstruction helps end it. The difficulties faced by Western militaries in Afghanistan and Iraq (and also in Lebanon) have demonstrated the limits of military power and reinforced the need for all instruments and agencies—be they governmental, intergovernmental, or nongovernmental—to be applied to mission success. The strategic partnership between NATO and the EU should thus be founded on a series of first principles concerning the generation of mission success in such places.

Unfortunately, from the EU side, such cooperation in the field is hardly convincing. The British leader of the EU training mission to Iraq has been effectively left without support because the EU attached more importance to the appearance of involvement than to substance. Moreover, the reticence of French, Germans, Italians, and Turks to support their American, British, Dutch, and Canadian NATO allies in southern Afghanistan has demonstrated the extent to which "solidarity" has become informal, further undermining the utility of both institutions. Consequently, risk sharing has become central to the NATO and EU dilemmas as too many members leave a few countries with a disproportionate security burden. Over time, no institution—let alone any interinstitutional relationship—can survive a basic lack of solidarity at the point of contact with danger.

NATO's core mission is to *cope* with the worst consequences of change in whatever form it takes. In contrast, the EU's core work is to ensure that these consequences are *managed* in a just and effective manner. In between is a whole raft of diplomatic and economic activity that points to the need for a direct EU-U.S. security relationship. Equally, whether one considers the EU's European Security Strategy or NATO's Strategic Concept, the security roles and missions of the two organizations are reasonably well delineated, with both committed to a broad approach to security. The two documents share basic tenets. Both NATO and the EU are devoted to creating a stable international environment, particularly in the Euro-Atlantic security environment. They both provide essential forums for security consultations on any issues that affect the vital, important, and general interests of their members, and both engage in conflict prevention and crisis management, including crisis response operations. However, only NATO is as yet formally committed to a territorial defense role, although much debate is taking place in the EU over such a role in the future. Furthermore, both NATO and the EU see themselves as having wide-ranging responsibilities to promote partnership, cooperation, and dialogue with other countries—increasingly globally, in NATO's case (albeit founded on the Euro-Atlantic community); and "in and around Europe," in the EU's case.

However, the meaning of broad security is changing as fast as the world it is intended to engage. The 2006 *NATO Handbook* states that the Alliance Strategic Concept comprises a broad approach to security, encompassing political, economic, social and environmental factors, as well as the Alliance's defense dimension; a strong commitment to transatlantic relations; maintenance of Alliance military capabilities to ensure the effectiveness of military operations; development of European capabilities within the Alliance; maintenance of adequate conflict prevention and crisis management structures and procedures; effective partnerships with non-NATO countries based on cooperation and dialogue; the enlargement of the Alliance and an open door policy towards potential new members; and continuing efforts towards far-reaching arms control, disarmament and non-proliferation agreements.[8]

With this language virtually mirrored in the European Security Strategy, complementarity and competitiveness sit side by side in the missions of the two organizations. The basic requirement for NATO-EU strategic synergy is also acknowledged in NATO's *Comprehensive Political Guidance* of November 2006:

Peace, security and development are more interconnected than ever. This places a premium on close cooperation and coordination among international organizations playing their respective, interconnected roles in crisis prevention and management. Of particular importance because of their wide range of means and responsibilities are the United Nations and the European Union. The United Nations Security Council will continue to have the primary responsibility for the maintenance of international peace and security. The European Union, which is able to mobilize a wide range of military and civilian instruments, is assuming a growing role in support of international stability.[9]

Unfortunately, for all the stated intent, the problems faced by both NATO and the EU are greatly complicated by the fact that the relationship between political intent and guidance and military planning and capabilities is fractured. This fracture in what is a political-military loop also exacerbates the fracture in the political-political loop because the gap between treaty language and the actuality it describes is too often designed to hide disagreement more than to reflect consensus or sound analysis. Again, until seriousness about security is reinjected into the political context in which both organizations work, it will be very hard to be confident that a true NATO-EU strategic partnership can be forged.

Consequently, both institutions lack strategic planning drivers, which creates a profound dilemma for the many members of both institutions that have little or no strategic tradition. Indeed, that is why a NATO-EU strategic consensus is so important, for it is probably the only way such states can justify the outlays and risks the contemporary quest for security does and will demand. The more traditional powers need to be sensitive to this dilemma, that is, what security investments should be made by such members, how to best support the two institutions, and how the use of their assets and capabilities by the two institutions should be organized to best effect. The inability to properly answer these questions goes a long way toward explaining the security weakness of much of Europe, and why the NATO first / EU first conflict has proved so debilitating. It is only to be hoped, inter alia, that Sarkozy's early intent to make the use of NATO and/or EU an issue of pragmatism is welcomed. His stated desire that France should rejoin NATO's integrated military structure is to be welcomed. George W. Bush's U.S. administration, but perhaps more important, Gordon Brown's U.K. government, need to match the French initiative with a gesture toward the European Security and Defense Policy, such as agreeing to a second Anglo-French Saint-Malo summit on the ESDP's future.

Political gestures aside, what is needed is an organizing focus and principle for the NATO-EU relationship that injects practical substance into their Strategic Partnership. In spite of the dangers of parasitical bureaucratic swamping, a NATO-EU Comprehensive Approach to security would enable NATO to create the needed security space in places like Afghanistan and would enable the EU to help fill it. Such an approach would imply some division of labor from time to time and, indeed, a direct EU-US security relationship, which is as it should be. But it would not in any way preclude EU-led operations. Rather, it would simply reflect certain basic facts of strategic life when it comes to power, projection, and performance.

A mere glance at the stabilization and reconstruction agenda reinforces the need for such an EU-NATO partnership, because a conscious cross-agency effort underlines the need to generate sustained state rebuilding by protecting and projecting national and transnational instruments and expertise. It is interesting to note that the EU is developing the British Post-Conflict Reconstruction Unit's database of experts. Such a resource will be essential to creating and sustaining critical state structures that have come to represent mission end states. These missions now include such complex goals as the balanced rule of law, effective education, legal commercial activity, sustainable humanitarian and health systems, open information, civilian-controlled armed forces, open economies, representative diplomacy, and sound and just governance. The work of NATO's provincial reconstruction teams is clearly being hampered in Afghanistan precisely because there are so relatively few civilians supporting the military effort. The EU is starting to implement its commitment to improve the effectiveness of the Afghan National Police Service. It is a beginning.

Better Organizing the Military Strategy

The West has what it has, and it must better organize what it has got: the military-operational reality of both NATO and the EU. How best, then, can it squeeze more effect out of the national capabilities from which the two institutions must draw, given the reality of the political-military pecking order at the heart of each? First and foremost, the primacy of big-state leadership needs to be acknowledged and accepted. Clearly, a new balance of power exists at the heart of both NATO and the EU, particularly in the realm of security and defense. Again, if this leadership/effect issue is not resolved, the big powers will simply step outside institutional frameworks to act.[10]

In the absence of a capabilities breakthrough, most NATO and EU members will have to pay the price of a marked reduction in military-strategic sovereignty for the two institutions to become effective and credible. Indeed, that is the essential equation that strategic diffidence has created; the more important the institution for security, and the less the defense investment from which it suffers, the greater the need for intense cooperation and thus the less members can expect military-strategic sovereignty. Thus, this implicit equation boils down to a military-operational paradox for both NATO and the EU—a paradox founded on the need to squeeze far more deployability and reusability (not just usability) out of existing force levels, structures, and capabilities. The facts again speak for themselves. While the British and French can deploy about 40 percent of their respective headline forces, most other Europeans are at about 8 to 10 percent, with some as low as 3 or 4 percent. The dilemma posed by the equation is thus the difficulty of finding a balance between specialization, pooling, and task sharing, the sine qua non of NATO and EU doctrine.

Naturally, for all but the United States, military-strategic sovereignty diminishes the higher up the conflict-intensity scale an engagement takes place. However, given the changing nature of the conflict-intensity scale, and with the advent of complex fourth-generation contingencies in which no natural planning thresholds exist, new thinking is needed even for the United States. Put simply, new planning thresholds are required with far lower levels of intended effectiveness at which pooling and specialization should commence. NATO and EU operational planning contingencies must now be prepared with that reality in mind. The current force structure, with its rigid teeth-to-tail ratios and inadequate logistics packages, seems the very antithesis of the flexible force-and-effects structures vital for sustained engagement with dangerous complexity over time and distance. For example, the gap between current force planning and operations is such that even the muscular British can only deploy one battalion out of the normal four as part of the 16 Air Assault Brigade in Afghanistan. Indeed, the British are one entire battalion short of being able to fulfill their current operational commitments. This basic failure of the political-military loop is vastly undermining both NATO and the EU as security actors.

This dilemma is compounded further by the planning horizon. It is becoming increasingly self-evident that the comforting illusions of the 1990s are fast disappearing. Such are the pace and nature of change in the world that both North Americans and Europeans now need once again to begin thinking about classical state threats to the Euro-Atlantic area. Given the change in the world forces answerable to both of them, NATO and the EU must retain an ability to reconstitute these forces for strategic effect. There is a very real danger that counterterrorism and counterinsurgency, important though they are, will come to dominate both Alliance and Union planning to the detriment of a balanced defense posture. Both NATO and the EU are thus in danger of preparing to fight the soon-to-be-last war. Put simply, the West needs both high and low military power to meet the challenges of high and low twenty-first-century politics, and the institutional flexibility in both NATO and the EU can make best use of it. At the very least, that will require intense cooperation between allies and partners, as well as tight synergy between NATO and the EU.

Indeed, the absence of a grand strategic consensus with the Russians and Chinese strongly suggests that former British prime minister Tony Blair's age of humanitarian interventionism is dead. More likely are structural interventions, whereby the West acts to shore up states that are vital to its own interests, such as Lebanon or Afghanistan, and prevent conflicts that could prove profoundly injurious to such interests. If *all* Europeans agree on the need to participate in such strategic stabilization, they will need far more robust, projectable, and protectable forces. If not, then NATO and the ESDP will simply fade away.

Better NATO-EU Mission Planning

By mid-2007, NATO was engaged on seven operations in Afghanistan (International Security Assistance Force, or ISAF), in Bosnia (Sarajevo Headquarters), in supporting the African Union in Darfur, in the Former Yugoslav Republic of Macedonia (Skopje Headquarters), in Iraq (NATO Training Mission 1), in Kosovo (KFOR), and in the Mediterranean (Operation Active Endeavour). By that time, the EU was also engaged in a dozen operations spanning three continents: significant military operations in Bosnia (EUFOR Althea) and in the Democratic Republic of Congo (EUFOR DR Congo); police missions in the Palestinian territories (EUPOL COPPS) and in Kinshasa (EUPOL Kinshasa); rule-of-law mission (of sorts) in Iraq (EUJUST Lex), and security-sector reform in the Democratic Republic of Congo (EUSEC DR Congo). Even as the EU was also preparing to enhance its role in Kosovo, subject to agreement over some form of final status, and to support peace efforts in Afghanistan, Europeans had engaged a 9,000-strong force in southern Lebanon as part of what is known as UNIFIL2. All these operations, however, highlight a range of issues that both NATO and the EU must resolve if forces under the command of either are to span the range of challenges and the spectrum of conflict intensity as both insist they must, particularly because there is only one set of Europeans and what elite forces exist are overstretched. Put simply, NATO and the EU do not talk to each other at any stage of the mission—and too often representatives of the two organizations have been actually prevented from coordinating properly on the ground. Indeed, NATO and the EU seem to conceive, plan, and execute operations as though the other institution did not exist.

Moreover, though the operations look reasonably strong on paper, the facts on the ground tell a very different story. Nor is this a purely

NATO-EU dilemma. For example, too many of NATO's ISAF forces supporting the provincial reconstruction teams in Afghanistan willfully refuse to support the British Operation Medusa, which is heavily engaged in counternarcotics, counterinsurgency, and counterterror missions in the south of the country.[11] In Kosovo, KFOR numbers some 16,946 NATO troops and 2,744 non-NATO troops. As the 2007 Ahtisaari Plan attests, it will be difficult to draw that force down significantly without ethnic trouble reigniting, and without meaningful progress on the final status of Kosovo, NATO forces will be locked in for some time to come—not least because the EU does not want to take over until the job is by and large done. Seemingly, the Union would rather the Alliance failed, which is a telling story in its own right. Using missions to play interinstitutional politics verges on dereliction of duty.

Consequently, the EU could and must do far more to expand the effect of civil-military and civilian security efforts in conflict zones in which NATO military forces are already heavily engaged. The EU makes much of its vaunted soft security capability, but this capability exists more on paper than on the ground. Indeed, before mission harmonization can take place, the EU must move decisively to end one of its enduring constraints: the difficult relationship within the EU between the European Council and the European Commission, which has done so much to effectively prevent a constructive dialogue with NATO. This unfortunate situation has exacerbated the tendency of the EU to play at operations and too often focus on media image and political spin rather than practical results. The bottom line is that if the issue of intra-Alliance and intra-Union risk and cost sharing is not resolved, then the creeping renationalization of the security and defense effort that is so undermining security effectiveness will gather pace. With the 2007 EU Lisbon Treaty calling for a new Office of the High Representative of the Union for Foreign Affairs and Security Policy that will merge the security responsibilities of the Council and Commission into one instrument, it is to be hoped that NATO will finally have a single telephone number to call on the other side of town. However, there have been many false dawns, and what is really needed is a NATO-EU security planning mechanism that goes beyond the EU Military Staff cell at NATO Headquarters, known as SHAPE. Indeed, the tasks required to achieve mission success now demand much more than mere operational planning. Instead, a new form of security planning is required founded on the effects-based approach designed to embrace a whole raft of vital partners.

Seeking Together the Capabilities Breakthrough

The figures on capabilities speak for themselves.[12] The British defense budget in 2006 amounted to $55.10 billion, or 26 percent of total defense spending for NATO Europe; defense was $45.3 billion in the French budget, or 21 percent of the total; and it was $35.7 billion in the German budget, or 17 percent of the total. Thus the biggest three NATO European member nations spent 64 percent of all defense expenditures by the European members of NATO—meaning, for each of the remaining states, an average defense spending of $3.56 billion per state a year, which is nothing like enough to generate the capabilities identified as vital by the *Comprehensive Political Guidance*. Moreover, the majority of such spending remains highly inefficient, with an excessive emphasis on personnel and organizational bureaucracies. It should be noted that the U.S. defense budget for 2006 was about $560 billion, or 264 percent of the entire NATO Europe combined defense budget (even if American outlays do not themselves often bear close examination).

Nor is the infamous transatlantic gap the only one likely to grow. According to current planning, by 2015 Britain and France together will represent 60 percent of European defense expenditures. The EU's own figures on EU's Headline Goal 2010 shortfalls confirm this imbalance:[13] of these shortfalls, 7 had been formally solved, 4 were showing signs of improvement, and 53 had not changed during the 2002–2005 period.[14] The majority of those shortfalls represent the failure of all EU member states with the notable exceptions of the British and French, who will have to exercise much stronger leadership over their European partners if this basic malaise is to be overcome.

Whether it is NATO's Prague Capability Commitment or the EU's Headline Goal 2010, the performance of Europeans in meeting agreed-on capability targets is at best modest, and this basic failing is profoundly undermining the military credibility of much of Europe. Indeed, the impact of this weakness is evident in the poor performance of many Europeans in both Iraq and Afghanistan. It is again important for Americans to make distinctions between Europeans on this subject; the transatlantic debate is too often presented as America versus Europe, but the reality of European military modernization reveals that the United States, Britain, and France are on one side and much of the rest of Europe is on the other. The British decision, in July 2007, to construct two F-35 Lightning II armed supercarriers, HMS *Queen Elizabeth* and HMS *Prince of Wales*, the two largest ships ever to serve the Royal Navy, will simply reinforce the divide between the European projection powers, Britain and France, the limited peacekeeping powers, led by Germany and Italy, and the protected powers, made up by many of the newer, smaller NATO and EU members.

Getting Procurement Right and Tight

Equally, the causes of the shortfalls that undermine the military credibility of both NATO and the EU are not solely a function of a lack of investment and strategic myopia. The poor way that most Europeans tend to use their defense budgets, with bloated personnel budgets and restrictive contract law, is often reinforced by excessive pressure from American defense contractors to sell equipment that is not needed and cannot conceivably meet the defense needs of Europeans—a pressure exacerbated by America's tendency to renege on promises to even its closest European allies. For example, the sort of barriers placed by Congress to prevent British operational sovereignty over its F-35 Lightning II aircraft damages bilateral relations, and by extension transatlantic relations.[15]

Indeed, the British experience with F-35 Lightning II will likely move European procurement forward through a strengthened European Defence Agency, which is unlikely in itself to mark a capabilities breakthrough because two essential dilemmas exist at the heart of the NATO and/or EU procurement mechanisms. First, most of the medium-sized to small defense investors in both NATO and the EU are intimidated by the upfront cost of increasingly expensive and complex military equipment, for which their leaders, personnel, and treasuries are not prepared. Second, there is little or no incentive for small countries to procure expensive military systems that will give them little political influence beyond what they already "enjoy." This latter stricture explains why 24 EU member-states, most of which are also NATO members, spend so little on defense and do it so badly.

Again, the politics of capabilities has driven too many NATO and EU members to conclude that they need to recognize only as much threat as they can afford. No amount of pushing from the United States and the more powerful European states will resolve this dilemma in the short term. The key to the resolution of this conundrum ought to be leadership from Germany, but its continuing and steadfast refusal to take its military-security responsibilities seriously is not only preventing a capabilities breakthrough in Europe but is also shifting the cost and responsibility for its own security onto the United States, Britain, France and, increasingly, the Netherlands. It is all the more ironic, therefore, that the Germans are happy to manufacture cutting-edge military equipment for others to use but that they are not prepared to use themselves. Too often the Germans talk Europe and transatlantic but act German.

Promoting New Strategic Partnerships

In late August 2006, former French president Jacques Chirac stated, "To seek to commit the Alliance to nonmilitary operations, in ad hoc partnerships, technological adventures, in insufficiently prepared enlargement could only distort its [NATO] vocation. NATO's very legitimacy is at stake as the military organizational guarantor of the collective security of the European and North American Allies."[16] The same can be said for the EU. Indeed, Kurt Volker, principal deputy assistant secretary of state for European and Eurasian affairs, put the partnership/enlargement dilemma of both organizations in perspective: "In this century, our security depends on meeting threats at strategic distance with a wide variety of partners. NATO is an Alliance with increasingly global partners—from the Mediterranean to the Pacific—who are committed to many of our strategic goals and want more ways to contribute to NATO's missions."[17]

The point is correct: If NATO and the EU are to fulfill the security responsibilities assigned to them by the citizens they are charged with protecting, then both the Alliance and Union must in some way play a role in the new deterrence and the new containment as part of what has been termed (for better or worse) Global Democratic Action. This does not mean a global NATO, and it certainly does not mean a global EU. However, if the Euro-Atlantic community is to maximize the effectiveness of security in this world, much of the challenge ahead will be to figure out how the two institutions can best work together in a global age. What is clear is that the great age of the twin enlargements is essentially over and that the concept of partnership, which for so long was intrinsically linked to the post–Cold War stability of Europe, must now change. Necessarily, a new strategic Partnership for Peace would be focused more on NATO than the EU. However, as the EU's strategic partnerships with Russia, China, and India attest, the Union has a strategic stabilizing role to play, particularly in the areas of trade, economics, and human rights.

Unfortunately, too many smaller members of both NATO and the European Union reject proposals for a global partnership between them because they believe they will be sidelined. Such concerns reveal a dangerous lack of strategic imagination. Predictably, the big powers will take whatever steps are needed to protect their interests and security. The Americans are already reenergizing a global web of security partners that include Australia, India, Japan, and South Korea. The British are reenergizing their security links with their Commonwealth partners like Australia, India, and South Africa, with which they share a common military culture. Indeed, Britain's decision to build the two supercarriers is a clear signal to its partners that it intends to return east of Suez for the first time since 1967.[18] NATO and the EU had better help enable that intention or get out of the way.

A glance at the 37 nations participating in ISAF demonstrates the need for an ongoing political and military dialogue with states that share the same security goals as NATO and the EU but that are not located in the Euro-Atlantic area. Indeed, in the new strategic environment, partnership will likely become as important as membership for both NATO and the EU. If the nations that invest little in defense simply seek to use the two institutions to constrain the more powerful from acting in pursuit of their security interests, then institutional-based Western security and defense will fail. It is as simple and straightforward as that. Rather, both NATO and the EU must become the essential security hubs of the West, multiplying the security of members and acting as focal points for the coordination of true strategic partners committed to global stability and security.

Agreeing on a Common Position on Putin's Russia

As stated by the *NATO Handbook*, "While differences remain on some issues which may take some time to resolve, the driving force behind the new spirit of cooperation is the realization that NATO member-states and Russia share strategic priorities and face common challenges, such as the fight against terrorism and the proliferation of weapons of mass destruction."[19] Russia supplies energy to the rest of Europe, but it is not a strategic partner of the West. Therein lays a dilemma that is becoming particularly acute as Russia moves toward the transfer of power from Vladimir Putin to himself in the guise of a spurious election. There is and can be no strategic consensus with Russia, as its attitude toward the Iranian nuclear program attests. Indeed, the manner in which the Russians seek a strategic relationship with China in the UN Security Council, and the purpose it betrays, confirms the extent of old thinking in Moscow—as does "Soviet lite" behavior in the "near abroad," especially toward Ukraine, Georgia, and the Kirghiz Republic (not to mention Chechnya).

The persistence of Moscow's provocative ways will soon make Russia once again a security priority.[20] Given that by 2020 an estimated three-quarters of Europe's energy needs are expected to come from Russia and that other source of "local" complexity, North Africa, this is a matter for profound concern.[21] At the very least, the West as the West must agree on a common position on dealing with Moscow, and NATO and the EU must be at the forefront of such efforts. Moscow seems only to understand a carrot-and-stick approach, and a common position through the NATO-Russia Council and the EU-Russia Strategic Partnership will remind Russia of the price it will pay for interference in the sovereign affairs of states that are members or partners of either or both organizations.

A BIT OF INSTITUTIONAL RELATIONSHIP COUNSELING

More in hope than expectation, NATO's *Comprehensive Political Guidance* states, "The role of the UN and EU, and other organizations, including as appropriate non-governmental organizations, in ongoing operations and future crises will put a premium on practical close cooperation and coordination among all elements of the international response."[22] A proper organization of EU-NATO relations is thus the foundation upon which the legitimate strategic effect of Europeans and North Americans must necessarily be founded in an age when regional instability is fast morphing into strategic instability. This is the case because such a working relationship between them is vital to the aggregation of strategic security effectiveness, of which military defense remains a vital component. Therefore, given the current dysfunctional state of the EU-NATO relationship, a new start is needed that emphasizes effectiveness. The timing is propitious. The NATO Strategic Concept may be rewritten by 2009, and the ambition implicit in the 2007

EU Lisbon Treaty suggests that the European Security Strategy will also need to be revisited. If the NATO-EU relationship is to move beyond estrangement into a new era of engagement, both organizations will need a new drive toward strategic preparedness founded on cohesion, cooperation, and convergence.

The first step is for NATO and the EU to be permitted to embark on a confidence-building program. Usefully, NATO's 60th-anniversary celebrations will take place in 2009, and their centerpiece, given the centrality of the Comprehensive Approach to both organizations, should be a NATO-EU strategic summit founded on making such an approach a reality rather than the exercise in bureaucratic futility it is fast in danger of becoming. The agenda would need to be carefully crafted, but an outline is immediately apparent. NATO and EU officials already meet on a regular basis at different levels of the command chain. Twice a year they meet at the foreign minister level, while at the ambassador level they meet at least six times a year and military talks take place roughly four times per year. Moreover, personnel supporting committees meet on a regular basis and staff as a matter of routine. At the risk of creating more bureaucracy, surely it is time to formalize the relationship through the creation of a NATO-EU Permanent Secretariat with a central mission to define and expand a common position on the Comprehensive Approach. Such an initiative would certainly help to mend the broken political-military loop, better promote the establishment of permanent military liaison arrangements, and thus better facilitate all-important cooperation at the operational level—particularly on the complex arrangements for the rotation of forces through the EU Battle Groups and the NATO Response Force, which have broken down of late.

Such an initiative would further help adapt both organizations to meet the challenges of the twenty-first century. Indeed, it has been eight years since the Washington Process began at the 50th-anniversary summit. Since then, the West has witnessed 9/11, the wars in Iraq and Afghanistan, and a whole range of other operations. Lessons aplenty have been learned, but a lack of flexibility in the NATO transformation model has promoted the ESDP as a cheaper alternative to the Alliance rather than a partner for it. This implicit competition needs to be brought to an end because it further complicates an already Byzantine European defense planning process that disaggregates rather than aggregates effect. One suggestion might be to harmonize the planning and guidance processes of NATO's Management Mechanism with that of the ESDP, particularly as it relates to the EU's Comprehensive Capability Development Process.

As part of that process of convergence, a joint NATO-EU audit of transformation could further help to cement trust and build up a fund of practical cooperation at the planning level. Both organizations preach the mantra of transformation but seem to mean different things. NATO emphasizes military effectiveness through a convergence on high-end, networked capability, whereas the EU implies security effectiveness by focusing on the better use of all civil-military instruments through the Comprehensive Approach. What is needed is smart transformation that enhances the natural strengths of NATO and EU members throughout the strategic stabilization task list and across the conflict-intensity spectrum. This is probably the only way to prevent a capability-capacity crunch because it will help to decrease conflict between the contrasting philosophies of the two organizations over how to achieve effectiveness.

At the very least, NATO and the EU need to face squarely up to the strengths and weaknesses of the Berlin-Plus process—what works and what does not. To that end, they should look jointly at the implications of an EU operational planning and command center at SHAPE that can better facilitate flexibility. At French instigation, the EU's MILEX 05 exercise was the Union's first command-post exercise in which an EU Operational Headquarters was effectively in position (located for the purpose of the exercise in Paris), with an EU Field Headquarters located in Ulm, Germany. Although on a relatively small scale, it is clear that France and Germany intend to proceed with such an architecture. The duplication is both apparent and wasteful, but the politics is well established. This issue needs to be addressed as a matter of urgency if the development of pointless parallel planning and processes is not to become a fact of life. In the event that should happen, arguments over which institution should be in the lead will doubtless proliferate in spite of the encouraging signals from President Sarkozy that France will take a "pragmatic" approach. The nature of bureaucratic politics will render such pragmatism problematic.

Steps have also been taken of late to ease inconsistencies between NATO and EU equipment programs and thus lessen the implicit competition between the Alliance's Prague Capabilities Commitment and the Union's European Capabilities Action Plan. The competition too often seems more about how to apportion blame over how badly each institution and its respective members have failed to fulfill capability goals. The sound of bucks being passed across Brussels is often deafening. However, in spite of the EU-NATO Working Group on Capabilities, the fact is that emerging planning and command stovepipes are helping to reinforce distinction and prejudice in procurement. Driven forward by Europe's largest defense contractor, EADS, backed more or less openly by the French and German governments, this is leading to the creation of Fortress Europe. It may not be a particularly well-constructed fortress, because its foundations are weakened by the anemic equipment budgets of most of the EU member states. However, the very real danger exists that such a structure will profoundly undermine the transformation and modernization of NATO forces because it presupposes equipment plans founded on the ESDP rather than NATO. National armament directors should thus be tasked to examine a closer working relationship between NATO's Conference of National Armament Directors, the Defense Investment Division, and the EU's European Defence Agency. This will help further to reduce conflict between the European Capabilities Action Plan and the Prague Capabilities Commitment processes. In particular, harmonization of initiatives should be pursued that enable strategic effectiveness. The main focus should be command, control, communications, and computer-based intelligence, surveillance, and reconnaissance; Allied Theater Ballistic Missile Defense; precision-guided munitions; and unmanned aerial vehicles—together with airlift and fast sealift.

The sense of parallel NATO and EU universes is reinforced by the current system of operational funding, which is causing tensions in both organizations. Again, NATO and the EU should *jointly* examine options to create common operational funds. At its most elegant, a "sinking fund" could be created that could be called on by Europeans of both organizations to fund operations. Such a fund would be established on the principle that the less a state does, the more it pays. Such a system would need to be based on a set of criteria; size of GDP, position on the OECD development index, level of defense expenditure, transformation investments and operational track record, and the like. It is equally self-evident that with robust operations likely in the Middle East, Asia, and Africa, both NATO and the EU need to recognize a fundamental principle that the greater the commitment to Alliance operations, the more the political representation. Neither

NATO nor the EU can escape the dictates of natural justice. Indeed, it is precisely the lack of such justice in Afghanistan that is doing so much damage to the Alliance. If solidarity collapses on contact with danger, there is little or no point for either organization to plan for a robust future. The less the action, the less the representation but the more the taxation must be the mantra for all operations today and in the future, whether they are under NATO or the EU flag. The bigger powers within both organizations must drive toward an accord on this contract, and then impose it on the others. Otherwise, spurious arguments over national caveats will strangle both NATO and the EU as strategic security actors.

It is easy for Americans to dismiss the notion of European strategic assets as fanciful. However, U.S. support for some constructive duplication would not be amiss. Indeed, the more truly autonomous strategic eyes, ears, and legs Europeans possess, the better allies they will likely become. This will require Americans to make a concerted effort to overcome an understandable contempt for such a notion, given past European performance. Moreover, Americans will also need to overcome the contradiction inherent in U.S. thinking that a stronger Europe must at the same time mean a dependent Europe. That is a nonstarter. One approach would be for Washington to propose a tripartite United States–NATO–EU dialogue over the future of Western strategic security architecture and to seek France as a copromoter.

The need to reflect the enhanced role of the EU implicit in the *Comprehensive Political Guidance* also needs to be reflected in defense financing. With non-NATO countries such as Sweden playing a constructive role in the generation of key enablers, such as strategic airlift, their inclusion in a proper strategic dialogue is a matter of urgency. To that end, it might be useful for NATO and the EU to look jointly at "creative" financing solutions to extend the dollar/euro spending by members of both organizations. For example, a joint study would be desirable on private financing initiatives that could involve the private financial sector in acquisition programs and help to spread the cost of investment across the life cycle of equipment. It might even be possible to create a new form of European lend-lease program involving leading Euro-Atlantic financial institutions.

Nor should NATO and the EU be afraid of looking to the future together. There are several issues that such a study could consider. It is self-evident that as the unit cost of equipment spirals, allied to the need for operational robustness that will be forced upon all members of both institutions, smaller states are going to have to make tough choices over specialization and niche building that might imply some limited form of defense integration. To assist what will be in effect ever more intense forms of effects-based interoperability, the EU and NATO could jointly look at the implications for force and operational planning. Again, given the importance that both Jaap de Hoop Scheffer of NATO and Javier Solana of the EU attach to the Comprehensive Approach and the bureaucratic swamp that could all too easily come to reflect the efforts of both institutions to generate interagency coordination for more effectiveness, the two entities should look jointly at the specifics of a strategic, comprehensive approach. In particular, they should consider strategy, tasks, and costs to see best where synergies could be found and conflict could be lessened.

Both NATO and the EU need to build on the practical work by looking at how cooperation works or fails in the field. Cost-effective cooperation should be built on field experience through EU-NATO crisis action teams. This will be particularly vital in places such as Afghanistan and Darfur, particularly when it comes to the enabling of third-party forces such as those of the African Union or the UN–African Union force proposed for Darfur.

Finally, the EU and NATO should look jointly beyond 2010, Battle Groups, and the NATO Response Force. The EU needs a Headline Goal 2020, and NATO needs to link its own transformative capabilities work with that of the EU in partnership and in practical harmony. A joint strategic horizons project would help to move that agenda forward and further boost the confidence building that is vital in their currently troubled relationship. All it will take is vision on the part of those who thus far have been spoilers to unlock the deep knowledge and extensive talent latent in both organizations. After all, NATO and the EU are there to protect citizens across the Euro-Atlantic community from the dark side of a world awash with dangerous change. It is about time they were permitted to get on with the job—before it is too late.

However, in 2007 the most pressing mission is Afghanistan. This is the current test case for the Comprehensive Approach. With a single operational and training framework urgently needed in Afghanistan, NATO and the EU should lead the way to bring all relevant institutions and actors together, under the auspices of the UN, particularly to improve the Afghan National Police Service, to civilianize the Provincial Reconstruction Teams, and to Afghanize the security mission. Afghanistan is not a theoretical test—it is here and now. It is evident that ISAF is reaching the end of its current operational phase and that the mission urgently needs adjustment and adaptation. Unless far better synergies develop at all levels of the NATO-EU relationship, the disaggregation of effectiveness that has too often marked this relationship will continue. Such a failure would not only further complicate an already complex mission but also increase the danger faced by both civilians and the military and thus render mission success more unlikely.

NATO AND THE EU: TERMS OF ENGAGEMENT OR ESTRANGEMENT?

Whether NATO and the EU face a phase of engagement or estrangement will depend on the strategic vision and political courage of leaders in North America and Europe over the next five years—the pivotal years of early-twenty-first-century strategic security. The questions implicit in this chapter are essentially simple: Are the West's leaders up to the difficult choices and agreements that will be needed during those years? Do they have the vision to overcome the contemporary political, bureaucratic, and economic barriers that constrain the common security effort? Is there enough political will to rescue the EU-NATO relationship from the bureaucratic morass into which it has fallen and elevate it to its true strategic context? Today, the answer to all four questions is No. Some ages may forgive mediocrity, but this is no such age.

Notes

1. Speech by Jaap de Hoop Scheffer, NATO secretary-general, Riga, July 14, 2006; www.nato.int/docu/speech/2006/s060714a.htm.

2. Venusberg Group, *Beyond 2010: European Grand Strategy in a Global Age* (Guetersloh, Germany: Bertelsmann, 2007), 62.

3. Julian Lindley-French, *European Security and Defence: A Chronology* (Oxford: Oxford University Press, 2007), 357.

4. "NATO and the EU: Time for a New Chapter," keynote speech by Jaap de Hoop Scheffer, January 29, 2007; www.nato.int/docu/speech/2007/s070129b.html.

5. NATO, *NATO Handbook* (Brussels: NATO, 2006), 18.

6. Venusberg Group, *Beyond 2010*, 3.

7. NATO, *NATO Handbook*, 28.

8. Ibid., 19.

9. NATO, *Comprehensive Political Guidance of the Riga Summit* (Brussels: NATO Headquarters, 2006).

10. See Julian Lindley-French, *British Strategic Leadership: Food for Thought* (Shrivenham: U.K. Defence Academy, 2006).

11. As the House of Commons Defence Select Committee stated, "We remain deeply concerned that the reluctance of some NATO members to provide troops for the ISAF mission is undermining NATO's credibility and also ISAF operations." House of Commons Defence Select Committee, *UK Operations in Afghanistan* (London: Her Majesty's Stationary Office, 2007), 19.

12. All figures were double checked against euro comparisons to establish dollar/euro parity based on the conversion rates for August 2, 2007, using the XE Universal Currency Converter (www.xe.com/ucc). For the figures themselves, see International Institute for Strategic Studies, *The Military Balance 2007* (Oxford: Oxford University Press, 2007).

13. This was according to the "Capability Improvement Chart I / 2006 of the EU's Headline Goal 2010 of 64 ESDP Capability Shortfalls and Catalogue Deficits covering Land, Maritime, Air, Mobility and ISTAR" (intelligence, surveillance, target acquisition, and reconnaissance).

14. See www.consilium.europa.eu/ueDocs/cms_Data/docs/pressData/en/esdp/89603.pdf.

15. The December 12, 2006, agreement was about far more than operational sovereignty. If the agreement had not been reached, the special relationship would have been dealt a blow that would have undoubtedly accelerated the development of the EU's ESDP as a competitive alternative.

16. Jacques Chirac, "Opening Address on the Occasion of the Ambassadors' Conference," Elysée Palace, Paris, August 28, 2006.

17. Kurt Volker, Testimony before the House International Relations Subcommittee on Europe, May 3, 2006; www.state.gov/p/eur/rls/rm/65874.htm.

18. In July 2007, Britain announced the construction of two supercarriers, *HMS Queen Elizabeth* and *HMS Prince of Wales*, as part of a $12 billion investment program for the Royal Navy. That expenditure is in turn part of a $24 billion overall investment program in the armed forces.

19. NATO, *NATO Handbook*, 209.

20. In August 2007 alone, Russia planted a flag on the seabed of the Arctic Ocean in an attempt to claim sovereignty over the oil and gas reserves in the region and flew missions over NATO territory and close to the U.S. base on Guam.

21. Venusberg Group, *Beyond 2010*.

22. NATO, *Comprehensive Political Guidance*.

CHAPTER NINE

RECASTING THE EURO-ATLANTIC PARTNERSHIP

Franklin D. Kramer and Simon Serfaty

Americans and Europeans can reflect with much satisfaction on the achievements of the past six decades. Built upon two institutional processes—one transatlantic and the other intra-European—they established an institutional architecture for the Euro-Atlantic partnership that waged and won the Cold War. NATO and the European Union have proved not only compatible but also complementary. For NATO and the EU to be cohesive and powerful required that their European members achieve reconciliation while regaining their strength in ever larger numbers—and that their relations with the United States be ever deepened. In late 2006, the NATO and EU summits held in Latvia and presided over by Lithuania respectively were, therefore, fraught with symbols. With those meetings, the 26 NATO countries, including 21 EU members, and the 27 EU members, including 21 NATO countries, demonstrated how far they had come in meeting the first significant challenge of the post–Cold War world: achieving stability and security for a free, safe, and gradually whole Europe.[1]

The success of that endeavor can be shown by the fact that, on a growing number of significant issues, U.S. relations with the European Union now matter more to the United States than bilateral relations with any EU member, and that on an ever larger number of issues, EU policies matter more than the policies of any of its members. But despite such satisfaction, there is recognition of the need for new efforts, including what remains to be done to approximate a Euro-Atlantic finality that approaches new modalities of U.S.-European relations for the organization of coordinated action—common or complementary—in the twice-changed security environment born out of the events of November 9, 1989, in Europe and September 11, 2001, in America.

Recasting the Euro-Atlantic partnership to meet the challenges of the twenty-first century will demand new approaches and concerted efforts by the members of the Euro-Atlantic community. Unlike the concept of stability in Europe, which the Alliance, by history and proximity, was well positioned to support, the challenges now faced by the Euro-Atlantic states and institutions—most pressingly those of failing states; radical militant Islam; energy security, including relations with Russia; and structural political and economic competition, including relations with China—are exceedingly complex and incompletely understood, offering few demonstrable short-term results and even fewer certain solutions.

Both the structures and capabilities of the Euro-Atlantic community will need revision if such challenges are to be met—and the development of new capacities will demand not only resources but also commitment on behalf of a renewed Euro-Atlantic consensus. For such a consensus to return, more will have to be done to recognize the dual historic achievements of European policies that permitted the rise of the EU with a decisive assist from the United States, and the triumph of NATO with a substantial assist from the European allies. These dual but complementary efforts have not only been poorly explained in recent years. They have also been missing as the institutions of the Euro-Atlantic community often failed to deliver what each new initiative seemed to promise, and each new crisis seemed to demand. This chapter sets out a way forward, recommending a broader strategic agenda and a more comprehensive institutional structure for more effective cooperation by the Euro-Atlantic countries.

THE MAIN AREAS OF CONCERN

By many measures, the Euro-Atlantic community has succeeded brilliantly. From within, the states of Europe and the United States form the most complete relationship in the world—a web of overlapping interests, compatible values, and shared goals. Relative to the world without, this is a community that includes 17 of the top 20 countries in the world, if measured in terms of gross domestic product per capita, and as many as 18 of the top 20 in terms of quality of life. Yet, by other standards, the Euro-Atlantic community also faces fundamental challenges that raise critical security, political, economic, and social concerns.

Traditional security concerns are increasingly bundled into circumstances that cannot be addressed by military power alone, however preponderant and capable that power might be. For the United States, Iraq and Afghanistan top the list of security issues that demand immediate attention. Yet Iraq and Afghanistan overlap into larger questions of stabilization and reconstruction, rogue regimes and failing states, and radical militant Islam and global terrorism. These questions are further linked to the issues presented by the proliferation of weapons of mass destruction, a subject dominated by (but hardly limited to) the ambitions and defiance of Iran and North Korea. For most Americans, having suffered the shock of 9/11 and the subsequent anthrax attacks, the potential significance of these and other rogue states acquiring these weapons is clear, despite the intelligence debacle of Iraq. Nevertheless, it is now widely agreed that U.S. military preponderance can be only one element of the comprehensive approach needed to counter this mixture of interrelated threats.

Additionally, the United States faces longer-term issues that have the potential to become critical and urgent concerns in the years ahead. Approximately 40 percent of U.S. energy comes from oil, a commodity whose susceptibility to economic and geopolitical instability has been regularly demonstrated in the past three decades. Natural gas, too, is increasingly subject to worldwide instabilities affecting U.S. allies and partners, as Russian (and Bolivian) actions regarding supply to neighbors have shown. Under such conditions, and with fossil fuels in finite supply, energy security must figure more prominently on the U.S. agenda. Energy security, however, cannot be separated from environmental issues, as the generation of carbon dioxide and other greenhouse gases from the consumption of fossil fuels portends an eventual climatic disaster. As a result, energy security achieved the wrong way may well lead to problems of an even greater magnitude, as climate problems overwhelm economic issues. Third, the United States faces concerns stemming from the changing structure of the world economy, particularly as a result of the swift and sustained rise of Asia.

These trends cannot fail to have consequences for the changing structure of the world order as well. The impact of the low-cost, high-quality producer on the global market, exemplified by the paradigmatic "Chinese manufacturer" and "Indian service provider," may divide the interests of American capital from American labor in ways not easily subject to remedy by regulatory mediation or multilateral negotiations. The path to adapting the U.S. economy to these new conditions without affecting current standards of living for future generations is not clear—and is a growing cause for public pressures that demand protection from these forces.

Europe, of course, also faces these issues, arguably even more acutely than the United States. For most European countries, the impact of radical militant Islam is not only an external issue but also one of domestic concern. Unlike the United States, Europe is within the range of Iranian missiles. When Russia puts its thumb on the gas pipeline and attempts to intimidate its neighbors, it is Europe whose energy is affected and security threatened. And while the Chinese and other Asian countries' invasion of the global markets has the potential to hurt the United States, Europe, which has been enduring relatively high unemployment and lower growth rates for the past two decades, is especially sensitive to such pain. In all these manifestations, Europeans face many of the same issues as Americans do. Reflective of this fact, the European Security Strategy put forth by the European Union and the U.S. National Security Strategy are remarkably, but not surprisingly, parallel.

In responding to the issues, however, the European and American processes are often different. This stems from an additional critical question faced by Europe—namely, the unfinished status of EU institutions. The Union (and the broader issues surrounding it) continues to raise serious questions of identity for Europeans, reflected in numerous levels of torn or shared sovereignty, parallel national and EU structures, and political steps that move erratically forward in some cases (like the euro) and back in others (like the Constitutional Treaty). The EU, which was originally an economic project with uncertain political consequences, has become far more a legislative and judicial sovereign entity (though not always with sovereign power), an influential diplomatic actor (though with parallel and often superior actors in member states), and even a military power (though with quite modest assertion so far). Thus, the Union is both sovereign in itself—a "supranational regional state," as argued by Vivien Schmidt[2]—and composed of sovereign member states, which have not given up their economic capacities, diplomatic endeavors, or control over security and military policy.

Therefore, unlike the United States, which has a basic single sovereignty in the international arena, the different actors within Europe can espouse substantively different positions on global issues—which is, of course, what they do and are likely to do for some time to come. With a European Union presidency, an EU high representative, and an EU bureaucracy all involved in key international issues in which national prime ministers, foreign ministers, and parliaments are also involved, European policy in international affairs can be quite complex. The "simplified" treaty negotiated in June 2007 as an alternative of sort to the defunct Constitutional Treaty may even accentuate that complexity as an appointed EU bureaucracy and the elected European Parliament representatives gain additional powers and authority. In the end, Europe now has a telephone number that the United States and other NATO allies that are not EU members can call, but the answer is often that of a voice mail system that directs callers to various national capitals in the Union and various administrative layers within the EU.

How then can Americans and Europeans, as well as their respective institutions, work together to ensure that tomorrow's solutions are effective? What should be the substantive focus of the Euro-Atlantic partnership? What do the complexity of European sovereignties and the potential for further change mean for transatlantic interaction? History has given us a starting point—a strong and powerful Alliance, together with a united and gradually stronger Europe, but how can those be used to shape a better and more orderly future?

THE QUESTION OF STRUCTURE

The question of how to structure Euro-Atlantic cooperation is critical to future effectiveness, because weak institutional structures significantly inhibit the generation and implementation of substantive solutions. *Qui fait quoi* (Who does what?) asked President Jacques Chirac in response to a German call for so-called finality in Europe.[3] Earlier, the French president had raised the same question in a broader context when he called for a "Charter" that would renew the transatlantic bargain of the Cold War years.[4] Though NATO has "survived" the clash over Iraq, and the EU has overcome the stall over the Constitutional Treaty—both among the most serious crises ever faced by either—

there is still little agreement and much dispute over the proper roles for NATO, the EU, and their individual members.

Admittedly, the desirability of a "more substantive political and strategic dialogue" between the United States and the EU, and the need for "closer relations between NATO and the EU" are now widely acknowledged. According to Chirac, these combine into a "vision for NATO" that reaffirms "the preeminent role" of the Atlantic Alliance as "a military organization, guarantor of the collective security of the Allies, and a forum where Europeans and Americans can combine their efforts to further peace."[5] The fundamental issue is whether to place the emphasis on "military organization"—as traditionally favored by France—or on a "forum where Europeans and Americans can combine their efforts to further peace"—a view favored by the United States.

Thus, at age 60, the Euro-Atlantic community still does not know where to assemble "for improvements in the NATO-EU strategic partnership as agreed by [both] organizations." Within the EU, there is still a marked predilection for the few over the many, and even issues with obvious security consequences, like Iran's nuclear program, are handled ad hoc, with a so-called EU-3 (Britain, France, and Germany) that, depending on this issue, might be reduced further for, say, Libya (as France did in mid-2007), or enlarged slightly for, say, Kosovo. Between the EU and the United States, whatever progress there has been is still defined by a marked tendency to remain narrowly focused on commercial issues at the expense of the strategic environment within which they now evolve.[6] And between NATO and the EU, two organizations that share 21 members, an impasse between Turkey, a non-EU member of NATO, and Cyprus, a non-NATO member of the EU, is enough to prevent a joint discussion of broader strategic issues facing the other 30 members of the Euro-Atlantic community.

The four separate dialogues between and among the Euro-Atlantic states—within NATO, within the EU, between the United States and the Union, and between the Union and NATO—need to be substantively and procedurally intertwined into a consultative forum that would group all 32 EU and NATO members, as well as the EU itself, because it is an entity of sovereign consequence. The NATO secretary-general would also be offered a seat at the table to enhance communication and implementation.[7]

The availability of such a Euro-Atlantic Forum would eliminate the need to define the respective competencies of the EU and NATO, as well as the role of individual states within each. There are no more trivial and debilitating types of questions than, for example, "whether NATO has the competence to engage in civilian tasks in support of its military missions"—especially because its member countries plainly have that competence—or "whether the EU has the capacity to undertake a military mission," when most of its members are also members of NATO, the most powerful military alliance in the world. Rather than being beset by such trivial self-imposed limitations, the new forum could, with all parties present, review, discuss, and ultimately decide upon the necessity of action, determine how best to implement it, and approve the appropriate implementing organization.[8] When, as surely will almost always be the case in the future, a combination of security, political, and economic measures are required, their implementation could be organized in a complementary rather than disjointed or even competitive fashion—among the member states and with or between their institutions.

The creation of this new forum would not mean that either NATO or the EU would be abandoning its distinct mission, structure, or even future. Indeed, the reverse is true; by restoring the needed consensus among the members of each institution, the forum would reinforce each institution's capacity for action, and by making it possible for each one to rely on the capabilities of the other it would also reinforce the efficacy of that action. For all 32 EU/NATO members would now be able to operate, through either institution or with both of them, in a coordinated fashion allowing maximization of effort and resources, eliminating the self-imposed limitations created by focusing on procedure over substance. The new forum would act as a strategic coordinator of the efforts of the Euro-Atlantic community, pooling all available security, political, and economic strengths. And when conflicting approaches were suggested, as would likely be the case, the forum would be available to enable members to arrive at consensus and cooperation.

Yet the creation of this appropriate new institutional structure is only the first step. As argued above, the Euro-Atlantic community's combined focus must move past traditional security questions to face the more difficult and complex issues raised by failing states, radical militant Islam, energy security, and structural global competition. These issues are discussed below.

THE NEW COMPREHENSIVE AGENDA

The fundamental joint agenda of America and Europe demands an effective and comprehensive international approach that goes beyond traditional security questions. Rigid distinctions between security, political, and economic aspects of global challenges act as barriers to achieving successful outcomes. NATO often fails to be effective because it is too limited to the military side—arguably less because of what it was meant to be after World War II than because of what it became during the Cold War. The EU, too, often has little political punch because its security dimension remains too limited. All too often, the United States fails to create adequate partnerships with its allies and partners—and, conversely, the latter fail to do so with the United States. New initiatives are necessary to generate the concepts, resources, and commitment necessary for success—and the proposed new forum needs to serve as a catalyst and driver in this process.

Failing States and the Problems of Stabilization and Reconstruction

The problem of failing states as a threat to peace is now well recognized in the security strategies of both the United States and Europe. But solutions have been elusive, and responses remain fundamentally ad hoc.

Afghanistan is representative of the problem. After September 2001, this was unanimously viewed as a legitimate war. After nearly six years of war, however, there is a consensus that progress in stabilization and reconstruction (S&R) is far from satisfactory. A report of the UN Security Council mission to Afghanistan concludes that "progress in 2006 …has not been as rapid as had been hoped …[and has] tempered the legitimate hopes of Afghans with signs of despondency and disillusionment." A midyear assessment in 2007 would not improve much on these conclusions.[9]

Regretfully, Afghanistan is not an aberration, and no Euro-Atlantic country can guarantee that its involvement in future interventions will necessarily resolve any given situation to the advantage of all. Thus, Bosnia is still far from an effectively functioning state; East Timor has had significant problems; Haiti remains a miasma. Conditions in Somalia and Iraq are worse.[10] The Kosovo situation has yet to be resolved and is turning into a major topic of discord with Russia. Each of these interventions has had significant international involvement, substantial resources, and long-term commitments. But none has had clear success.

To be sure, there are examples of positive results—the interventions in Bosnia and Kosovo put an end to significant killings, and, despite the difficulties since then, those instances had great benefit for that reason alone. But Bosnia and Kosovo also both show the difficulty of moving from humanitarian efforts—"halting the killing"—to the broader requirements of creating a functioning polity; and other cases, such as Somalia and Iraq, show that interventions do not even always result in the end of killing (though, of course, nonintervention can result in a great deal more, as in Rwanda and now Darfur).

There is little doubt that S&R efforts inherent in dealing with failing states require more than military power, which is to say that S&R capabilities are of no lesser importance to preventing and ending a war than coercion is central to waging and winning it. To that end, cooperation of the military with civilians, within and among participating countries, as well as between the institutions to which they belong, is a key element of the future ability to deal with failing states and manage the instabilities that they suffer or create. NATO secretary-general Jaap de Hoop Scheffer embraced this need when asking the 26 NATO members for the authority to develop a civilian capacity for NATO beyond, and even separate from, its Response Force's high-intensity capability. The U.S. Department of Defense also officially views stability operations, including political and economic requirements, as a task on a par with war fighting.[11] Yet, for such recognition of the multidimensional nature of S&R tasks, there is little to show, as the above list of interventions demonstrates, by way of actual results, in terms of building up functioning, standalone countries.

Needless to say, failing states differ from one another, and the demands of S&R efforts will likewise be different in their particulars. To bring about more successful interventions, there needs to be a far greater appreciation of the political situation in each state in question, compared to that of past cases, as well as the related regional circumstances for each of those states, compared to those of other regions. Concomitant with this is a necessity to understand how to provide the internal parties with enough incentives to make peace and stability in their interest. This requires a carefully coordinated approach in which security, political, and economic efforts are properly prioritized and implemented.

A major Euro-Atlantic initiative that gives greater attention to what factors and approaches make a difference in the outcome of a range of intervention scenarios could provide important grounding relevant to succeeding in specific contexts. Simply continuing to pursue with greater vigor the ad hoc approach that has characterized past interventions suggests that future outcomes will only be, if not precisely failures, then "nonsuccesses." The first great task of the Euro-Atlantic community is to generate a more effective approach to failing states and S&R.

One fundamental requirement of such efforts is that there be an integrated approach among the international outside intervening parties and among both security and nonsecurity activities. Thus, the goal is for the 32 Euro-Atlantic countries to make effective use of both NATO and the EU and individual national capabilities on these issues—to invest the respective resources of these institutions and countries in joint S&R initiatives that are sufficiently flexible and sufficiently well endowed with relevant capabilities to respond to local and regional conditions. Almost certainly, other institutions and countries will also be associated with such efforts for legitimacy as well as for capabilities and relevant resources, and the Euro-Atlantic approach needs to recognize the probability of such a multidimensional effort.

Radical Militant Islam

The issue of radical militant Islam—the force that generated 9/11 and the Madrid and London bombings in March 2004 and July 2005, respectively, and has been an underlying source of domestic and external tensions and apprehensions ever since—presents the Euro-Atlantic community with the challenge of creating a long-term and multifaceted response to an ideology that will use violence, but also political and economic activities, to advance its agenda.

The Euro-Atlantic community's response to this challenge—reflected in the concepts of democracy and individual rights, including tolerance for the practice of religion—is completely valid. This approach, which was a central feature of the failed EU Constitutional Treaty, is incorporated in most national constitutions, as well as in the UN Declaration of Human Rights, and it is largely accepted worldwide.[12] It also hardly needs stating that the Euro-Atlantic community possesses great political, economic, security, and social strengths with which to counter the spread of radical militant Islam. The issue is how to bring all these capabilities to bear; anti-European and anti-American sentiments outside the Euro-Atlantic community create an environment that will demand the most creative approaches.

In waging the related battle of ideas, the Euro-Atlantic community must again face a central dilemma of the Cold War: promoting democracy and human rights, on the one side, versus establishing stability, on the other. The Cold War strategy did not simply abandon democracy promotion to ensure stability—rather, it made use of intelligent diplomacy, combining the efforts of private with public institutions. In early 2007, President Gerald Ford's passing recalled the brilliance of the Helsinki Final Act, which framed the democratic aspirations of many then–Warsaw Pact nations while providing a platform for the West. It is true, of course, that during the Cold War not every possible action was taken in favor of democracy—but the fact is that democracy promotion and the generation of stability existed simultaneously as coordinated, common, and central values. To be sure, there were flaws and inconsistencies in the policies pursued by or on behalf of Euro-Atlantic countries, but ultimately these policies worked and delivered democratic governance and values while ensuring unprecedented security and stability for a group of 32 states that is now nearly three times as large as the initial 12 members of the Atlantic Alliance, and over five times larger than the initial 6 members of the European Economic Community. It should again be a task of the Euro-Atlantic community to promote both these goals—stability and democratic change—in this new century.

In a globalized and interconnected world, withdrawal from the struggle with radical militant Islam is not an option, and isolation from the consequences of that struggle in any one country or region is not likely to be viable either. Admittedly, radical militant Islam is, as noted above, an internal issue for many European countries, and, accordingly, so is the solution to that issue. As already shown too many times since 9/11, and to paraphrase an earlier revolutionary, even if you are not interested in radical militant Islam, it is interested in you. The Euro-Atlantic community needs a shared commitment to meet radical militant Islam head-on—but head-on in an effective, resourced, and strategic fashion.

The critical issues raised by radical militant Islam simply transcend a battle of ideas with the Euro-Atlantic West. Equally central are issues rooted in the history of European and American relations with countries and regions where Islam prevails. There is more to such considerations than the Arab-Israeli conflict, however important the conflict has been in Islam's perception of the Euro-Atlantic West over the past six decades. A Euro-Atlantic Forum would also permit coordinated action on issues of primary interest to the Muslim interlocutors of the Euro-Atlantic community, especially with regard to the Greater Middle East.

The forum would also allow for a far more effective dialogue concerning Turkey. EU membership for Turkey is a distant prospect at best, which carries consequences not only for the future of EU-NATO institutional relations but also for EU and NATO relations with the Middle East and even Russia. What would be the consequences of a triple play of negative scenarios for this important NATO member—a breakdown of current negotiations with the EU, a precipitate U.S. withdrawal from Iraq, and a nuclear Iran? With each of these outcomes quite plausible before the end of the decade, each with different measures of probability but conceivably all in a rapid sequence, such a scenario should be examined.

As the discussion of Turkey suggests, not that all 32 Euro-Atlantic countries respond to the same concerns and traditions in the Greater Middle East region—but, for the most part, they do have common goals, or at least overlapping aspirations, for the region. Predictably, their differences often create distinct priorities and vulnerabilities, but effective consultation about these differences can help overcome the obstacles that would otherwise stand in the way of common or at least compatible policies. Having successful Euro-Atlantic policies with regard to the Greater Middle East is a matter of sheer interest. No region in the world is more important but also more volatile—more disruptive, dangerous, unstable, expensive, and intrusive; indeed, for the next several decades, no other region will offer the same potential for exporting chaos and war on a global scale. Because of this unusual combination—vital significance and explosive potential—it is there that the Euro-Atlantic community will meet its most demanding test, but it is also there that it can least afford to fail that test.

It will take a long time to resolve this problem, and it will require a comprehensive, adaptable approach. Politics must lead, but economic and development strategies will be crucial, and security activities—external and internal—will also play an important role. The proposed new forum of the NATO and EU countries plus the European Union itself and with the NATO secretary-general would have the appropriate resources to coordinate such a comprehensive and even integrated effort mobilizing the political, economic, and security assets of the Euro-Atlantic community.

Weapons of Mass Destruction

The Iran nuclear question dominates the concerns of the Euro-Atlantic community as a whole regarding the issue of weapons of mass destruction, but the prospects of al Qaeda or an affiliate acquiring such weapons—as well as North Korea—are also important concerns. Fears of the "worst weapons in the hands of the worst people" go beyond technical questions of nonproliferation, however; they overlap with the issues of how to deal with rogue states and radical militant Islam.

Again, there is no forum in which to bring the countries of the Euro-Atlantic community together to discuss such issues. Iran and North Korea, for example, have each been addressed by ad hoc groupings, and each case has moved on to the United Nations Security Council. In neither case does the prospect of successful negotiations, leading these countries to abandon their nuclear ambitions, appear likely, and in the case of Iran especially they may face time constraints that force decisions before negotiations have run their course. Dealing with countries that fail to abide by international norms is of great consequence for the Euro-Atlantic community. The failure to do so in a coordinated fashion in the case of Iraq cut deeply into the cohesion of the community on many issues, and was an important contributor to some of the failures in the Iraq engagement. In the case of Iran and North Korea, the prospect of using force to eliminate nuclear programs also raises deep political and military issues that deserve significant discussion. In all cases, these issues raise crosscutting political, military, and economic questions that demand a common approach by the countries of NATO and the EU.

There have been a variety of suggested approaches to the Iranian nuclear problem. Sanctions have long been on the table. Then-chairman of the Senate Armed Services Committee Senator John Warner specifically called for a "ring of deterrence" that would surround Iran if and when needed.[13] In late 2006, then–French president Chirac began to envision ways in which Iran would be prevented from ever using its nuclear capabilities, in or outside its region, his goal being to discourage Iran from proceeding with its plans by reminding its government of the consequences of first use for the entire country.[14] Thus, a common approach to "containment" or "containment-plus" of a nuclear Iran might include such steps as a coordinated set of bilateral security commitments that would be made by each of the three Euro-Atlantic nuclear powers (the United States, Britain, and France) to any and all of the countries that would feel threatened by Iran's acquisition of such weapons. These Euro-Atlantic countries, acting on behalf of the broader Euro-Atlantic community, could also invite other nuclear powers to make a comparable commitment as well. Such assurances might go a long way toward halting whatever momentum Iran's acquisition of nuclear capabilities will otherwise create with regard to proliferation. In addition, the Euro-Atlantic community could rely on its political and economic leverage to isolate a nuclear Iran with a comprehensive strategy of sanctions, thus exacting a price for the fulfillment of a goal that would have been made visibly worthless. In this case, too, countries outside the Euro-Atlantic community would also be invited to join, possibly in a UN framework that would provide global legitimacy. The point is not to anticipate what the decision will be, and how and when it would be enforced. The point is that given the need for some sort of decision, there should be some discussion of how best to form a consensus that will be conducive to action when the time comes.

In the emerging multipolar security system, many other pivot states deserve anticipatory discussion in the context of some of the issues that loom ahead, some with particular weapons of mass destruction issues. In South Asia, Pakistan is such a pivot state, a potential reincarnation of Iran in the late 1970s—though currently working with the United States, but not wholly satisfactorily, on some important aspects of counterterrorism. Its internal politics are uncertain—with democratic claims vying with Army institutionalism and each with Islamic radicalism, including in the relatively ungoverned northwest areas. All these issues added to its nuclear capacities raise serious questions, for the United States and other Euro-Atlantic countries.

There are other examples, to be sure, and, no less surely there is no lack of other contingencies that might result from assassination, major terrorist attacks, natural disasters, severe energy shortages, territorial conflicts, and more (or worse). In thinking about, and preparing for, such contingencies, the goal is not the creation of another layer of rigid and discursive bureaucracy. At a time of considerable volatility and under conditions of growing complexity, the goal instead is for more effective joint planning by 32 likeminded NATO and EU members that already abide by a collective discipline that has served them well in the past and will continue to serve them well so long as these institutions are properly used and, to that end, recast. This contingency planning could also involve specific outside groups (think tanks and universities in the countries involved) with specialist knowledge, access to relevant national and multilateral agencies, and the ability to reach across constituencies and borders. Formal and informal networks could also be used to nurture public support for a range of policy options through substantive debate of the issues involved. A Euro-Atlantic Council of Experts representing some of the countries most directly affected would act as an early warning before follow-up meetings of relevant officials.

Energy Cooperation

The world, whatever its levels of economic development, depends on the availability of reasonably priced and readily available energy, a requirement that has generated issues tied to rising costs, security of supply, and environmental impact. As is the case for the other issues discussed above, there is no integrative forum where the countries of NATO and the EU can cooperate to meet these challenges. In November 2006, NATO's Riga communiqué took the step of proposing "to consult on the most immediate risks in the field of energy security" and to "support a coordinated, international effort to assess risks to energy infrastructure."[15] The EU, too, has devoted much time to achieving an allegedly united policy on such a vital issue.[16] There is nothing intrinsically wrong in these separate approaches other than the obvious point that neither the proposed NATO study nor the alleged EU policy amounts to an action plan—and even if the study were completed or the policy adopted, and action plans developed accordingly, the problems of assuring energy supply at a reasonable price would not be met.

Moreover, even in terms of security, the problem of protecting energy supply goes far beyond those of securing critical infrastructure in developed nations. As a report by senior U.S. chief executive officers and retired four-star officers noted,

In light of military threats to the global oil infrastructure, the U.S. should, where appropriate: Encourage burden sharing with U.S. allies and partners, including producing and consuming nations, in defense of global oil flows; foster formal and informal security arrangements on multilateral, regional, and bilateral bases;... provide diplomatic support as well as counterterrorism training and military aid so that oil-producing nations can better assist in protecting petroleum supplies; [and] offer assistance to producing countries in their efforts to develop attractive investment climates backed by stable civil societies.[17]

Although this report was explicitly U.S.-centric, there is precedent for NATO to undertake some of the proposed activities. However, most of the recommended actions are not operations that are or can be undertaken by NATO. For example, military, counterterrorism, and other types of security aid to countries are generally arranged on a bilateral basis. Many NATO countries have been patrolling in the Gulf, but either under UN auspices or on an ad hoc basis. While NATO does have the Partnership for Peace and the Istanbul Cooperation Initiative, which include key security-minded countries that are not NATO members, neither the partnership nor the initiative has a mandate for dealing specifically with energy security.

Even more important, numerous energy security issues do not lend themselves to military action. The very tight supply-demand situation in the oil markets has led to an overall rise in prices in the past several years, with periodic spikes to levels of serious concern. How to allocate oil in crisis circumstances is a question on which the countries that have worked together to develop stockpiles under the auspices of the International Energy Agency have had substantial discussions. But plans to deal with an immediate crisis that would necessitate opening stockpiles into the market do not deal with the much more important issue of how to ensure sufficient supply at reasonable prices over the longer term.

Similar to the issue raised by the inelasticity of the oil market is the issue of an enforced cutoff of supply, currently punctuated by concerns over Russian energy policies. Russia supplies about a third of Europe's gas requirements and a quarter of its oil. These numbers are expected to rise significantly over the next two decades, notwithstanding occasional warnings that Gazprom may not have enough gas to satisfy both existing contracts and domestic demand. In the context of this substantial dominance, numerous voices have raised the question of whether the Euro-Atlantic community should predetermine a collective response if, say, supplies to one country, including a non-EU, non-NATO country, were cut off by the Russian government, as was done temporarily to Ukraine in early 2006.[18] The Euro-Atlantic countries cannot afford any misunderstanding about their commitment and intent; questions raised by recent Russian behavior are worth appropriate answers, or at least sufficient reflection to permit prompt answers should Russia take more damaging steps.

The vital issue of energy dependence is intimately tied to other Russia-related issues that extend beyond energy and raise traditional security questions—from missile deployment to Kosovo. In recent years, Europe's attempts to develop a common policy on Russia have not been effective, as was seen at the EU-Russia summit in Samara in mid-May 2007. Though most of the new leaders in the major EU members would now agree that there is a need for a firmer engagement of Russia, there is little agreement on what the terms of engagement should be—economic, political, and institutional—and there is even less agreement on what the tests of the new firmness ought to be. But, again, planning what to do, in a crisis, though obviously quite important, does not resolve the substantive issues that generated the crisis in the first place and require pre-crisis consultation and preparation. As with other issues, a longer-term strategic approach is required to achieve a better understanding of each other's views on Russia, share more of the analysis on each other's energy needs and concerns that such needs might not be met, evaluate policy alternatives for serious contingencies, and make the required commitments for addressing those contingencies together—and yet there is no appropriate forum for the states of the Euro-Atlantic community to formulate such cooperation, from state to state together with each of the main institutions to which they belong or which they hope to join.

Environmental concerns similarly lack a Euro-Atlantic forum for discussion. The Kyoto Accord, the U.S. decision not to join, and the question of whether the Kyoto protocols are in any way alleviating the nearly universally acknowledged threat of global warming is well known. Though there has been some progress on these issues, the states of Europe and the United States, as well as Canada, have much more to do to address an issue that is being "discovered" with growing urgency by citizens at local levels.[19] That is especially the case if the agreement reached at the June 2007 Group of Eight Summit is to be conducive to an effective "Kyoto II" treaty. A first step is to put the issue on the agenda of the Euro-Atlantic community and to undertake its review in the context of discussions seeking consensus, rather than in the context of negotiations that generate countervailing pressures. The proposed new Euro-Atlantic Forum would be an appropriate coordinating body for such discussions.

Global Structural Economic Competition

One of the fundamental challenges facing the Euro-Atlantic community is posed by economic competition from parts of the world whose technical competencies now match those of the West, but whose labor and, often, capital costs are much lower and are expected to remain lower for many years to come. As noted above, these challengers are generally characterized as the "Chinese manufacturer" and the "Indian service provider," but the reality is that increased educational levels, spreading technical competencies, and enhanced transportation, communication, and information capabilities have made much of the world competitors in what until only recently were largely Western preserves. The situation is analogous to that faced in the United States during the 1950s and 1960s when much industry moved from the northern "Rust Belt" to the southern "Sun Belt." Over the long term, the U.S. economy as a whole benefited from these changes, and the northern states developed new sources of jobs replacing those that moved. But in the shorter term, the dislocations created significant local hardship, and some areas never recovered.

In the international arena, companies aiming to maximize profits will seek low-cost production. Likewise, new companies that can be low-cost producers will move into industry. The lower wages and capital costs to be found in developing countries almost guarantee that there will be continuing disruptions of ongoing enterprises in developed countries. The ultimate scale of such disruptions is not yet clear, and the exact timing and pace of these shifts is difficult to predict. Over the long term, the benefits to the world are clear enough—lower costs benefit consumers and, if the developing world generates a per capita gross domestic product even remotely approaching that of the developed world, the developing world will find much to purchase from the developed world.

But the rub is what is meant by the "long term." If it takes more than 50 years—and it almost certainly will—for the developing world to start to meet developed-world income levels, what will be the impact on industry and jobs in the developed world? The results are likely to be problematic, given the fact that the developing world has a significant surplus of labor, mostly on rural land, whose movement into industry is likely to keep labor costs in those countries quite low. In addition, developing countries face issues of instituting the costly social welfare requirements of the developed world, such as labor standards, health care, and pensions.

There is also an important national security aspect to these questions. Research and development tends to conjoin with manufacturing, and as and if industry settles away from the Euro-Atlantic community, research and development, which might be expected to breed innovation to keep developed countries competitive, may also display changing patterns. The West has had the benefit of all technological change over the past 800 years, but what will happen when technology develops elsewhere again is less than fully clear, and clarity, when it finally comes, may prove to be less than fully satisfying.

There are no easy solutions to these issues, but currently the Euro-Atlantic community lacks any substantial forum in which even to contemplate them in a useful fashion. The proposed forum of EU and NATO countries, plus the two institutions to which they belong or with which they are closely associated, could fulfill that need. In the meantime, this group of 32 countries would also benefit from further efforts in two priority areas of desirable deliverables. First, a joint commitment to a Transatlantic Market by a date certain, which had been repeatedly proposed by some in the European Parliament and the U.S. Congress, as well as by leading experts and corporate leaders, was a major achievement of the EU-U.S. Summit of May 2007, and it must be completed.[20] A road map that singles out the remaining barriers to transatlantic trade and investment, and picks a target date—2015—for their removal, will help assert the nonpartisan legitimacy of this goal.

Second, past the failed Doha round of global trade negotiations, closer EU-U.S. cooperation is needed to influence China and to establish a viable long-term economic framework. In addition to ongoing efforts by the main Euro-Atlantic economies to coordinate their respective messages on Chinese protection of foreign companies' intellectual property, opportunities for more and more open cooperation exist on state aid, market access, dumping, and developing more transparent and open financial markets. The common goal is to urge China to behave as a full-time economic stakeholder in the global marketplace. The global competitive market system will not be sustainable and mutually beneficial without a globally institutionalized mechanism explicitly designed to protect it—but no such mechanism can emerge without a joint U.S.-EU effort to that end, including coordinated or parallel but unambiguous advocacy of a quick appreciation of the Chinese and other Asian currencies.

CONCLUSION

The Euro-Atlantic community faces new and different challenges in the twenty-first century. A new focus and new organizations will be necessary to meet those challenges. Making the problems of failing states, radical militant Islam, energy and the environment, and global structural economic competition the focus of the community's effort and creating a new forum in which to discuss and act upon those issues will enable the community to achieve the same success in the twenty-first century as it did in meeting the challenges of the Cold War. For these challenges to be met, the terms of engagement between the states of Europe, organized as a Union but with NATO, and the United States, through the Atlantic Alliance but with the EU, must be renewed.

To this effect, a Euro-Atlantic Summit of all NATO/EU heads of state and government should be held at an appropriate time, but hopefully no later than in November 2009, the 20th-anniversary summit of the fall of the Berlin Wall—a historically decisive event fraught with powerful meaning for all members of the Euro-Atlantic community. Though remaining explicitly distinct from either the EU or NATO, a Euro-Atlantic Summit would introduce the two sides of the Atlantic to the new expanded consultative body between the 32 EU/NATO countries, together with the EU and with the participation of the NATO secretary-general. A Joint Declaration from the U.S. Senate and the European Parliament, released in the context of the Euro-Atlantic Summit, would also help give added legitimacy to such an initiative.

The Euro-Atlantic Forum would not be designed for summit meetings only, and in practice such summits would continue to be on top of a consultative pyramid that would include all sorts of intermediate levels designed to encourage and facilitate consultation among these

32 countries at lower official levels or even through different nongovernmental venues. The forum might also become common practice for interministerial meetings that would associate EU members to non-EU members of NATO, and NATO members to non-NATO members of the EU—as well as relevant EU and NATO institutional representation. Thus, the EU high commissioner for foreign policy could have a deputy for defense issues, who might also be the EU representative at the related NATO defense interministerial, also extended to permit participation by the defense ministers of non-NATO, EU members.[21]

The emphasis on consultation and coordination would be extended to areas that either institution might view as needed and beneficial for its own sake. For example, a new Strategic Concept for NATO, based on the *Comprehensive Political Guidance* endorsed in Riga in November 2006,[22] could parallel a comparable EU effort for a new European Security Strategy. Neither document would be easy to draft, either for the 26 NATO allies or for the 27 EU members. But a commitment to doing so by a date certain, and an interest in making these documents converge through related discussions among all the 32 countries involved, would be a significant step toward reasserting the allies' interest in renewing their consensus in the post–Cold War, post-9/11, post-Iraq, and even post-Bush world.

The postwar Founders who embraced the causes on whose behalf the Cold War was waged and won left us with an awesome institutional structure within which it proved possible to start building a Europe that would be, at last, whole and free. The next few years will tell whether the new generation of political leaders who assumed their responsibilities late in the first decade of the twenty-first century will show the will and resilience to move on with the final refashioning and refurbishing of the Euro-Atlantic community inherited from their bold and steadfast predecessors.

Notes

1. Besides the United States and Canada, the non-EU members of NATO are Iceland, Norway, and Turkey. The non-NATO members of the EU are Austria, Cyprus, Finland, Ireland, Malta, and Sweden.

2. See chapter 4 in this volume by Vivien A. Schmidt.

3. Jacques Chirac, "Dialogue avec des jeunes et des intellectuels de l'université Humboldt en Allemagne," speech at Humboldt University, Berlin,

June 26, 2000. Joschka Fischer, "From Confederacy to Federation: Thoughts on the Finality of European Integration," speech at Humboldt University, Berlin, May 12, 2000.

4. Address by President Jacques Chirac to a Joint Session of Congress, February 1, 1996. Remarkably, only about 30 House members and 25 senators attended Chirac's speech. Steven Erlanger, "Chirac Offers a Vision of NATO," *New York Times*, February 2, 1996.

5. Jacques Chirac, "France's Vision for NATO," *Christian Science Monitor*, November 28, 2006.

6. There are more than three dozen U.S.-EU agreements and at least 15 regulatory agreements that produce constant and daily meetings and repeated conversations between relevant officials on issues of concern on either side of the Atlantic—but predictably, these issues are mostly, though not exclusively, not part of the traditional security agenda.

7. See Stan Sloan, *NATO, the European Union, and the Atlantic Community: The Transatlantic Bargain Challenged* (Lanham, Md.: Rowman & Littlefield, 2005), 254.

8. Because this Euro-Atlantic Forum would be a coordinating group, it could not bar any of the sovereign EU or NATO member from going forward with decisions of their own, if they so preferred, but coordination would be the fundamental approach not the afterthought.

9. Report of the Security Council Mission to Afghanistan, S/2006/935, November 11–16, 2006.

10. See James Dobbins, *America's Role in Nation-Building: From Germany to Iraq* (Santa Monica, Calif.: RAND, 2003).

11. See U.S. Department of Defense Directive 3000.05.

12. However, in some places, this is more as a normative goal than actuality. E.g., the Chinese Communist government has issued a White Paper on democracy, although the actual Chinese practice is considerably less than democratic.

13. Senator John Warner, remarks at the Atlantic Council 2006 Award for Distinguished International Service dinner, April 26, 2006.

14. Elaine Sciolino, "Chirac's Iran Gaffe Reveals a Strategy: Containment," *New York Times*, February 3, 2007.

15. Riga Summit Declaration, issued by the Heads of State and Government participating in the meeting of the North Atlantic Council in Riga on November 29, 2006, paragraph 45.

16. See, e.g., European Commission, "A European Strategy for Sustainable, Competitive, and Secure Energy," Green Paper, March 8, 2006.

17. Securing America's Future Energy, "Recommendations to the Nation on Reducing U.S. Oil Dependence," December 2006, 54.

18. The Polish defense minister raised the issue in the context of the proposed pipeline being built from Russia to Germany, which will bypass Poland. One of the coauthors proposed in a pre-Riga conference in September 2006 that a sufficient "limitation on one be treated as a limitation on all," which could trigger a support mechanism. Senator Richard Lugar proposed that the NATO treaty be considered the basis for a collective response in an important speech just before Riga. See also Katinka Barysch, *Russia, Realism and EU Unity*, Policy Brief (London: Centre for European Reform, 2007).

19. See Julianne Smith and Derek Mix, "The Transatlantic Climate Change Challenge," *Washington Quarterly* 31, no. 1 (Winter 2007–2008): 139–154.

20. See James Elles, "The Transatlantic Market: A Reality by 2015," in *Visions of the Atlantic Alliance: The United States, the European Union, and NATO*, ed. Simon Serfaty (Washington, D.C.: CSIS Press, 2005), 131–151.

21. Daniel Keohane, *Europe's New Defense Agency*, Policy Brief (London: Centre for European Reform, 2004).

22. NATO, *Comprehensive Political Guidance of the Riga Summit* (Brussels: NATO Headquarters, 2006).

INDEX

Page numbers followed by t *refer to tables; page numbers followed by* n *refer to note and note number.*

ABOUT THE AUTHORS

Hans Binnendijk is currently the Theodore Roosevelt Chair in National Security Policy and founding director of the Center for Technology and National Security Policy at the National Defense University. He previously served on the National Security Council as special assistant to the president and senior director for defense policy and arms control (1999–2001). He has also served as director of the Institute for National Strategic Studies at the National Defense University (1994–1999), director of the Institute for the Study of Diplomacy at Georgetown University (1991–1993), deputy director and director of studies at the International Institute for Strategic Studies in London, and editor of *Survival* (1988–1991). His most recent book is *Seeing the Elephant: The U.S. Role in Global Security* (with Richard Kugler; Potomac Books, 2006).

Michael Brenner is professor of international affairs at the University of Pittsburgh and a fellow at the Center for Transatlantic Relations of the Paul H. Nitze School of Advanced International Studies at Johns Hopkins University. He is a prolific writer on European-American relations and American foreign policy, and his most recent work includes *Toward a More Independent Europe* (Egmont Papers, 2007); *The European Union, United States & "Liberal Imperialism"* (American Consortium on European Union Studies, 2006); and *Reconcilable Differences: French-American Relations in a New Era* (with Guillaume Parmentier; Brookings Institution Press, 2002).

Benoît d'Aboville served as the French ambassador in Prague (1993–1997) and Warsaw (1998–2002), and as the ambassador, permanent representative, to NATO (2002–2005). Since October 2005, he has been at the Cour des Comptes, the French national court of audit. Previously, he served in the French Ministry of Foreign Affairs in Washington (1969–1973) and Moscow (1973-1976), on the Planning Staff of the Quai d'Orsay (1976–1977), and in the Office of the Foreign Minister (1977–1978) as deputy assistant secretary for arms control and political military affairs (1978–1986) and as deputy political director (1986–1989). He also served as French consul-general in New York (1989–1993).

Jolyon Howorth is Jean Monnet Professor (ad personam) of European Politics at the University of Bath. Since 2002, he has been visiting professor of political science at Yale University. His previous appointments were at the University of Paris III (Sorbonne-Nouvelle), University of Wisconsin–Madison, and Aston University. He has held visiting professorships at Harvard University and the Institut d'Etudes Politiques. He has published extensively in the field of European politics and history, especially on security and defense policy and transatlantic relations, including, most recently, *Security and Defence Policy in the European Union* (Palgrave, 2007); *Defending Europe: The EU, NATO and the Quest for European Autonomy* (edited with John Keeler; Palgrave, 2003); and *European Integration and Defence: The Ultimate Challenge?* (Institute for Security Studies of the European Union, 2000).

Franklin D. Kramer is a Distinguished Research Fellow at the Center for Technology and National Security Policy at the National Defense University. He has served as assistant secretary of defense for international security affairs (1996–2001), principal deputy assistant secretary of defense for international security affairs (1979–1981), and special assistant to the assistant secretary of defense for international security affairs (1977–1979). He is the chairman of the board of the World Affairs Council of Washington, chairman of the Committee on Asian and Global Security of the Atlantic Council and on the Executive Committee of its board, and a Capstone Professor at the George Washington University's Elliott School of International Affairs. He has been a partner with the Washington law firm of Shea and Gardner.

Ivan Krastev is chairman of the Board of the Centre for Liberal Strategies in Sofia, Bulgaria. He is director of the Open Century Project of the Central European University in Budapest, Hungary and executive director of the International Commission on the Balkans. He is also editor in chief of the Bulgarian edition of *Foreign Policy*. In the last decade he has been visiting fellow at St. Anthony College, Oxford; Woodrow Wilson Center for International Scholars in Washington, D.C.; Collegium Budapest, Wissenschaftskolleg, Berlin; Institute of Federalism, University of Fribourg, Switzerland; Institute for Human Sciences, Vienna; and Remarque Forum, New York. His latest publications in English include *The Anti-American Century* (editor, with Alan McPherson, Central European University Press, 2007) and *Shifting Obsessions. Three Essays on Politics of Anti-Corruption* (Central European University Press, 2004).

Richard L. Kugler most recently was Distinguished Research Professor at the Center for Technology and National Security Policy of the National Defense University. A specialist on U.S. national security strategy and NATO, he has over 35 years of experience at the Department of Defense and the RAND Corporation, and with the U.S. federal Senior Executive Service. He was one of the original architects of NATO enlargement and the NATO Response Force, as well as other U.S. and NATO strategic initiatives. He holds a PhD from the Massachusetts Institute of Technology. He is the author of 17 books in his field, including, most recently, *Policy Analysis in National Security Affairs: New Methods for a New Era* (Center for Technology and National Security Policy, 2007) and *Seeing the Elephant: The U.S. Role in Global Security* (with Hans Binnendijk; Potomac Books, 2006).

Julian Lindley-French is professor of military art and science at the Royal Military Academy of the Netherlands, senior associate fellow of the Defence Academy of the United Kingdom, and senior scholar at the Centre for Applied Policy at the University of Munich. He was formerly director of the International Security Policy Training Course at the Geneva Centre for Security Policy. He was born in Sheffield, Yorkshire, in 1958. He has also served as deputy director of the International Centre for Security Analysis at King's College, London, and was senior research fellow at the EU Institute for Security Studies in

Paris. His most recent books include *The North Atlantic Treaty Organization: The Enduring Alliance* (Routledge, 2007) and *A Chronology of European Security and Defence 1945–2007* (Oxford University Press, 2007).

Vivien A. Schmidt is Jean Monnet Professor of European Integration and professor of international relations at Boston University. She is currently Franqui Interuniversity Chair for Foreign Scholars, held jointly at the Free University of Brussels and the University of Louvain (January to June 2007) and also visiting professor at the Institut d'Études Politiques in Paris. She has been a professor at the University of Massachusetts and visiting professor at the Institute for Advanced Studies in Vienna, the European University Institute in Florence, the Max Planck Institute for the Study of Societies in Cologne, and the Universities of Paris and Lille, and has been a visiting scholar at Nuffield College, Oxford University, and at Harvard University, where she is currently a faculty affiliate in the Center for European Studies. Her many books include, most recently, *Democracy in Europe: The EU and National Polities* (Oxford University Press, 2006); *The Futures of European Capitalism* (Oxford University Press, 2002); and the two-volume *Welfare and Work in the Open Economy* (with F. W. Scharpf; Oxford University Press, 2000).

Simon Serfaty is a professor of U.S. foreign policy at Old Dominion University in Norfolk, which designated him as eminent scholar of the university in May 2001. From 1972 to 1993, he was a research professor at the Paul H. Nitze School of Advanced International Studies at Johns Hopkins University, serving as director of the Johns Hopkins Center of European Studies in Bologna (1972–1976), director of the Washington Center of Foreign Policy Research (1978–1980), and executive director of the Foreign Policy Institute (1984–1991). In 2003, he became the first holder of the Zbigniew Brzezinski Chair in Global Security and Geostrategy at CSIS, where he had directed the Europe Program for the previous 10 years. His many books include, most recently, *Architects of Delusion: Europe, America, and the Iraq War* (University of Pennsylvania Press, 2008); *The Vital Partnership: Power and Order* (Rowman & Littlefield, 2005); *Visions of the Atlantic Alliance* (editor; CSIS Press, 2005); and *La tentation impériale* (Odile Jacob, 2004).